365 Easy
Low-Calorie
Recipes

365 Easy
Low-Calorie
Recipes

Sylvia Schur
and
Dr. Vivian Schulte, R.D.

A JOHN BOSWELL ASSOCIATES BOOK

 HarperPerennial
A Division of HarperCollins*Publishers*

Dear Reader:

We welcome your recommendations for future 365 Ways books. Send your suggestions and a recipe, if you'd like, to Cookbook Editor, HarperCollins Publishers, 10 East 53rd Street, New York, NY 10022. If we choose your title suggestion or your recipe we will acknowledge you in the book and send you a free copy.

Thank you for your support.

Sincerely yours,
The Editor

Design: Nigel Rollings
Index: Maro Riofrancos

LIBRARY OF CONGRESS CATALOG CARD NUMBER 89-46115

ISBN 0-06-016309-7

93 10 9

Acknowledgments

We salute the contemporary dieter, a new kind of cook who sets high goals for great meals prepared in quick time, low in calories and rich in quality and style. Awareness of changes in food tastes, in choices of mostly fresh ingredients, and expectation of fun and style in low-calorie foods were our challenges in writing these recipes.

Our thanks go to Robyn Rosenthal for careful calorie calculations and editorial research and to Lillie Charlton for caring recipe testing. Our appreciation to Judith McNichol for her skillful, patient, manuscript preparation, and to all the staff of Creative Food Service, cognizant tasters and commentators.

Contents

Smart Choices for Slimming Down

Try one new recipe from this book each day. By the end of 365 days, you will have achieved a new food repertoire, new eating pleasure, and a new eating style.

By the year 2010, this may be the way most people eat. As diet experts, we talk about such behavior modification. This diet book creates it simply, effortlessly, with one new recipe experience a day, or as many as you choose. You need not count calories—they are all counted for you. You need not weigh portions—they are all measured for you. You have the satisfaction of home-prepared meals with a minimum of fuss, in little time, with maximum taste and freshness.

Prepare these snacks, salads, soups, main dishes, desserts, healthful grains, and indulgent cookies as and when you want them. Balance your recipes and menus as you like, while you keep in mind the total number of calories designed to bring your weight to the level you want—1,000 to 1,200 calories for weight loss for small and light-framed people, 1,800 calories for larger, heavier frames.

These recipes provide stimulating variety in contemporary dishes with great potential for attractive plate arrangements. You will enjoy the fun of some fool-the-eye dishes, the flavors in broad variety, the range of textures designed to maximize the pleasure of smaller portions.

The recipes in general are planned so that you can allot 20 percent of the calories—and nutrients—for breakfast, 30 percent for lunch, 40 percent for dinner, and 10 percent for snacks. If you choose to "graze" instead of enjoying larger meals, consider your total nutritional needs for the meal you are replacing and enjoy smaller portions of desirable foods throughout the day.

In developing and testing the recipes, we reduced fats and oils to far lower levels than usual. Since fats have 9 calories per gram compared with 4 calories per gram for carbohydrates and proteins, reduction in fats carries a double bonus in calorie reduction. In most ordinary recipes, larger quantities of oil are used.

We include a large variety of vegetables and fruits, grains, and pastas that substitute other flavorful ingredients for the usual oil. Having tasted these, recipes with larger amounts of oil begin to seem excessive.

All the recipes are low on fat, sugar, and calories, moderate in salt, and wholesome in fiber content. You will find that portions are modest—that's as it should be if you want to take pounds off effectively and quickly.

All main dishes are under 300 calories. Many of them way under. They allow for an accompaniment or two and still come out to 480 calories.

Most desserts are under 150 calories. (In fact, only two are over.) And many can be enjoyed at under 100 calories.

After you reach the weight you want, stick to the principles of these recipes:

- Limit total fats. Using more unsaturated oils, you'll reduce cholesterol problems too.
- Eat plenty of fiber in whole grains, fruits, and vegetables.
- Eat regular meals, even if they are small ones.
- Choose sensible portions.
- Make calories count for good nutrition.
- Take pleasure in every bite, eat slowly, and savor the flavors.
- Sit down at the table to eat.
- Use salt and sugar in moderation.
- Stock your refrigerator with low-calorie snacks, with plenty of lean protein and vegetables.

Enjoy the 365 adventures in easy low-calorie recipes ahead!

Chapter 1

Snacks and Starters

Many of us enjoy a series of little meals instead of fewer big ones. The most frequently eaten meal in America, in fact, is the snack. Just consider that these are part of your total daily eating plan, and make the snacks you choose count as significant food.

These recipes offer satisfying little meals or snacks with lots of variety and change of pace. They can help you lose weight because they help you feel better—emotionally as well as physically.

There are more recipes in this chapter than in any other because you will want to munch more often. Many need no cooking; some are quickly microwaved. Enjoy an inventive range of taste sensations, in tasty lean dishes that make every calorie count. Some of the recipes that follow are for one, and some for two or for a party.

Calories per portion in this chapter range from 6 to 110—with most under 50 calories. If you want to enjoy a variety of snacks instead of one main dish, mix and match your choices for good balance.

---

1 LOW-CAL POTATO CHIPS
Prep: 5 minutes   Cook: 50 minutes   Makes: 70 chips
Calories per 5 chips: 20

You'll never go back to the commercial chips after you've tasted these. They're wonderfully crisp and chewy. Great with chicken or meat too!

2 large baking potatoes　　　　　　　**Paprika**
　Salt or seasoned salt

1. Preheat oven to 300°. Scrub and very thinly slice potatoes (easily done in a food processor or on a mandoline if you have one). Spread out potato slices in a single layer on a large wire rack set over a baking pan.

2. Season lightly with salt and paprika. Place in oven and bake for 50 minutes, or until potato chips are crisp and brown. To speed crisping after chips begin to brown, place on paper plate and microwave on high 1 minute. Store in a bag or tin.

2   NACHOS

Prep: 1 minute   Cook: 20 seconds   Serves: 2
Calories per serving: 66

4 corn tortilla chips
1 ounce low-fat Monterey jack
cheese with jalapeño, cut
into 4 thin slices

2 teaspoons prepared salsa,
mild, medium, or hot to
your taste

1. Place tortilla chips on a paper plate. Put a slice of cheese on each chip.

2. Microwave on high for 20 seconds, until cheese just begins to melt. Top each with ½ teaspoon salsa.

DIPS

Six dashing dips make raw veggies taste satisfying and different—quick-to-make, low-calorie party additions.

3   CUCUMBER-YOGURT DIP

Prep: 3 minutes   Cook: none   Makes: 1½ cups
Calories per tablespoon: 7

1 medium cucumber, peeled,
seeded and chopped
(1 cup)
½ cup plain low-fat yogurt

1 garlic clove, crushed
through a press
2 tablespoons chopped fresh
mint or dill
Salt and pepper

Combine cucumber, yogurt, garlic, and mint and stir together. Season with salt and pepper. Cover and refrigerate until ready to serve.

4   CRABMEAT DIP

Prep: 4 minutes   Cook: none   Makes: 1½ cups
Calories per tablespoon: 12

½ cup low-fat sour cream
½ cup plain low-fat yogurt
1 3½-ounce can crabmeat
2 teaspoons chopped fresh
chives

1 teaspoon grated lemon zest
1 teaspoon tarragon
Salt and pepper

In a medium bowl, combine sour cream, yogurt, crabmeat, chives, lemon zest, and tarragon. Mix well to blend. Season with salt and pepper. Cover and refrigerate until well chilled.

5 GUACAMOLE

Prep: 3 minutes   Cook: none   Makes: 1⅓ cups
Calories per tablespoon: 20

1 ripe avocado
 Juice of 1 small lime
½ onion, finely chopped
1 small tomato, peeled,
   seeded, and chopped

¼ fresh hot red or green chili
   pepper, peeled, seeded,
   and chopped
 Salt and pepper

1. Cut avocado in half and twist to release from seed. Scoop pulp with spoon into shallow soup bowl. Mash avocado with fork. Mash in lime juice.

2. Add onion, tomato, and hot pepper. Mix well. Season with salt and pepper. Put in serving bowl or half of the scooped-out avocado shell.

6 CREAMY HERB DIP

Prep: 5 minutes   Cook: none   Serves: 10
Calories per 2-tablespoon serving: 43

Serve this tangy dip with an assortment of vegetables. Refer to the chart.

½ cup plain low-fat yogurt
½ cup low-fat sour cream
¼ cup heavy cream
 Mustard, curry powder, or
   mixed herbs

Dippers: green or red
   pepper sticks, celery ribs,
   Belgian endive leaves,
   snow peas

1. Combine yogurt, sour cream, and sweet cream. Stir until smooth. Cover and refrigerate "crème fraîche" to use as needed.

2. Remove 2 tablespoons of "crème fraîche." Combine with 1 teaspoon mustard or ½ teaspoon curry powder or mixed herbs to taste. Dip vegetable sticks in seasoned mixture of your choice.

7 SAGE CHEESE DIP

Prep: 2 minutes   Cook: none   Makes: 1 cup
Calories per tablespoon: 9

½ cup low-fat cottage cheese
½ cup plain low-fat yogurt
2 tablespoons chopped onion

1 teaspoon sage
1 tablespoon chopped parsley
 Salt and pepper

1. Combine cottage cheese, yogurt, onion, sage, and parsley in a food processor or blender. Puree until smooth. Season with salt and pepper.

2. Scoop into small bowl. Cover and refrigerate until serving time.

8   GREEN GODDESS DIP

Prep: 10 minutes   Cook: none   Chill: 1 hour   Makes: 1½ cups
Calories per tablespoon: 22

½ **cup reduced-calorie**
   mayonnaise
½ **cup plain low-fat yogurt**
¼ **cup chopped fresh spinach**
¼ **cup chopped watercress**

¼ **cup chopped parsley**
3 **scallions, sliced**
¼ **teaspoon tarragon**
1 **tablespoon lemon juice**
   Salt and pepper

1. Place mayonnaise, yogurt, spinach, watercress, parsley, scallions, tarragon, and lemon juice in a bowl. Stir vigorously until well combined. Season with salt and pepper.

2. Cover and refrigerate 1 hour, or until ready to use.

Dippers

Asparagus: Snap off tough end, clean bottom of stalk with vegetable peeler. 3 asparagus stalks = 16 calories.

Belgian endive: Trim base of head; separate leaves. 1 medium head Belgian endive (about 12 leaves) = 8 calories.

Broccoli florets: Trim from tough stalk, wash or blanch 1 minute. ½ cup florets = 20 calories.

Carrot: Scrape, cut into sticks, and chill in ice water. 1 medium carrot = 32 calories. 6 or 8 strips (1 ounce) = 12 calories.

Cauliflower florets: Cut from stalk, wash, chill in ice water with a little lemon juice. ½ cup cauliflower = 14 calories.

Celery: Cut into sticks and chill in ice water. 1 medium celery rib = 5 calories.

Green Beans: Snap top end, pull strings, blanch 1 minute. ½ cup green beans = 17 calories.

Green or red pepper: Wash, halve, and seed, cut into strips. ½ green pepper = 11 calories.

Jicama: Peel portion to be used, slice thin. 3 slices jicama = 6 calories.

Snow peas: Pull off tough strings, open if desired, fill with dip. ½ cup = 30 calories.

Turnip: Wash, peel where necessary, cut into thin wedges. ½ cup = 20 calories.

9   ARTICHOKES COOKED IN MARINADE

Prep: 12 minutes   Cook: 30 minutes   Serves: 4
Calories per serving: 54

These delicious, super-tender artichokes need no butter enhancement. They provide satisfying eating pleasure at about 50 calories.

2 **whole artichokes (7 ounces each)**
2 **tablespoons white wine vinegar**
2 **teaspoons olive oil**

1 **garlic clove, cut in half**
½ **small dried hot pepper, or 4 peppercorns**
¼ **teaspoon salt**

1. Trim artichoke stem flat and pull off any bruised outer leaves. Cut off top third of artichoke and trim ends of remaining leaves with scissors.

2. Place in pot just large enough to hold artichokes side by side. Pour 1 tablespoon vinegar and 1 teaspoon oil across top of each artichoke.

3. Add boiling water to cover, garlic, hot pepper, and salt. If artichokes float, place a heavy heatproof plate on top to hold them down. Cover pot with a tight lid, bring to a boil, and cook about 30 minutes, until tender. Let artichokes cool in liquid.

4. Drain artichokes and cut in half lengthwise. Scoop out hairy choke. Serve warm, at room temperature, or chilled. (To refrigerate, place upside down in bowl, basting with a little of cooking marinade.)

10   EGGPLANT CAVIAR

Prep: 10 minutes   Cook: 30 to 40 minutes   Makes: 2 cups
Calories per tablespoon: 15

A tasty, creamy spread of eggplant to serve on lettuce or endive, or spread on Sesame Crackers (page 16).

1 **medium eggplant**
1 **tablespoon lemon juice**
1 **large tomato, peeled and finely chopped**
1 **medium onion, finely chopped**

1 **garlic clove, minced**
2 **tablespoons chopped parsley**
2 **tablespoons olive oil**
¾ **teaspoon salt**
¼ **teaspoon pepper**

1. Preheat oven to 400°. Pierce eggplant in 2 or 3 places with the tip of a knife. Put eggplant in an ovenproof skillet or baking dish and bake for 30 to 40 minutes, until very soft. Let cool.

2. Peel eggplant and discard skin. Place eggplant in a medium bowl and mash to a puree.

3. Add lemon juice, tomato, onion, garlic, parsley, and oil. Mix well. Season with salt and pepper. Cover and refrigerate until chilled.

4. Serve as a dip or as an appetizer salad on lettuce leaves.

11   BAGEL CRISPS
Prep: 45 seconds   Cook: 15 minutes   Serves: 2
Calories per serving: 83

Is it the chewy texture or the wonderful bready flavor that makes these thin bagel rings so appealing? Add ground pepper for extra flavor appeal. Serve with light cream cheese or low-fat ricotta cheese if desired.

1   **medium bagel**
    Water

Optional: Freshly ground
    black pepper

1. Preheat oven to 325°. Using a sharp serrated knife, cut bagel crosswise into 4 slices.

2. Brush cut surfaces lightly with water. Sprinkle with pepper, if desired.

3. Place bagel slices on a cookie sheet and toast in oven until crisp and golden, about 15 minutes. Store in a paper bag.

12   ONION-TOMATO TART WITH ANCHOVIES AND OLIVES
Prep: 12 minutes   Cook: 30 minutes   Makes: 15 pieces
Calories per piece: 32

The French version of pizza with our twist of genius to bring down the calorie count.

4   **sheets phyllo dough**
1   **tablespoon olive oil**
3   **medium onions, thinly**
    sliced
2   **medium tomatoes, thinly**
    sliced

½   **can (1 ounce) anchovies**
2   **ounces pitted black olives,**
    quartered (2 tablespoons)
2   **tablespoons chopped fresh**
    basil
    Freshly ground pepper

1. Cover phyllo dough with a damp kitchen towel to prevent drying out and let come to room temperature. Unfold and separate each sheet of pastry and place on a 10 x 15-inch jelly roll pan. Brush with olive oil. Fold edges under to make a standing rim. Cover again with a damp towel.

2. Preheat oven to 400°. In a large nonstick skillet heat oil. Add onions and cook over moderate heat, stirring occasionally, until translucent, about 5 minutes. Spread onions evenly over pastry.

3. Arrange tomatoes over onions and criss-cross anchovies on top in a diamond pattern. Put a piece of olive at each diamond point. Sprinkle with basil and season with pepper.

4. Bake tart for 25 minutes, or until pastry is brown and crisp. Serve in 3-x-3¼-inch rectangles (5 cuts on 15-inch side, 3 on 10-inch side).

13 CINNAMON FRUIT CRISPS

Prep: 1 minute   Cook: 30 seconds   Serves: 1
Calories per serving: 92

Crunch on this wholesome cereal snack with the added touch of flavor.

½ **cup cereal squares with fruit
    centers**

1 **tablespoon water**
½ **teaspoon cinnamon**

1. Place cereal squares in a small microwavable bowl. Sprinkle with water and toss. Sprinkle cinnamon over cereal and toss again.

2. Place in microwave and cook on medium-high power for 30 seconds. Serve warm. Store in a dry place to retain crispness.

14 CLAMS IN TOMATO

Prep: 2 minutes   Cook: none   Serves: 1
Calories per serving: 51

Two zesty mouthfuls of clam, tomato, and horseradish—a gutsy and satisfying snack.

1 **plum tomato**
2 **tablespoons canned minced
    clams, drained**

1 **teaspoon prepared white
    horseradish**
Lemon wedge

1. Cut tomato in half lengthwise. Scoop out seeds.

2. Place 1 tablespoon minced clams in each tomato half. Top each with ½ teaspoon horseradish and a squirt of lemon juice.

15 CRABMEAT LETTUCE BUNDLES

Prep: 4 minutes   Cook: none   Serves: 4
Calories per roll: 41

A light and savory pick-me-up for crabmeat fans.

1 **6-ounce can crabmeat**
2 **teaspoons reduced-calorie
    mayonnaise**

2 **dashes of hot pepper sauce**
1 **teaspoon lemon juice**
4 **lettuce leaves**

1. Drain crabmeat and toss with mayonnaise, hot sauce, and lemon juice.

2. Divide crab among lettuce leaves. Fold sides in, then roll up leaves to encase crabmeat. Cut each roll in half.

16   ENDIVE "SPOONS" WITH CAVIAR
Prep: 2 minutes   Cook: none   Serves: 4
Calories per serving of 2: 11

Tangy endive is the perfect foil for these briny fish eggs. An elegant snack or appetizer.

8 endive leaves	4 teaspoons caviar
4 teaspoons low-fat sour cream	1 teaspoon chopped chives

1. On the wide end of each leaf of endive, place ½ teaspoon of the sour cream.

2. Top each leaf with ½ teaspoon caviar and a sprinkling of chives.

17   CELERI REMOULADE
Prep: 5 to 10 minutes   Cook: none   Serves: 4
Calories per serving: 65

This classic salad of unique sharp flavor makes a great snack as well as appetizer.

1 celeriac (celery root), peeled and coarsely grated (2 cups) (food processor does fine)	¼ cup plain low-fat yogurt
	1 tablespoon Dijon mustard
	Salt and pepper
¼ cup reduced-calorie mayonnaise	4 Boston lettuce leaves
	8 red bell pepper strips

1. Place grated celeriac, mayonnaise, yogurt, and mustard in a bowl. Stir until blended. Season with salt and pepper.

2. Place 1 lettuce leaf on each of 4 plates. Spoon celeri remoulade onto lettuce, dividing evenly. Garnish each serving with 2 red pepper strips.

18   BROCCOLI WITH LEMON-MUSTARD COTTAGE DIP
Prep: 3 minutes   Cook: none   Serves: 1
Calories per serving: 98

When the munchies strike, here's a satisfying portion with plenty of flavor, and big enough to share. (If you do share, divide the calories, too.)

¼ pound broccoli tops	1 tablespoon lemon juice
¼ cup low-fat cottage cheese	1 teaspoon Dijon mustard

1. Wash, drain, and dry broccoli. Cut into 1- to 1½-inch florets. Place in a microwavable bowl, add ¼ cup water, cover, and microwave on high 1½ minutes. Drain and rinse under cold running water; drain well.

2. In a small bowl, combine cottage cheese, lemon juice, and mustard. Blend well. Serve as a dipping sauce with broccoli.

---

19   TUNA SALAD SUSHI
Prep: 6 minutes   Cook: none   Serves: 8
Calories per 3 pieces: 64

A low-calorie snack approach for tuna—refreshing as a stop at a sushi bar.

1 3¼-ounce can chunk-style water-packed tuna	1 tablespoon reduced-calorie mayonnaise
1 tablespoon finely chopped onion	½ teaspoon soy sauce
2 tablespoons finely chopped celery	8 outer leaves of Boston lettuce
	2 scallions

1. In a small bowl, combine tuna, onion, celery, and mayonnaise. Mix with a fork to blend well. Season with soy sauce.

2. Rinse lettuce leaves and pat dry. Quarter the scallions lengthwise.

3. Spread 1 tablespoon tuna mixture along one side of each lettuce leaf and place a piece of scallion on each. Roll up each leaf and cut into thirds.

---

20   HERBED YOGURT CHEESE
Prep: 5 minutes   Standing time: 4 hours   Serves: 8
Calories per 1-ounce serving: 61

Let this tasty fresh cheese ripen overnight and enjoy it as a snack spread any time.

2 tablespoons chopped fresh parsley	¾ teaspoon salt
2 tablespoons minced fresh chives	1 quart plain low-fat yogurt
1 teaspoon coarsely cracked pepper	

1. Stir parsley, chives, cracked pepper, and salt into yogurt.

2. Moisten a coffee filter or double layer of cheesecloth. Place filter in top of a drip coffee maker, or cheesecloth in a sieve. Add yogurt, fold top ends over, and let drip at room temperature 4 hours or overnight. When cheese stops dripping and feels firm enough to hold its shape, turn out of filter or cheesecloth and refrigerate. Use as a soft spread.

21   PITA PIZZA

Prep: 5 minutes   Cook: 3 to 5 minutes   Serves: 4
Calories per serving: 85

You won't believe the calorie count when you taste these palate-pleasing pizzas. Ideal for a snack or a whole lunch with a green salad.

2 **4-inch whole wheat pita breads**	1 **teaspoon oregano** **Dash of garlic powder**
¼ **cup tomato sauce**	2 **ounces low-fat mozzarella**
2 **tablespoons chopped fresh chives or scallion green**	**cheese, grated (about ½ cup)**

1. Split the pita breads in half to make 4 flat rounds. Place in toaster until crisp.

2. Spread 1 tablespoon tomato sauce over each pita round. Top with chives. Sprinkle with oregano and garlic powder. Top with mozzarella cheese.

3. Set pizzas under broiler about 4 inches from heat and broil until cheese bubbles, 3 minutes.

22   LEAN BROCCOLI QUICHE

Prep: 20 minutes   Cook: 25 minutes   Makes: 25 pieces
Calories per piece: 47

Make this quiche part of your party fun. It's as good to talk about as it is to eat, with its filling of broccoli, mushrooms, and low-calorie cheese. Even the egg in the custard is made leaner by the addition of extra egg whites. All this in a light phyllo crust.

4 **sheets phyllo dough**	1 **cup low-fat ricotta cheese**
1 **10-ounce package frozen chopped broccoli, thawed**	¾ **cup skim milk**
2 **medium onions, chopped**	1 **teaspoon chervil or curry powder**
2 **tablespoons defatted chicken broth**	¼ **teaspoon salt**
¼ **pound mushrooms, sliced**	¼ **teaspoon white pepper**
2 **medium egg whites**	½ **cup grated Alpine Lace cheese (2 ounces)**
2 **medium whole eggs**	

1. Preheat oven to 425°. Open phyllo sheets out on a nonstick 10 x 15-inch jelly roll pan or cookie sheet. Fold edges inside the pan to make a smooth rim. Cover dough with a damp paper towel to prevent it from drying and becoming brittle.

2. Squeeze broccoli dry and scatter over phyllo dough.

3. Place chopped onion in a small glass measure with 1 tablespoon of broth and microwave on high 1 minute. If moist, cook a little longer to dry. Scatter over broccoli. Place mushrooms in a dish in microwave with remaining 1 tablespoon broth and cook on high 2 minutes, or until lightly browned and dried; scatter over onion.

4. Beat egg whites until light and foamy. Add whole eggs, ricotta, skim milk, chervil, salt, and white pepper to egg whites. Beat to combine. Pour custard over vegetables in pan. Sprinkle cheese over top.

5. Bake in bottom third of oven until pastry is golden and custard is set, about 20 minutes. Cut into rectangles, 2 x 3 inches. Serve warm or at room temperature.

23 PICKLED GREEN BEANS
Prep: 3 minutes   Cook: 10 minutes   Marinate: 24 hours   Serves: 10
Calories per serving: 29

No hesitation about making return trips for these tangy nibbles.

1 **pound green beans**	½ **teaspoon salt**
1 **cup cider vinegar**	1 **garlic clove, chopped**
2 **tablespoons sugar**	¼ **cup coarsely chopped fresh**
2 **teaspoons mixed pickling**	**dill**
spices	

1. Wash beans well. Snip off ends. Heat 1 quart water to boiling, add beans, and cook about 5 minutes, until just tender but still bright green. Drain, reserving ½ cup cooking liquid.

2. In a small nonreactive saucepan, combine vinegar, sugar, pickling spices, salt, garlic, and dill. Add reserved liquid. Stir well. Cook over medium heat 5 minutes.

3. Place beans in a 2-quart jar or bowl. Pour vinegar mixture over beans, cover, and refrigerate, tossing occasionally, 24 hours or longer.

24 TOMATO SLICES WITH MOZZARELLA
Prep: 4 minutes   Cook: none   Serves: 4
Calories per serving: 39

A pick-me-up that is filling without piling on the calories.

2 **medium tomatoes**	2 **tablespoons chopped fresh**
Salt and pepper	**basil**
¼ **pound low-fat mozzarella**	
cheese	

1. Core tomatoes and cut each into 4 thick slices. Season lightly with salt and pepper.

2. Cut mozzarella into 8 thin slices. Place a piece of mozzarella on each tomato slice. Top each with ¾ teaspoon chopped basil.

25   PICKLED SALMON

Prep: 6 minutes   Cook: 5 minutes   Marinate: 24 hours   Serves: 8
Calories per serving: 43

Spear these with a toothpick for a real taste treat.

1 garlic clove, minced
1 medium onion, finely
    chopped
½ cup white wine vinegar
¼ cup water
¼ cup dry white wine
2 teaspoons mixed pickling
    spices

1 tablespoon sugar
½ teaspoon salt
1 pound fresh salmon,
    skinned, boned, and cut
    into 1-inch cubes

1. In a medium nonreactive saucepan, combine all ingredients except salmon. Heat to boiling, reduce to simmer, and cook for 5 minutes.

2. Put salmon cubes in a narrow 3½–4 cup bowl and pour hot vinegar mixture over. Let stand at room temperature until cool.

3. Cover and refrigerate 24 hours or longer.

26   PICKLED SHRIMP

Prep: 15 minutes   Cook: 3 to 4 minutes   Marinate: 24 hours
Serves: 10   Calories per serving: 51

A satisfying favorite for snacking or as a meal starter.

1 pound raw shrimp
½ cup dry white wine
½ cup water
2 bay leaves, broken in half
2 scallions, sliced
¼ cup lemon juice
1 teaspoon tarragon

1 tablespoon Worcestershire
    sauce
Dash of salt
Dash of pepper
Dash of hot pepper sauce
1 tablespoon olive oil

1. Peel and devein shrimp, leaving tails on.

2. In a deep nonreactive skillet or saucepan, combine wine, water, and bay leaves. Heat to boiling. Add shrimp and cook 3 to 4 minutes. Drain, reserving broth. Discard bay leaves.

3. In a bowl, combine reserved shrimp stock with scallions, lemon juice, tarragon, Worcestershire, salt, pepper, hot sauce, and olive oil. Stir well. Add shrimp and toss to coat evenly.

4. Cover bowl and refrigerate, tossing occasionally, for 24 hours, or up to 3 days.

27 LOBSTER MEDALLIONS
Prep: 5 minutes   Cook: 1½ minutes   Serves: 4
Calories per serving: 65

For a savory treat, reach into the freezer for a lobster tail, defrost, and cook in the microwave. Slice and serve to 4 appreciative friends as a snack or appetizer.

1 **frozen rock lobster tail, about 4 ounces**	**Dash of hot pepper sauce**
¼ **cup reduced-calorie mayonnaise**	**Dash of nutmeg**
1 **teaspoon lemon juice**	1 **tablespoon diced red bell pepper**

1. Place frozen lobster tail on a microwavable plate. Cover with plastic wrap and cook on high 1 minute 30 seconds to defrost and cook. Let stand for a few minutes until cool enough to handle.

2. Slit underside of lobster shell, snap back, and remove meat. Cut lobster tail into 8 slices, or medallions.

3. In a medium bowl, combine mayonnaise, lemon juice, hot sauce, nutmeg, and red pepper. Stir to mix well. Add lobster medallions and toss to coat. Serve with picks.

28 CLAMS AND OYSTERS ON THE HALF SHELL
Prep: 2 minutes   Cook: 5 minutes   Serves: 2
Calories per serving: 68

12 **littleneck clams or small bluepoint oysters**	2 **lemon wedges**
1 **cup club soda**	**Hot pepper sauce**

1. Scrub clams or oysters under running water to remove any grit from shells.

2. To open easily, place in a small shallow baking pan. Add club soda and set in a 250° oven for about 5 minutes, or until shells open slightly. Pry off top shell and cut around edges between halves with a sturdy small knife.

3. Chill on ice and serve 6 pieces per portion, with lemon wedges and hot pepper sauce on the side.

29   SESAME CRACKERS

Prep: 10 minutes   Cook: 20 minutes   Makes: about 4 dozen
Calories per cracker: 37

A crisp cracker to be enjoyed by itself or as a base for any of the spreads.

1 **cup quick-cooking oatmeal**
1 **cup oat flakes, crumbled**
1 **cup whole wheat flour**
¼ **cup bran cereal, crushed**
½ **teaspoon salt**

½ **cup vegetable oil**
1 **cup unsweetened apple**
   juice
   Sesame seeds, for topping

1. Preheat oven to 325°. Lightly grease an 11 x 15-inch cookie sheet. In a large bowl, combine oatmeal, oat flakes, whole wheat flour, bran, and salt. Add oil and apple juice and mix to make a stiff dough.

2. Roll out dough between 2 sheets of wax paper to 10½ x 14½-inch rectangle. Remove top sheet of wax paper. Invert dough onto cookie sheet. Peel off remaining sheet of wax paper. Sprinkle with sesame seeds and press into dough with rolling pin or palm of hand.

3. With a small sharp knife or ravioli wheel, cut dough into 2-inch squares. Bake 20 minutes, or until crackers are crisp and brown. Let cool before removing from baking sheet.

30   POPCORN

Prep: none   Cook: 3 to 5 minutes   Serves: 4
Calories per serving: 27

Fluffy popcorn is a dieter's good friend—27 calories to a cupful. This makes popping worth doing, in a microwave, electric popper, or plain covered pan.

1 **1-ounce bag plain**
   microwave popping corn,
   no oil added, or 2
   tablespoons plain
   popping corn

Salt or dried herbs

1. Microwave corn as directed on package, or place 2 tablespoons unpopped kernels in electric corn popper or in a small heavy saucepan with 2 tablespoons boiling water. Cook over high heat, shaking pan frequently, about 3 minutes, until popped.

2. Sprinkle hot popcorn with salt or herbs to taste.

PEPPY POPCORN

Prepare 1 quart popcorn as above. Sprinkle with ⅛ teaspoon cayenne. Toss well to distribute.

31 FRESH MICRO-CORN

Prep: 2 minutes   Cook: 8 minutes   Serves: 4
Calories per serving: 96

Steamed in its own goodness, corn makes a giant filling snack. You'll never miss the butter!

4 ears of corn

1. Pull husks back. Take off all the silk and discard. Rewrap ears in husks and tie with string.

2. Place on a microwavable glass dish.

3. Cook at high heat for 4 minutes. Turn over and cook 4 minutes longer.

4. When cool enough to handle remove husks. Season with hot sauce for zesty flavor.

32 SALMON SLICES IN LIME JUICE

Prep: 10 minutes   Cook: none   Marinate: 45 minutes   Serves: 8
Calories per serving: 34

A most elegant treat. Delicious as is, or serve on Sesame Crackers (page 16) at an extra 37 calories per cracker.

½ **pound fresh salmon,
    skinned and boned**
3 **tablespoons fresh lime juice**
½ **small onion, minced**
⅛ **teaspoon coarsely cracked
    white pepper**

2 **tablespoons chopped fresh
    dill, or 2 teaspoons dried
    dill weed**
Dash of dry mustard
Parsley sprigs or watercress

1. Chill salmon in freezer for 15 minutes, then slice paper thin. Spread slices on a ceramic or glass dish.

2. Sprinkle salmon with lime juice, onion, pepper, dill, and dry mustard. Cover with plastic wrap.

3. Refrigerate salmon 30 minutes or overnight, basting occasionally with the marinade. Garnish with parsley or watercress to serve.

33   TOMATO BAGNA CAUDA
Prep: 3 minutes   Cook: 3 minutes   Makes: 1 cup
Calories per tablespoon: 9

Bagna cauda, or "hot bath," is usually made with garlicky olive oil. Our bright low-calorie version is good hot or cold. Keep in the refrigerator to use as wanted.

1 cup tomato sauce	¼ teaspoon basil
1 tablespoon anchovy paste	Dash of pepper
2 garlic cloves, crushed	
through a press	

In a very small saucepan or fondue pot, combine all ingredients. Mix to blend well. Cook over moderate heat for 3 minutes, stirring. Serve warm as a dip for any vegetables.

34   TURKEY ROLL-UPS
Prep: 3 minutes   Cook: none   Serves: 6
Calories per serving: 52

Chewy and tangy—to be eaten with the fingers or on a toothpick.

2 tablespoons low-fat cream	⅛ teaspoon pepper
cheese	4 thin 1-ounce slices cooked
1 tablespoon Dijon mustard	turkey breast
¼ teaspoon salt	4 scallions

1. Combine cream cheese, mustard, salt, and pepper. Spread cream cheese mixture over each of the turkey slices.

2. Cut each scallion in half. Place both halves on each turkey slice. Roll up. Cut each roll into thirds. Allow 2 pieces per serving.

35   SLIM BEEF WITH PEPPERCORN SAUCE
Prep: 2 minutes   Cook: none   Serves: 1
Calories per serving: 62

An elegant and sophisticated appetizer or snack, yet quick, simple, and low in calories.

1 slice lean rare roast beef	½ teaspoon Dijon mustard
(about 1 ounce)	1 tablespoon plain low-fat
1 teaspoon green	yogurt
peppercorns, in brine	Dash of basil or thyme

1. Trim any excess fat from beef. Refrigerate until slightly chilled. Cut very thin slices diagonally across the grain.

2. Mash green peppercorns and mustard together, then stir in yogurt and basil.

3. Place beef on plate, top with sauce, and enjoy.

---

36   SPINACH PUFF

Prep: 5 minutes   Cook: 2 minutes   Serves: 1
Calories per serving: 36

Whip up a soufflé-like snack in about 6 minutes to pamper yourself with something good to taste—and good for you!

½ **cup cooked spinach, well**
    drained
1 **slice onion, cut up**
1 **tablespoon Parmesan cheese**

   Dash of nutmeg
1 **medium egg white**
½ **teaspoon lemon juice**

1. In a food processor, combine spinach, onion, Parmesan, and nutmeg. Puree until smooth.

2. Beat egg white with lemon juice until stiff. Fold in spinach.

3. Pour mixture into an 8-ounce glass custard cup or microwavable soufflé dish or coffee cup, buttered on bottom only. Microwave on high 2 minutes, or until puffed and set. Let cool slightly and enjoy pronto.

---

37   WATERCRESS CANAPES

Prep: 4 minutes   Cook: none   Makes: 8
Calories per canapé: 26

Herbed and full of flavor—a perfect snack.

½ **cup low-fat cottage cheese**
¼ **teaspoon tarragon**
¼ **teaspoon dried dill weed**
2 **tablespoons minced fresh**
    chives

¾ **cup chopped watercress**
   Salt and pepper
8 **rye Melba toast crackers**

1. In a small bowl, combine cottage cheese, tarragon, dill weed, chives, and watercress. Mix to blend well. Season with salt and pepper.

2. Place a generous tablespoon of the cheese mixture on each Melba cracker.

38   CHINESE CABBAGE PICKLE
Prep: 10 minutes   Pickling: 1 to 2 days   Makes: about 4 cups
Calories per ¼ cup serving: 8

Here's a zesty pickle that is ready after only 1 day.

1 small head cabbage, preferably Chinese celery cabbage	4 slices fresh ginger
	1 garlic clove, halved
	1 tablespoon salt
2 dried hot red peppers, or 4 drops hot pepper sauce	1¼ cups boiling water
	1¼ cups cider vinegar

1. Cut cabbage into bite-size pieces; there should be 4 cups. Halve peppers lengthwise and discard stems and seeds. Cut in thin long strips. Peel ginger and finely chop.

2. Combine cabbage, pepper strips or hot sauce, ginger, and garlic in a quart jar.

3. Dissolve salt in boiling water, cool, then combine with vinegar and add to jar. Cover jar tightly.

4. Let jar stand 1 day, enjoy, then refrigerate the remainder. Pickle is ready after 1 day, better after 2, and it will keep well refrigerated for up to 2 weeks.

39   STUFFED CHERRY TOMATOES
Prep: 5 minutes   Cook: none   Serves: 4
Calories per serving: 42

Brightly colored bite-size low-calorie container for a zesty filling.

8 cherry tomatoes	½ teaspoon curry powder
1 medium hard-cooked egg, chopped	1 teaspoon chopped chives
	Salt and pepper to taste
1 tablespoon reduced-calorie mayonnaise	8 small parsley sprigs

1. Cut off tops of tomatoes and scoop out seeds. Place seeds in bowl. Add egg and mash well with a fork.

2. Add mayonnaise, curry powder, and chives. Mix well. Season with salt and pepper.

3. Fill tomato shells with curried egg mixture. Top each tomato with a sprig of parsley.

40   CARAWAY-STUFFED CELERY
Prep: 3 minutes   Cook: none   Serves: 4
Calories per serving: 15

A crunchy snack with lots of flavor.

4 **celery ribs**	1 **teaspoon seasoned salt**
4 **ounces low-fat cottage**	1 **teaspoon caraway seeds**
cheese (about ½ cup)	

1. Clean celery and trim off ends.

2. In a small bowl, combine cottage cheese, seasoned salt, and caraway seeds.

3. Fill hollow of each celery rib with 2 tablespoons of the cottage cheese mixture.

4. Cut each rib into 4 pieces.

41   SARDINES ON CUCUMBER
Prep: 6 minutes   Cook: none   Serves: 5
Calories per serving of 2: 54

Score the cucumber by running the tines of a fork down the sides, then cut diagonally for longer slices, with petal-like edges.

1 **3¾-ounce can sardines**	**Salt and pepper**
1 **small onion, finely chopped**	1 **medium cucumber,**
2 **celery ribs, finely chopped**	**unpeeled**
2 **teaspoons reduced-calorie**	10 **parsley sprigs**
mayonnaise	

1. Drain and discard oil from can of sardines. Put sardines in a bowl and mash with a fork. Add onion, celery, and mayonnaise. Mix well. Season with salt and pepper.

2. Cut cucumber diagonally into 10 slices about ¼ inch thick. Place equal amounts of sardine mixture on each cucumber slice. Top with a sprig of parsley.

42   CUCUMBER SLICES WITH GOLDEN CAVIAR

Prep: 2 minutes   Cook: none   Serves: 4
Calories per serving: 27

Simply delicious—cool and colorful ridged cucumber slices with savory caviar or anchovy topping.

½ **medium cucumber**
2 **tablespoons golden (whitefish) or red caviar, or 12 thin anchovy strips**

1 **tablespoon low-fat yogurt**

1. Run tines of fork down side of cucumber, all around. Cut into 12 slices about ⅜ inch thick.

2. Top each slice with ½ teaspoon caviar or 1 curled strip of anchovy.

3. Dot each slice with a dab of yogurt. Allow 3 slices per serving.

43   MINI-LITE S'MORES

Prep: 1 minute   Cook: 45 seconds   Serves: 1
Calories per serving: 41

When the yen for something sweet hits, try 4 tiny bites of a favorite you may remember from childhood camping days.

4 **mini-bear graham crackers, or ½ regular graham cracker broken into 4 pieces**

4 **mini-marshmallows**
4 **semisweet chocolate morsels**

1. Set mini-graham crackers on a paper dish. Top each with a small marshmallow and press a chocolate morsel into each marshmallow.

2. Microwave on medium 45 seconds, until chocolate is shiny and marshmallows are beginning to melt. Eat warm.

44   GARLIC-HERB OAT BITES

Prep: 2 minutes   Cook: 22 minutes   Makes: 3 cups
Calories per ¼ cup: 53

Crunch away and know that you are adding health while lowering weight.

3 cups cubed (½-inch) oat
    bran bread
2 tablespoons butter or
    margarine
1 garlic clove, crushed

1 teaspoon fines herbes or
    Italian herb mix
¾ teaspoon salt
⅛ teaspoon cayenne

1. Preheat oven to 300°. Spread bread cubes on a 10 x 15-inch jelly-roll pan.

2. In a small saucepan, melt butter or margarine. Add garlic, herbs, salt, and cayenne. Stir well and cook over low heat 2 minutes.

3. Drizzle seasoned butter over bread and toss. Bake 20 minutes, stirring every 10 minutes. Store in an airtight container.

SPREADS

Tasty spreads are handy toppings for a lettuce leaf, a thin slice of bread, a rice cracker, or a tomato slice. Make a batch to store in the refrigerator, for when the munchies call. Use a tablespoon at a time. These average about 18 calories a tablespoon, as compared with, say, peanut butter at 94 calories per tablespoon.

45   FIVE-SPICE CHEESE SPREAD

Prep: 2 minutes   Cook: none   Serves: 8
Calories per serving: 23

Invest in a jar of Chinese five-spice powder, or combine equal parts of cinnamon, ginger, cloves, nutmeg, and star anise and grind in a coffee mill. Great with poultry, too.

1 cup smooth low-fat cottage
    cheese
1½ teaspoons Chinese five-spice
    powder

1½ tablespoons unsweetened
    applesauce

Combine all ingredients. Place in a covered jar and refrigerate.

46   CLAM SPREAD
Prep: 3 minutes   Cook: none   Makes: 1½ cups
Calories per tablespoon: 12

1   **7-ounce can minced clams**
½   **cup low-fat ricotta cheese**
½   **teaspoon lemon juice**

⅛   **teaspoon pepper**
⅛   **teaspoon garlic powder**

Drain clams. Mix well with remaining ingredients. Store in covered container in refrigerator.

47   HERBED COTTAGE CHEESE
Prep: 3 minutes   Cook: none   Makes: 1¼ cups
Calories per tablespoon: 10

Flavorful cheese spread—super for topping radish or cucumber slices or Sesame Crackers (page 16).

¼   **cup plain low-fat yogurt**
1   **cup low-fat cottage cheese**
1   **tablespoon chopped parsley**
1   **tablespoon minced chives**

1   **teaspoon tarragon**
½   **teaspoon salt**
    Dash of pepper

1. In a small bowl or a blender, combine all ingredients. Blend with a fork or in blender until smooth.

2. Place in a bowl. Cover and refrigerate until chilled.

48   TOMATO AND MOZZARELLA CHEESE SPREAD
Prep: 1½ minutes   Cook: none   Makes: 1 cup
Calories per tablespoon: 8

This tasty snack has satisfying contrasts of flavor texture and color—and good food values as well.

2   **tomatoes, medium-ripe,**
    roughly cut up
2   **ounces part-skim mozzarella**
    cheese

1   **teaspoon chopped basil**
    leaves
    Salt and pepper

In a blender or small food processor, combine tomatoes, cheese, and basil. Puree until fairly smooth. Season with salt and pepper.

49   SHRIMP SPREAD ON ENDIVE LEAVES

Prep: 3 minutes   Cook: none   Serves: 4
Calories per serving: 30

Combine leftover cooked shrimp, a little tomato sauce, horseradish, and lemon juice for a tasty spread to serve on endive leaves.

½ **cup cooked and shelled shrimp**
2 **tablespoons light ketchup**
1 **teaspoon prepared white horseradish**

1 **teaspoon lemon juice**
8 **Belgian endive leaves, or 2 celery ribs cut into 4 pieces**

In a food processor or blender, combine shrimp, ketchup, horseradish, and lemon juice. Puree until fairly smooth, about 1 minute. Serve on endive "spoons" or celery pieces.

Chapter 2

Soups and Sandwiches

Like a happy couple or a pair of good friends, soups and sandwiches complement each other while maintaining their individual identities.

Soups are great diet meals, high in water content, with an infinite variety of flavors and textures. They are comfort foods. Choose the best ingredients of the season to make soups with year-round variety. Make soup your meal, or a light starter.

The texture of your soup may be smooth, thickened with vegetable puree rather than heavy cream or sauces, or it may be thick with chunks of vegetables or pasta, beans, rice, fish, or poultry. Soup may be pastel in hue, a riot of bright colors, or ruddy with tomato or beets. Enjoy soup hearty and hot in the winter, cool and refreshing in the summer. Calories range from 16 for Chicken Broth and 37 for light and tasty Gingered Watercress Soup with crunchy chestnuts, to 147 for a Curried Tuna Bisque and 179 for Chicken in a Pot, with high points for flavor and satisfaction, both meals in themselves.

Here is also a whole new world of sandwiches, to accompany the soups or stand on their own. The fillings are vegetables and beans, as well as meat, fish, and poultry. The style is often open-face and thin, closer to Danish smørrebrød than New York deli fare. Some are low enough in calories so that you can enjoy two at about 300 calories—the cost of one ordinary sandwich.

In making your own sandwich variations, switch to purchased reduced-calorie mayonnaise at about 50 calories a tablespoon, instead of 101 for regular mayonnaise. Or make our Low-Fat Dressing, at only 18 calories per tablespoon, which is high in protein instead of fat. Use this as a spread for bread in place of mayonnaise or butter.

Grill your beefburger on a slice of bread for juicy new flavor, and skip the cheese topping. Be generous with mustard, instead. Enjoy a turkey burger made with ground turkey or use ground chicken meat. Cold leftover fish makes a great sandwich; beans mash into a new kind of burger, high in fiber. Enjoy hot sandwiches in zap time, in a choice of microwave-heated specialties.

SOUPS

---

50 CHICKEN BROTH

Prep: 12 minutes   Cook: 1½ hours   Serves: 10; makes 2 quarts
Calories: 16 per ¾-cup serving

This heavenly broth can be savored on its own, but it provides the base for many other soups and recipes. To store for easy usage, freeze some of soup in 1- to 2-cup containers, and use some to fill ¼-cup ice cube molds.

1 4-pound stewing hen or chicken, quartered, with giblets
3 quarts cold water
1 large onion, stuck with 5 whole cloves
3 celery ribs with leaves, halved

1 large carrot, peeled and thickly sliced
1 medium parsnip, peeled and quartered
4 large parsley sprigs with stems attached
8 peppercorns
Salt

1. Rinse chicken and giblets and place in a stockpot. Discard liver or reserve for another use. Bring to a boil over medium heat, skimming several times to remove foam from surface.

2. Add onion with cloves, celery, carrot, parsnip, parsley, and peppercorns. Reduce heat to medium-low and simmer, partially covered, 1½ hours.

3. Drain broth into a large bowl or clean pot. Refrigerate, then scrape congealed fat off top of soup. Store in covered container in refrigerator for up to 3 days, or freeze for up to 3 months. If using as soup, season with salt before serving.

---

51 LEMONY DILLED BEET SOUP

Prep: 4 minutes   Cook: 5 minutes   Serves: 4
Calories per serving: 65

Equally good hot or cold, this tangy soup is popular all year.

1 16-ounce can sliced beets, liquid reserved
1 10¾-ounce can beef broth
1¼ cups water
2 tablespoons minced fresh dill, or 1½ teaspoons dried dill weed

2 tablespoons fresh lemon juice
1 teaspoon grated lemon zest
1 tablespoon sugar
Salt and pepper
4 teaspoons low-fat sour cream
Dill sprigs, for garnish

1. Place beets and half their liquid in a food processor or blender. Puree until smooth. Transfer to a nonreactive medium saucepan.

2. Add beef broth, water, and 1 tablespoon minced fresh dill or ¾ teaspoon dried. Simmer 5 minutes.

3. Add lemon juice, lemon zest, sugar, and remaining dill. Stir to dissolve sugar. Season with salt and pepper. Ladle at once into 4 soup bowls and garnish each with 1 teaspoon sour cream and a sprig of dill, or refrigerate until chilled before serving.

52   CHILLED FRUIT SOUP
Prep: 3 minutes   Cook: 5 minutes   Chill: 1½ hours   Serves: 4
Calories per serving: 130

1 16-ounce can pitted sour cherries, liquid reserved	½ cup low-calorie cranberry juice
1 cinnamon stick	1 teaspoon sugar
2 whole cloves	4 dried apricots, quartered
½ cup orange juice	

1. Place liquid from can of cherries in a nonreactive medium saucepan. Add cinnamon stick and cloves. Simmer over medium heat 5 minutes. Remove from heat and let cool.

2. Stir orange juice, cranberry juice, and sugar into cherry juice. Add cherries and apricots. Cover and refrigerate until well chilled, at least 1½ hours.

53   FRESH ASPARAGUS SOUP
Prep: 2 minutes   Cook: 4 minutes   Serves: 4
Calories per serving: 41

This is a smooth, luxurious soup that has a deceptive richness.

¾ pound fresh asparagus	¼ teaspoon black pepper
5 cups water	Dash of cayenne
1 teaspoon salt	2 tablespoons Light Crème
1½ cups chicken broth	Fraîche (page 143) or plain low-fat yogurt

1. Break tough ends off asparagus. Cut remainder into 1-inch pieces. In a large saucepan, bring water and salt to a boil over high heat. Add asparagus and cook until tender, 3 to 5 minutes. Drain into a colander set over a bowl. Measure out and reserve 2 cups cooking liquid.

2. Place asparagus and reserved cooking liquid in a food processor or blender. Puree until smooth. Pour puree into a medium saucepan. Stir in chicken broth, black pepper, and cayenne and bring to a boil. Remove from heat and stir in Light Crème Fraîche or yogurt.

54 CHICKEN IN A POT

Prep: 10 minutes   Cook: 30 minutes   Serves: 4
Calories per serving: 179

Here's a hearty soup that's a meal in a bowl.

4 7-ounce chicken breast halves, skinned	1 medium white turnip
3 cups chicken broth	1 bay leaf
2 medium celery ribs	4 parsley sprigs plus 2 tablespoons minced parsley
1 large carrot	
1 medium leek, well rinsed	Salt and pepper

1. Place chicken breasts in a large saucepan or flameproof casserole. Add chicken broth and bring to a boil. Reduce heat to medium-low, cover, and simmer 10 minutes.

2. Meanwhile, cut celery in half crosswise; then split each half lengthwise. Peel carrot; cut in same fashion as celery. Trim leek to 5 or 6 inches of white and tender green and quarter lengthwise. Peel and quarter turnip.

3. Add vegetables, bay leaf, and parsley sprigs to chicken broth. Simmer 20 minutes, or until chicken is white throughout but still moist and vegetables are tender. Discard parsley sprigs and bay leaf. Season with salt and pepper.

4. To serve, place 1 chicken breast half and a portion of each vegetable in each of 4 soup plates. Garnish with minced parsley and serve with a knife, fork, and spoon.

55 CHINESE EGG DROP SOUP

Prep: 2 minutes   Cook: 5 minutes   Serves: 4
Calories per serving: 34

3 cups chicken broth	½ teaspoon soy sauce
2 teaspoons cornstarch	2 tablespoons minced scallion greens
2 slices fresh ginger	
1 medium egg, beaten	

1. Skim any fat from chicken broth. In a small bowl, combine 3 tablespoons chicken broth with cornstarch. Stir to blend well.

2. Place remaining chicken broth in a medium saucepan. Add ginger and bring to a boil. Stir in cornstarch mixture and cook, stirring, until soup thickens slightly, about 1 minute.

3. Gradually add egg to boiling soup in a thin stream, stirring soup with a fork to break up strands of egg. Add soy sauce and scallion; discard ginger and serve.

56   GAZPACHO

Prep: 10 minutes   Cook: none   Chill: 1 hour   Serves: 4
Calories per serving: 71

3   medium tomatoes (1 pound)
1   medium cucumber
1   medium green bell pepper
2   cups tomato juice
½   cup coarsely chopped red
      onion

1   garlic clove, crushed
2   tablespoons lemon juice
½   teaspoon salt
¼   teaspoon pepper
3   dashes of hot pepper sauce

1. Cut 2 tomatoes into quarters; chop 1 tomato. Peel and seed cucumber. Cut half into chunks; finely dice remainder. Cut half of green pepper into chunks; finely dice remainder.

2. In a blender or food processor, combine quartered tomatoes, cucumber and pepper chunks, tomato juice, red onion, garlic, lemon juice, salt, pepper, and hot sauce. Puree until smooth. Transfer to a covered container and refrigerate until chilled, at least 1 hour.

3. To serve, place one fourth of diced cucumber and green pepper and chopped tomato in each of 4 soup bowls. Ladle chilled gazpacho over vegetables. Serve chilled.

57   HEARTY FISH CHOWDER

Prep: 10 minutes   Cook: 13 to 20 minutes   Serves: 4
Calories per serving: 145

Enjoy a delicious soup meal with this zesty chowder, a salad, and some fresh fruit for dessert.

1   cup bottled clam juice
1   cup tomato juice
1   cup water
¼   cup dry white wine
2   scallions, thinly sliced
1   garlic clove, minced
4   ounces fennel bulb or
      2 celery ribs, cut into
      ½-inch dice
1   medium carrot, cut into
      ½-inch dice

1   4-ounce red potato,
      scrubbed, cut into ½-inch
      dice
½   teaspoon fennel seeds
¼   teaspoon saffron threads,
      crumbled, or paprika
¾   pound skinless, boneless
      cod or halibut, cut into
      ¾-inch dice
Salt and pepper

1. In a large saucepan, combine clam juice, tomato juice, water, wine, scallions, garlic, fennel, carrot, potato, fennel seeds, and saffron. Bring to a boil, reduce heat to a simmer, and cook, partially covered, until fennel, carrot, and potato are tender, 10 to 15 minutes.

2. Add fish and simmer until just opaque throughout, 3 to 5 minutes. Season with salt and pepper.

58   CREAMY CORN AND CLAM CHOWDER

Prep: 5 minutes   Cook: 10 minutes   Serves: 4
Calories per serving: 138

1 tablespoon butter or
   margarine
½ cup finely chopped onion
1 tablespoon flour
1 7½-ounce can minced clams,
   liquid reserved

1 cup fresh, canned, or frozen
   corn kernels
1½ cups skim milk
¼ teaspoon thyme
⅛ teaspoon cayenne

1. Melt butter in a medium saucepan over medium heat. Add onion and cook until soft and translucent, about 3 minutes.

2. Stir flour into butter. Cook, stirring, for 1 minute to make a roux. Add reserved liquid from clams and stir well to combine with roux. Add corn, clams, skim milk, thyme, and cayenne. Simmer 5 minutes.

59   ESCAROLE SOUP

Prep: 5 minutes   Cook: 10 minutes   Serves: 4
Calories per serving: 44

3 cups chicken broth
½ head escarole (½ pound),
   shredded
1 medium egg

1 tablespoon grated Parmesan
   cheese
   Salt and pepper

1. In a medium saucepan, bring broth to a boil over medium-high heat. Add escarole and cook for 2 minutes, until just tender.

2. Reduce heat to medium-low. Beat egg and cheese together in a cup. Add to broth in a slow, thin stream, beating with a fork to break up shreds. Season with salt and pepper. Simmer for 1 minute.

60   FRESH MUSHROOM BISQUE

Prep: 10 minutes   Cook: 11 minutes   Serves: 4
Calories per serving: 79

2 teaspoons butter or
   margarine
1 medium onion, chopped
½ pound mushrooms, coarsely
   chopped
1 cup chicken broth

1½ cups skim milk
¼ teaspoon thyme
¼ teaspoon salt
⅛ teaspoon pepper
   Pinch of nutmeg

1. In a large nonstick skillet, melt butter over medium heat. Add onion and cook until softened but not browned, about 3 minutes. Add mushrooms and cook, stirring, 3 minutes longer.

2. Scrape onion and mushrooms into a food processor or blender. Add chicken broth and ½ cup milk and puree until smooth. Return to saucepan. Add remaining milk, thyme, salt, pepper, and nutmeg. Simmer 5 minutes. Serve hot.

61 CURRIED TUNA BISQUE
Prep: 10 minutes   Cook: 8 minutes   Serves: 4
Calories per serving: 147

½ cup chicken broth
2 scallions, sliced
2 celery ribs, sliced
1 plum tomato, peeled,
   seeded, and diced
½ tart green apple, peeled and
   diced

1 tablespoon curry powder
2 3½-ounce cans tuna packed
   in water, drained
2½ cups skim milk
1 teaspoon lemon juice
½ teaspoon salt
¼ teaspoon pepper

1. In a medium saucepan, combine chicken broth, scallions, celery, tomato, and apple. Cook over medium heat, stirring occasionally, 7 minutes. Add curry powder and cook 1 minute longer.

2. Place mixture in a food processor or blender. Add 1 can of tuna and half the milk. Puree until smooth.

3. Scrape puree back into saucepan. Add remaining can of tuna and milk and stir to separate tuna into chunks. Season with lemon juice, salt, and pepper. Heat to just below a boil and serve hot.

62 ZUCCHINI BISQUE
Prep: 10 minutes   Cook: 10 to 15 minutes   Serves: 4
Calories per serving: 58

2 medium zucchini (1 pound
   total)
1 large leek (½ pound)
3 cups chicken broth

¼ cup buttermilk or plain low-
   fat yogurt
Salt and pepper
1 tablespoon chopped parsley

1. Trim zucchini and cut into thick slices. Trim leek to remove root and very tough green leaves near top. Split lengthwise almost to root end and rinse very well in several changes of cold water; drain. Cut leek into thick slices.

2. In a medium saucepan, bring chicken broth to a boil. Add zucchini and leek. Reduce heat to medium-low and simmer, partially covered, until vegetables are tender, 10 to 15 minutes.

3. Transfer to a food processor or blender and puree until smooth. Return to saucepan and stir in buttermilk or yogurt. Season with salt and pepper. Heat until hot but do not boil. Serve, garnished with a sprinkling of parsley.

63 ONION SOUP
Prep: 3 minutes   Cook: 10 to 15 minutes   Serves: 4
Calories per serving: 73

1 **pound onions, thinly sliced**
3 **cups beef broth**
2 **teaspoons Worcestershire sauce**

¼ **cup finely diced low-fat Gruyère or Swiss cheese**

1. In a medium saucepan, combine onions and beef broth. Simmer until onion is soft and translucent, 10 to 15 minutes.

2. Stir Worcestershire sauce into hot soup. Ladle into bowls and sprinkle 1 tablespoon cheese over each serving.

64 GINGERED WATERCRESS SOUP
Prep: 4 minutes   Cook: 3 minutes   Serves: 4
Calories per serving: 37

1 **large bunch watercress (4 ounces)**
4 **cups chicken broth**
1 **teaspoon minced fresh ginger**

1 **6-ounce can sliced water chestnuts, rinsed and drained**

1. Rinse watercress and discard tough stems. In a medium saucepan, bring chicken broth to a boil over medium-high heat. Add watercress and ginger. Cook until watercress is wilted but still bright green, about 2 minutes.

2. Add water chestnuts and serve at once.

65 HERBED TOMATO SOUP WITH YOGURT
Prep: 5 minutes   Cook: none   Chill: 1 hour   Serves: 4
Calories per serving: 75

3 **cups vegetable tomato juice**
1 **tablespoon chopped fresh basil, or ½ teaspoon dried**
1 **teaspoon chopped fresh oregano, or ½ teaspoon dried**

1 **tablespoon chopped chives**
1 **tablespoon chopped parsley**
1 **garlic clove, crushed**
½ **cup plain low-fat yogurt Salt and pepper**

1. Place all ingredients except salt and pepper in a blender or food processor. Blend for 30 seconds.

2. Transfer to a covered container and refrigerate until chilled, at least 1 hour. Season with salt and pepper before serving.

66 MANHATTAN CLAM CHOWDER
Prep: 10 minutes   Cook: 9 to 12 minutes   Serves: 4
Calories per serving: 91

1 16-ounce can tomatoes,
    crushed, juice reserved
1½ cups water
2 medium celery ribs,
    chopped (1¼ cups)
1 medium onion, chopped
    (⅔ cup)
1 medium red potato (4
    ounces), finely diced

⅓ cup finely diced green bell
    pepper
¼ teaspoon thyme leaves
1 7½-ounce can minced clams,
    liquid reserved
1½ teaspoons lemon juice
    Salt and pepper

1. In a medium nonreactive saucepan, combine tomatoes with their juice, water, celery, onion, potato, bell pepper, and thyme. Bring to a boil, reduce heat to medium, and simmer uncovered until vegetables are just tender, 7 to 10 minutes.

2. Add clams with their liquid and lemon juice. Simmer 2 minutes. Season with salt and pepper and serve hot.

67 GARDEN VEGETABLE SOUP
Prep: 15 minutes   Cook: 20 to 25 minutes   Serves: 4
Calories per serving: 64

Here's a soup that's loaded with nutrition but lean on calories. Serve with two Sesame Crackers (page 16) for a fine lunch.

2 medium celery ribs with
    leaves, diced (1⅓ cups)
1 large onion, chopped (1 cup)
1 large carrot, diced (⅔ cup)
1 small zucchini, diced(½ cup)
1 medium red potato
    (4 ounces), diced
1 garlic clove, minced

2½ cups chicken broth
½ teaspoon salt
¼ teaspoon pepper
2 tablespoons chopped fresh
    dill, or 2 teaspoons dried
    dill weed
1 tablespoon minced parsley

1. In a large saucepan, combine celery, onion, carrot, zucchini, potato, garlic, chicken broth, salt, pepper, and 1 tablespoon dill. Bring to a boil, reduce heat to medium-low, and simmer, partially covered, until vegetables are tender, 20 to 25 minutes.

2. Ladle into 4 soup bowls and sprinkle with remaining dill and the parsley. Serve hot.

68 SIMPLY SCALLOP SOUP
Prep: 10 minutes   Cook: 12 minutes   Serves: 4
Calories per serving: 67

2 medium celery ribs, diced
  (1 cup)
1 medium carrot, scraped and
  diced (½ cup)
4 shallots or 1 small red onion,
  minced (½ cup)
1 bay leaf

2½ cups water
½ pound bay scallops or
  quartered sea scallops
1½ tablespoons lemon juice
½ teaspoon salt
⅛ teaspoon pepper
¼ cup minced parsley

1. In a medium saucepan, combine celery, carrot, shallots, bay leaf, and water. Simmer over medium heat, covered, until carrots are tender, about 10 minutes.

2. Add scallops, lemon juice, salt, and pepper. Simmer, covered, 2 minutes, or until scallops are just opaque throughout.

3. Remove bay leaf and ladle soup into bowls. Garnish each serving with 1 tablespoon minced parsley.

SANDWICHES

69 BEANBURGER MELT
Prep: 5 minutes   Cook: 4 to 5 minutes   Serves: 4
Calories per serving: 134

1 cup canned kidney beans,
  drained and rinsed
2 tablespoons minced onion
1 tablespoon finely chopped
  green bell pepper

1 tablespoon ketchup
1 teaspoon Dijon mustard
2 English muffins
4 teaspoons shredded low-
  calorie American cheese

1. In a medium bowl, mash beans coarsely. Add onion, green pepper, ketchup, and mustard. Blend well.

2. Split each English muffin in half and toast in toaster.

3. Preheat broiler. Spread one fourth of bean mixture over each English muffin half. Set 4 to 6 inches from heat and broil 3 minutes, until beans are hot and bubbly.

4. Sprinkle cheese over muffins and return to broiler 1 to 2 minutes, until cheese melts. Serve hot.

70 DEVILED EGG SALAD ON RYE TOAST

Prep: 5 minutes   Cook: 12 minutes   Serves: 4
Calories per serving: 142

3 eggs
1 medium celery rib, finely
    diced (½ cup)
2 tablespoons reduced-calorie
    mayonnaise

¼ teaspoon powdered mustard
⅛ teaspoon salt
    Several dashes of cayenne
4 thin slices rye bread

1. Put eggs in a small saucepan and add cold water to cover by 1 inch. Set over medium-low heat and cook 12 minutes, or until eggs are just hard-cooked. Drain and cool briefly in a bowl of cold water. Peel eggs at once. If not using immediately, store peeled eggs in refrigerator in bowl of cold water to cover for up to 2 days.

2. In a medium bowl, mash eggs with a fork. Add celery, mayonnaise, mustard, salt, and cayenne. Mix to blend well.

3. Toast bread in toaster. Divide egg mixture into 4 equal parts. Spread 1 portion of deviled egg salad over each slice of toast.

71 CHEESE PUFF

Prep: 4 minutes   Cook: 10 minutes   Serves: 2
Calories per serving: 141

1 medium egg
1 1-ounce slice low-fat Swiss
    cheese, cut up
1 scallion, quartered

¼ teaspoon salt
⅛ teaspoon pepper
    Dash of hot pepper sauce
2 slices white toast

1. Preheat oven to 375°. Break egg into blender or food processor. Add cheese, scallion, salt, pepper, and hot sauce. Whirl briefly to chop scallion and blend egg with cheese.

2. Spoon egg mixture onto toast, dividing evenly. Spread almost to edges.

3. Place on baking sheet and bake for 10 minutes, or until puffed and golden. Serve immediately.

MICROWAVE CHEESE PUFF

Follow directions for Cheese Puff through step 2. Place bread slices on a microwavable plate and cover with a glass bowl. Microwave at 70 percent power for 1½ minutes, or until puffed. Serve immediately.

72   TARRAGON CHICKEN DIJON ON SPROUTED WHEAT BREAD

Prep: 3 minutes   Cook: none   Serves: 1
Calories per serving: 167

2 teaspoons low-fat cottage cheese
1 teaspoon Dijon mustard
½ teaspoon tarragon
1 slice sprouted wheat bread

2 thin slices cooked chicken (2 ounces total)
Salt and pepper
4 thin strips red bell pepper

1. In a small bowl or cup, blend together cottage cheese, mustard, and tarragon. Spread over bread.

2. Place chicken slices on top and season lightly with salt and pepper. Garnish sandwich with red pepper strips.

73   BAGEL STRETCH

Prep: 4 minutes   Cook: 1 minute   Serves: 2
Calories per serving: 148

Share a bagel with a friend and enjoy a chewy, crunchy sandwich, even on a diet.

1 bagel
2 ounces low-fat cream cheese
2 tablespoons diced red radishes

2 tablespoons diced green bell pepper
1 tablespoon minced chives

1. Split bagel in half and toast in toaster. Set halves aside on 2 lunch plates.

2. Blend together cream cheese, radishes, bell pepper, and chives. Spread half of cream cheese salad over each bagel half.

74   TURKEY BURGER HEROS

Prep: 4 minutes   Cook: 11 to 12 minutes   Serves: 4
Calories per serving: 203

¾ pound ground turkey
¼ cup minced onion
1 tablespoon ketchup
1 tablespoon Dijon mustard
1 tablespoon dry sherry

¼ teaspoon salt
⅛ teaspoon pepper
2 French bread rolls, split in half

1. Preheat broiler. In a medium bowl, combine turkey, onion, ketchup, mustard, sherry, salt, and pepper. Mix until well blended.

2. Divide turkey mixture into 4 equal parts. Form each portion into an oval patty, roughly the shape of the French roll and about ½ inch thick.

3. Broil turkey burgers 4 to 6 inches from heat, turning once, until browned outside and cooked through but still juicy inside, about 5 minutes per side.

4. Set French roll halves under hot broiler until lightly toasted, 1 to 2 minutes. Top each roll half with a turkey burger.

75   BEEFBURGER ON TOAST

Prep: 4 minutes   Cook: 5 minutes   Serves: 4
Calories per serving: 218

¾ **pound ground round**
2 **tablespoons red pepper relish**
¼ **teaspoon salt**
⅛ **teaspoon pepper**

4 **slices firm-textured white bread**
2 **tablespoons deli-style mustard**

1. In a small bowl, combine beef, pepper relish, salt, and pepper. Mix until well blended.

2. Toast bread in toaster. Spread 1½ teaspoons mustard over each slice. Divide beef mixture into fourths and spread one portion over each slice of bread, covering to edges.

3. Preheat broiler. Set beefburgers 4 to 6 inches from heat and broil until browned outside and cooked through but still juicy, about 5 minutes.

76   FISH FILLET SANDWICH

Prep: 4 minutes   Cook: 2 minutes   Serves: 1
Calories per serving: 138

If you have any leftover white fish fillet—baked, steamed, broiled, or microwaved—feel free to use that instead of the flounder prepared here in step 1.

1 **teaspoon Dijon mustard**
1 **teaspoon plain low-fat yogurt**
1 **3-ounce flounder fillet**
1 **slice white bread**

1 **arugula or Boston lettuce leaf**
1 **tablespoon minced parsley**
1 **lemon wedge**

1. Mix together mustard and yogurt. Spread over fish. Place on microwavable plate and microwave on high 1 minute. Let stand 1 minute longer.

2. Toast bread and place arugula or lettuce on it. Top with flounder fillet and garnish with minced parsley. Serve lemon wedge on side to squeeze over fish, if desired.

77   PROVENÇALE HERO
Prep: 10 minutes   Cook: none   Marinate: 2 hours   Serves: 4
Calories per serving: 141

This sandwich is great for picnics or any take-along lunch. It is prepared ahead, and the salad-like filling moistens the bread as it stands.

1 12-ounce loaf French bread, about 12 inches long
1 large tomato, diced (½ cup)
1 small cucumber, thinly sliced (⅔ cup)
4 black olives, sliced
½ cup diced red or green bell pepper
4 flat anchovy fillets, rinsed and patted dry
¼ cup Light French Dressing (page 140) or bottled

1. Cut top off bread loaf; set aside. Scoop and pull out soft center of bread. Reserve for crumbs or discard.

2. In a small bowl, combine tomato, cucumber, black olives, bell pepper, and anchovies. Add French dressing and toss to coat well. Spoon salad into hollowed-out bread loaf.

3. Place top back on bread and wrap loaf well in plastic wrap. Set aside at room temperature for at least 2 and up to 4 hours. Before serving, cut into 4 equal portions.

78   TOMATO AND MOZZARELLA SANDWICH WITH BASIL AND BALSAMIC VINEGAR
Prep: 5 minutes   Cook: 2 minutes   Serves: 4
Calories per serving: 147

4 1-ounce slices Italian bread, cut about ¾ inch thick
1 garlic clove, cut in half
2 teaspoons extra-virgin olive oil
4 ½-inch-thick large tomato slices
4 teaspoons shredded fresh basil, or ½ teaspoon dried
Salt and pepper
2 teaspoons balsamic vinegar
4 ½-ounce slices mozzarella cheese

1. Preheat broiler. Toast bread under broiler for 30 to 60 seconds, or toast in toaster. Rub top sides of each slice with cut garlic. Brush each slice with ½ teaspoon olive oil.

2. Place a slice of tomato on each piece of garlic toast. Sprinkle 1 teaspoon basil over each slice of tomato and season with salt and pepper. Drizzle ½ teaspoon balsamic vinegar over each sandwich.

3. Top each sandwich with a slice of mozzarella cheese. Set 4 to 6 inches from heat and broil until cheese just melts, 1 to 2 minutes.

79 ASPARAGUS RAFT
Prep: 5 minutes   Cook: none   Serves: 1
Calories per serving: 123

1 teaspoon mustard
1 teaspoon reduced-calorie
   mayonnaise
½ teaspoon lemon juice
1 thin 4-inch-square slice
   pumpernickel bread

1 lettuce leaf
5 cooked asparagus spears,
   fresh, frozen, or canned
1 cherry tomato, cut into 3
   slices
   Salt and pepper

1. Blend together mustard, mayonnaise, and lemon juice. Spread over pumpernickel bread. Place lettuce leaf on top.

2. Trim asparagus spears to 4 inches, if necessary. Arrange on top of bread and set tomato slices on top. Season with salt and pepper.

80 APPLE CHEDDAR MELT
Prep: 4 minutes   Cook: 1½ minutes   Serves: 4
Calories per serving: 170

The microwave oven is a great tool for dieters. When making sandwiches, though, be sure not to overcook them, because the bread can become dry and tough.

1 medium apple (6 ounces)
3 ounces low-fat cheddar
   cheese
4 teaspoons reduced-calorie
   mayonnaise

4 thin slices pumpernickel
   bread

1. Quarter apple and remove core but do not peel. Cut each apple quarter into 3 thin slices.

2. Cut cheddar cheese into thin slices and then into strips, so they can be used to cover bread.

3. Spread 1 teaspoon mayonnaise over each slice of bread. Arrange one fourth of apple slices over each slice. Top with cheese strips.

4. Place bread slices on a microwavable paper towel on a plate and cook at 70 percent power 1½ minutes, or until cheese melts. Repeat with remaining sandwiches.

81   CHILI IN A PITA
Prep: 5 minutes   Cook: 45 seconds   Serves: 1
Calories per serving: 182

Here's a lot of sandwich for very few calories.

1   6-inch pita bread
⅓   cup Chili con Carne with
      Vegetables (page 88)
2   tablespoons shredded
      lettuce

1   tablespoon chopped tomato
1   tablespoon chopped
      cucumber

1. Split pita partially open. Fill with chili. Wrap in microwavable paper towel and set on a plate. Microwave at 70 percent power 45 seconds, or until hot.

2. Remove sandwich from microwave. Top chili with shredded lettuce, chopped tomato, and cucumber.

82   SAUERKRAUT AND SMOKED TURKEY SANDWICH
Prep: 7 minutes   Cook: none   Serves: 4
Calories per serving: 157

1   cup sauerkraut
½   medium apple, cored and
      coarsely chopped (⅓ cup)
½   teaspoon caraway seeds
2   scallions, thinly sliced

4   slices pumpernickel bread
4   1-ounce slices smoked
      turkey
4   teaspoons minced parsley

1. Drain sauerkraut well. Add apple, caraway seeds, and scallions. Blend well.

2. Place about ⅓ cup sauerkraut mixture on each slice of bread and spread to edges. Top each sandwich with a slice of smoked turkey and garnish with a sprinkling of parsley.

83   RATATOUILLE AND CHEESE MELT ON FRENCH BREAD
Prep: 3 minutes   Cook: 1 minute   Serves: 2
Calories per serving: 147

½   cup Ratatouille (page 104)
1   crisp French roll (3 ounces),
      halved lengthwise

2   tablespoons shredded low-
      fat mozzarella cheese

1. Spread ¼ cup ratatouille over each roll half. Sprinkle 1 tablespoon shredded cheese over each sandwich.

2. Place on a microwavable paper towel on a plate and microwave on high 1 minute, until sandwich is warm and cheese is melted.

84   CHICKEN FRANKS IN CABBAGE BLANKETS

Prep: 7 minutes   Cook: 6 to 7 minutes   Serves: 4
Calories per serving: 116

4 **large cabbage leaves**	4 **chicken frankfurters**
4 **teaspoons water**	4 **teaspoons mustard of choice**
Salt	4 **teaspoons relish**

1. Cut around core of cabbage to remove 4 nice whole leaves. Shave off ridge from back of each leaf. Place leaves on a microwavable plate, sprinkling them with water and seasoning them lightly with salt. Cover with a microwavable paper towel and microwave on high 3 minutes, or until leaves are wilted.

2. As soon as cabbage leaves are cool enough to handle, place a chicken frank near the base of each leaf. Spread 1 teaspoon mustard and 1 teaspoon relish over each frank. Turn up bottom of each cabbage leaf, fold in sides, and roll up to seal frank inside.

3. Place cabbage rolls on a plate, cover with plastic wrap, and microwave on high 3 to 4 minutes, or until hot throughout.

85   GRILLED COTTAGE CHEESE AND TOMATO SANDWICH

Prep: 3 minutes   Cook: 1 to 2 minutes   Serves: 1
Calories per serving: 105

Here's a low-calorie version of a grilled cheese and tomato sandwich that is surprisingly satisfying.

¼ **cup low-fat cottage cheese**	**Salt and pepper**
2 **tablespoons diced tomato**	1 **slice five-grain bread**
¼ **teaspoon fines herbes, or**	
⅛ teaspoon thyme and	
⅛ teaspoon basil	

1. Preheat broiler. In a small bowl, blend cottage cheese with diced tomato and fines herbes. Season with salt and pepper.

2. Spread cottage cheese mixture over bread, covering to edges. Set 4 to 6 inches from heat and broil 1 to 2 minutes, until bubbling and golden.

86   MUFFIN PIZZA MELT
Prep: 4 minutes   Cook: 2 to 3 minutes   Serves: 4
Calories per serving: 187

½ cup chunky tomato sauce
4 fork-split English muffins
½ teaspoon oregano
½ cup shredded low-fat
      mozzarella cheese
      (2 ounces)

4 teaspoons grated Parmesan
      cheese

1. Preheat broiler. Spread 1 tablespoon chunky tomato sauce over each English muffin half. Season evenly with oregano, crumbling leaves as you sprinkle.

2. Top each muffin with a sprinkling of 1 tablespoon mozzarella and ½ teaspoon Parmesan cheese.

3. Set pizza muffins 4 to 6 inches from heat and broil until cheese is melted and bubbling, 2 to 3 minutes.

87   HOT TUNA ON RYE
Prep: 5 minutes   Cook: 2 to 3 minutes   Serves: 4
Calories per serving: 176

1 7-ounce can water-packed
      tuna, drained
⅓ cup finely chopped onion,
      (½ medium)
⅓ cup finely diced red bell
      pepper (½ medium)

¼ cup reduced-calorie
      mayonnaise
⅛ teaspoon salt
      Dash of pepper
4 thin slices rye bread

1. In a medium bowl, combine tuna, onion, red pepper, mayonnaise, salt, and pepper. Mix until well blended.

2. Preheat broiler. Toast rye bread in toaster. Divide tuna mixture in 4 equal parts and spread 1 portion over each slice of toasted rye. Set 4 to 6 inches from heat and broil until hot and lightly browned at the edges, 2 to 3 minutes.

88 BARBECUED CHICKEN IN A BREAD BASKET

Prep: 4 minutes   Cook: 1 minute   Serves: 2
Calories per serving: 138

1 6-inch strip French bread	1 tablespoon barbecue sauce
3 ounces barbecued or roast chicken breast meat	½ cup shredded lettuce

1. Split bread strip in half horizontally. Scoop out soft inside part and reserve for crumbs or discard. Place chicken in hollow. Drizzle 1½ teaspoons sauce over each sandwich.

2. Place sandwiches, cut sides up, on a microwavable paper towel. Cover tops with plastic wrap. Microwave on medium (50 percent power) for 1 minute, or until warmed through.

3. Unwrap, sprinkle shredded lettuce over chicken, and serve hot.

89 GREEK SALAD-STUFFED PITAS

Prep: 5 minutes   Cook: none   Serves: 4
Calories per serving: 145

¾ cup diced cooked green beans	1 tablespoon extra-virgin olive oil
½ cup sliced cucumber	1 tablespoon chicken broth or water
½ cup diced tomato	
2 scallions, sliced	1½ tablespoons chopped fresh mint, or ¾ teaspoon dried
1⅓ cups shredded lettuce	¼ teaspoon salt
¼ cup crumbled feta cheese (1 ounce)	¼ teaspoon pepper
2 tablespoons red wine vinegar	4 small whole wheat pita pockets

1. In a medium bowl, combine green beans, cucumber, tomato, scallions, lettuce, and feta cheese.

2. In a small bowl, whisk together vinegar, oil, broth, mint, salt, and pepper. Pour over salad and toss to coat.

3. Split pita breads open at one end. Fill with Greek salad and serve at once.

SMØRREBRØD

These small, open-face sandwiches are virtually works of art in Denmark, where they are nibbled for lunch and for midafternoon snacks. These are all made on thin slices of bread, and some are so low in calories that you can allow yourself a selection of two.

---

90   SCRAMBLED EGG SANDWICH
Prep: 3 minutes   Cook: 1 minute   Serves: 1
Calories per serving: 243

1 whole medium egg
1 medium egg white
   Salt and pepper
   Dash of nutmeg
1 tablespoon skim milk

½ teaspoon butter or
   margarine, softened
2 thin square slices
   pumpernickel bread

1. In a small bowl, beat whole egg and egg white with salt and pepper to taste and nutmeg. Whisk in milk.

2. Rub a shallow 4-inch-square microwavable dish or shallow storage container with butter. Pour in eggs, cover with plastic wrap, and microwave at 70 percent power for about 1 minute, or until just set. If not set in center, stir eggs from center toward edge, rotate dish, and cook 30 seconds longer. Let stand for 30 seconds.

3. Set egg on bread. Cut in half and serve warm or at room temperature.

---

91   MARINATED MUSHROOM SANDWICH
Prep: 5 minutes   Marinate: 15 minutes   Cook: none   Serves: 1
Calories per serving: 117

2 large mushrooms (2 ounces)
¼ cup Light French Dressing
   (page 140) or bottled
1 thin 4-inch slice
   pumpernickel bread

1 tablespoon low-fat sour
   cream
2 strips red bell pepper

1. Trim off ends of mushroom stems. Wipe mushrooms with a damp paper towel and cut into thin slices. Place in a small bowl, add French dressing, and toss gently to coat. Let stand at room temperature, tossing occasionally, 15 minutes to 1 hour.

2. Remove mushrooms with a slotted spoon. Arrange slices decoratively on bread, overlapping as necessary. Top with a dollop of sour cream and garnish with red pepper strips.

92   PICKLED SHRIMP SANDWICH
Prep: 3 minutes   Cook: none   Serves: 1
Calories per serving: 145

1 **tablespoon reduced-calorie
     mayonnaise**
1 **thin 4-inch square black
     bread**

¼ **cup Pickled Shrimp
     (page 14)***
2 **fresh dill sprigs or parsley**

1. Spread mayonnaise over bread. Cut slice in half.

2. Arrange shrimp decoratively on bread pieces, overlapping slightly. Garnish with fresh dill.

*You can also make this sandwich with ordinary cooked shrimp, in which case flavor with a squeeze of lemon before garnishing with dill.

93   ASPARAGUS AND CHEESE SANDWICH
Prep: 3 minutes   Cook: none   Serves: 1
Calories per serving: 142

1 **thin 4-inch slice
     pumpernickel bread**
1 **teaspoon Dijon mustard**
1 **thin slice Alpine Lace cheese
     (¾ ounce)**

4 **cooked asparagus spears,
     fresh, frozen, or canned**
1 **lemon slice, halved**

1. Cut bread in half. Spread ½ teaspoon mustard over each piece. Cut cheese in half in same fashion as bread. Set cheese on bread.

2. Trim asparagus spears as necessary and arrange over cheese. Garnish sandwich with lemon slice halves.

94   SARDINES ON RYE DELI-STYLE
Prep: 4 minutes   Cook: none   Serves: 1
Calories per serving: 163

2 **teaspoons reduced-calorie
     mayonnaise**
1 **teaspoon Dijon mustard
     Dash of hot pepper sauce**
1 **thin slice rye bread**

1 **thin slice red onion, cut in
     half**
6 **small Brisling sardines, well
     drained**
1 **lemon wedge**

1. Combine mayonnaise, mustard, and hot sauce. Spread over rye bread. Cut bread in half.

2. Place one red onion slice half on each piece of bread. Arrange 3 sardines on top of each. Squeeze lemon over sardines before serving.

95 STRAWBERRY AND CREAM CHEESE SANDWICH

Prep: 3 minutes   Cook: none   Serves: 1
Calories per serving: 138

Here's a delightful tea sandwich, in the same vein as a date-nut and cream cheese sandwich—a real treat with a reasonable calorie count.

6 large strawberries
2 tablespoons whipped low-
     fat cream cheese

1 slice whole wheat bread

1. Hull strawberries and cut in half lengthwise.

2. Spread cream cheese over bread. Arrange strawberry halves decoratively over cream cheese, overlapping as necessary. Cut sandwich in half.

96 SMOKED TURKEY AND CRANBERRY SAUCE SANDWICH

Prep: 5 minutes   Cook: none   Serves: 2
Calories per serving: 128

1 tablespoon low-fat sour
     cream
1 teaspoon prepared white
     horseradish
2 thin slices black bread

2 1-ounce slices smoked
     turkey
4 teaspoons low-calorie whole
     cranberry sauce

1. Combine sour cream and horseradish. Spread over both slices of bread. Arrange turkey on bread. Cut each slice in half.

2. Top each piece of bread with 1 teaspoon cranberry sauce.

97 WATERCRESS AND SWISS SANDWICH

Prep: 4 minutes   Cook: none   Serves: 1
Calories per serving: 182

2 teaspoons reduced-calorie
     mayonnaise
2 teaspoons Dijon mustard

1 slice wheat bran bread
1 1-ounce slice Swiss cheese
4 watercress sprigs

1. Blend together mayonnaise and mustard. Spread over bread slice.

2. Place cheese on bread. If slice is larger than bread, fold edges under. Cut sandwich in half. Arrange 2 sprigs of watercress on top of each piece.

98   TUNA AND CUCUMBER SANDWICH ON RICE ROUNDS

Prep: 5 minutes   Cook: none   Serves: 4
Calories per serving: 153

The crispy rice cake, a dieter's lifesaver, makes an interesting base as a substitute for bread.

1   7-ounce can water-packed tuna, drained
1   medium cucumber, peeled, seeded, and cut into small dice (¾ cup)
1   tablespoon soy sauce
¼   cup reduced-calorie mayonnaise
4   rice cake rounds

1. Break up tuna and mix with cucumber. Add soy sauce and mayonnaise and mix well.

2. Spread one fourth of tuna-cucumber mixture over each rice cake. Serve at once.

Chapter 3

Chicken and Turkey: The Calorie Miser's Meats

From a dieter's point of view, the ideal chicken is built of breast meat only, and it's skinless. It is also a young bird. In a modest 3½-ounce portion, there is a difference of 50 calories between chicken with skin and without; another 10-calorie difference between light meat and dark. A broiler chicken portion of about ¼ pound boneless meat raw, about 3½ ounces cooked, adds up to a lean 166 calories. The same portion size, in roaster meat with skin on, adds up to 248 calories. What's more, the broiler light meat without skin has 31.5 grams of protein in a 3½-ounce portion, while the roaster has 27 grams of protein. You can readily see why we have used boneless breast of chicken, in sizes that come from young birds, about 4½ ounces per half-breast, as our standard.

If you love dark meat (and we agree, it is juicier and more flavorful) that difference comes to only about 10 calories per portion—if you remove the skin and pockets of fat. Removing the skin and fat is the larger calorie saving. Yes, chicken does brown without the skin, and it is juicy and tender if cooked to doneness, as directed—not overcooked.

Similar differentials apply to turkey meat. Turkey breast meat, available in the fresh meat case, uncooked, is lean and low in calories, delicious prepared as scallopini or rolled. And ground turkey—or ground chicken—is a light alternative to ground beef, at only 7 percent fat.

99   BROILED HERBED CHICKEN BREASTS

Prep: 5 minutes   Marinate: 30 minutes   Cook: 20 to 25 minutes   Serves: 4   Calories per serving: 212

2 **tablespoons white wine vinegar**	½ **teaspoon thyme**
2 **tablespoons extra-virgin olive oil**	½ **teaspoon salt**
½ **teaspoon tarragon**	¼ **teaspoon pepper**
	4 **7-ounce chicken breast halves, skinned**

1. In a medium bowl, combine vinegar, olive oil, tarragon, thyme, salt, and pepper. Pierce each chicken piece several times with a fork and add to bowl. Turn to coat. Marinate at room temperature, turning once or twice, 30 to 60 minutes.

2. Preheat broiler. Set chicken, bone side up, about 6 inches from heat and broil 10 minutes. Turn, baste with any marinade remaining in bowl, and broil 10 to 15 minutes longer, until chicken is white throughout but still moist.

100   CHICKEN PAPRIKASH

Prep: 10 minutes   Cook: 25 minutes   Serves: 4   Calories per serving: 242

Traditional in flavor and low in calories, this ruddy chicken dish is delicious with rice.

4 **4½-ounce skinless, boneless chicken breast halves**	2 **tablespoons imported sweet paprika**
Salt and pepper	1 **cup chicken broth**
1 **tablespoon olive oil**	2 **tablespoons plain low-fat yogurt**
2 **medium onions, sliced**	1 **tablespoon low-fat sour cream**
1 **garlic clove, minced**	
1 **tablespoon flour**	

1. Season chicken lightly with salt and pepper. Heat oil in a large nonstick skillet. Add chicken breasts and cook over medium-high heat, turning once, until lightly browned, 3 to 5 minutes. Remove chicken to a plate.

2. Add onions to skillet, reduce heat to medium, and cook until softened and translucent, about 3 minutes. Add garlic and cook 1 minute longer. Add flour and paprika. Cook, stirring constantly, 1½ minutes. Add chicken broth and bring to a boil, whisking occasionally.

3. Reduce heat to a simmer and return chicken to pan, along with any juices that have collected on plate. Simmer, partially covered, 10 minutes, or until chicken is white throughout but still moist.

4. Stir yogurt and sour cream into sauce. Season with salt and pepper. Cook until heated through, but do not allow to boil.

101 CHICKEN CACCIATORE

Prep: 20 minutes   Cook: 15 minutes   Serves: 4
Calories per serving: 226

1 pound skinless, boneless
    chicken breasts
Salt and pepper
1 tablespoon olive oil
¼ cup chicken broth
1 medium onion, chopped
½ medium green bell pepper,
    diced

¾ cup sliced mushrooms
1 garlic clove, minced
1 16-ounce can Italian-style
    tomatoes with puree
2 tablespoons dry white wine
¼ cup minced parsley
1 teaspoon basil
½ teaspoon oregano

1. Season chicken breasts lightly with salt and pepper. Heat olive oil in a large nonstick skillet over medium-high heat. Add chicken and sauté, turning once, until lightly browned, about 3 minutes. Remove chicken and set aside.

2. Add onion to skillet. Cook, stirring occasionally, until onion is softened and translucent, 2 to 3 minutes. Add pepper, mushrooms, and garlic; cook 3 minutes longer. Add tomatoes with puree and stir, breaking up tomatoes with spoon. Add wine, parsley, basil, and oregano.

3. Cut chicken into 1-inch dice and return to skillet, along with any juices that have collected. Reduce heat to medium-low. Simmer, uncovered, stirring occasionally, until chicken is just cooked through and sauce is thickened slightly, about 5 minutes. Season with salt and pepper before serving.

102 BAKED BARBECUED CHICKEN

Prep: 10 minutes   Cook: 1 hour   Serves: 4
Calories per serving: 270

1 tablespoon vegetable oil
1 medium onion, chopped
2 garlic cloves, minced
½ cup ketchup
¼ cup cider vinegar
1 tablespoon Worcestershire
    sauce

3 tablespoons brown sugar
1 tablespoon chili powder
1½ teaspoons cumin
½ teaspoon salt
⅛ to ¼ teaspoon cayenne
1 2½-pound chicken,
    quartered and skinned

1. Preheat oven to 350°. Heat oil in a nonreactive small saucepan. Add onion and cook over medium heat until softened, about 3 minutes. Add garlic and cook 1 minute longer. Add ketchup, vinegar, Worcestershire, brown sugar, chili powder, cumin, salt, and cayenne. Simmer barbecue sauce, stirring occasionally, 10 minutes.

2. Arrange chicken in a baking dish just large enough to hold pieces in a single layer. Pour barbecue sauce over chicken and bake uncovered about 45 minutes, until chicken is tender and white to the bone but still moist.

103 BROILED TARRAGON CHICKEN WITH WHITE WINE

Prep: 5 minutes   Marinate: 30 minutes   Cook: 20 to 25 minutes
Serves: 4   Calories per serving: 191

Use a dry white wine to marinate the chicken. A small (6-ounce) glass of it to sip at dinner will cost you only 80 calories.

¼ **cup dry white wine**
1 **tablespoon olive oil**
¾ **teaspoon tarragon**
½ **teaspoon salt**

¼ **teaspoon pepper**
4 **7-ounce chicken breast halves, skinned**

1. In a medium bowl, combine wine, olive oil, tarragon, salt, and pepper. Add chicken and turn to coat. Marinate at room temperature, turning once or twice, 30 to 60 minutes.

2. Preheat broiler. Set chicken, bone side up, about 6 inches from heat. Broil 10 minutes. Turn, baste with marinade, and broil 10 to 15 minutes longer, until chicken is white throughout but still moist.

104 CHICKEN BREASTS IN DIJON YOGURT SAUCE

Prep: 5 minutes   Cook: 20 to 25 minutes   Serves: 4
Calories per serving: 280

Dijon mustard and yogurt combine in a low-effort sauce that's high in flavor. Set off the tangy chicken with simply steamed zucchini or spinach.

1 **tablespoon vegetable oil**
4 **4½-ounce skinless, boneless chicken breast halves**
2 **medium onions, finely chopped (1 cup)**

2 **garlic cloves, minced**
1 **cup chicken broth**
2 **tablespoons Dijon mustard**
1 **cup plain low-fat yogurt**
  Salt and pepper

1. Heat oil in a large nonstick skillet. Add chicken breasts and cook over medium-high heat, turning once, until lightly browned, 2 to 3 minutes per side. Remove chicken to a plate and set aside.

2. Add onion and garlic to skillet and reduce heat to medium. If pan seems dry, add 1 to 2 tablespoons chicken broth. Cook until onion is translucent, about 3 minutes. Add chicken broth and bring to a boil. Whisk in mustard until blended.

3. Return chicken along with any juices on plate to skillet. Reduce heat to low, cover, and simmer 12 to 15 minutes, turning chicken once or twice, until white throughout but still moist. Transfer chicken to a heated platter and cover with foil to keep warm.

4. Boil sauce in skillet 2 to 3 minutes to reduce slightly. Put yogurt in a small bowl and gradually whisk in ⅓ cup hot sauce. Stir yogurt mixture into remaining sauce in skillet. Simmer until hot, about 1 minute, but do not let sauce boil, or yogurt will curdle. Season with salt and pepper. Pour sauce over chicken and serve.

105 BROILED DEVILED CHICKEN BREASTS

Prep: 5 minutes   Cook: 20 to 25 minutes   Serves: 4
Calories per serving: 214

2 tablespoons vegetable oil	¼ teaspoon hot pepper sauce
2 tablespoons water	Dash of Worcestershire
1 tablespoon cider vinegar	sauce
1 teaspoon chili powder	4 7-ounce chicken breast
½ teaspoon dry mustard	halves, skinned
½ teaspoon salt	

1. In a wide shallow bowl, combine oil, water, vinegar, chili powder, mustard, salt, hot sauce, and Worcestershire. Blend well. Add chicken pieces and turn to coat.

2. Preheat broiler. Set chicken, bone side up, about 6 inches from heat. Broil 10 minutes. Turn and baste with seasoned oil. Continue to broil 10 to 15 minutes, until chicken is white throughout but still moist.

106 BROILED CHICKEN BREASTS OREGANATA

Prep: 5 minutes   Cook: 20 to 25 minutes   Serves: 4
Calories per serving: 213

If you enjoy Italian flavors, try this recipe. Serve with a tossed green salad and a slice of toasted Italian bread for a simple and satisfying supper.

2 tablespoons olive oil	¼ teaspoon pepper
2 garlic cloves, crushed	4 7-ounce chicken breast
¾ teaspoon oregano	halves, skinned
½ teaspoon salt	

1. In a wide shallow bowl, combine olive oil, garlic, oregano, salt, and pepper. Dip chicken pieces in seasoned oil, turning to coat.

2. Preheat broiler. Set chicken, bone side up, about 6 inches from heat and broil 10 minutes. Turn, baste with seasoned oil, and broil 10 to 15 minutes, until chicken is white throughout but still moist.

107 CHICKEN FAJITAS

Prep: 8 minutes   Marinate: 1 hour   Cook: 8 to 12 minutes
Serves: 4   Calories per serving: 272

Here's a flavorful and tender grilled chicken set off with a tasty guacamole and served in a corn tortilla.

4 4½-ounce skinless, boneless, chicken breast halves	½ teaspoon thyme
	¼ teaspoon oregano
	¾ teaspoon salt
1 small onion, halved	¼ teaspoon pepper
2 garlic cloves, smashed	¼ teaspoon hot pepper sauce
⅓ cup orange juice	4 corn tortillas
1½ tablespoons white wine vinegar	¼ cup Guacamole (page 5)
	½ cup shredded lettuce

1. Cut each chicken breast lengthwise into 3 strips. Place in a medium bowl.

2. In a food processor or blender, combine onion, garlic, orange juice, vinegar, thyme, oregano, salt, pepper, and hot sauce. Puree until smooth. Pour over chicken in bowl; toss strips to coat. Cover and marinate, tossing occasionally, 1 to 2 hours at room temperature, or up to 12 hours refrigerated.

3. Prepare a hot fire in a grill or preheat broiler. Set chicken strips about 5 inches from heat and grill or broil, turning and basting with marinade several times, 8 to 12 minutes, or until just white throughout but still moist.

4. To serve, place 3 strips of grilled chicken on each tortilla. Top each with 1 tablespoon Guacamole and 2 tablespoons shredded lettuce, roll up, and eat.

108 CHINESE-STYLE BARBECUED CHICKEN

Prep: 15 minutes   Marinate: 30 minutes   Cook: 25 minutes
Serves: 4   Calories per serving: 227

1 2½-pound chicken, quartered	2 tablespoons rice wine vinegar or cider vinegar
1 tablespoon peanut oil	2 tablespoons soy sauce
2 garlic cloves, minced	1 teaspoon honey
2 tablespoons dry sherry	Dash of cayenne

1. Rinse chicken pieces and pat dry. In a medium bowl, combine oil, garlic, sherry, vinegar, soy sauce, honey, and cayenne. Stir to mix well. Add chicken pieces and turn to coat. Marinate at room temperature, turning once or twice, 30 to 60 minutes.

2. Prepare a medium-hot fire in a grill or preheat broiler. Set chicken about 6 inches from heat and grill or broil, turning and basting with marinade every 10 minutes, until browned outside and white to the bone but still moist, about 25 minutes.

109 CHICKEN SCALLOPINI WITH MUSHROOMS AND VERMOUTH

Prep: 10 minutes   Cook: 8 to 9 minutes   Serves: 4
Calories per serving: 242

4 4½-ounce skinless, boneless
    chicken breast halves
  Salt and pepper
1½ tablespoons olive oil

½ pound mushrooms, sliced
3 tablespoons dry vermouth
2 tablespoons chopped
    parsley

1. Open up chicken breast halves and pound between wax paper until evenly flattened to about ¼ inch. Season with salt and pepper.

2. In a large nonstick skillet, heat 1 tablespoon olive oil over medium-high heat. Add chicken and cook, turning once, until lightly browned and just cooked through, 3 to 4 minutes. Remove to a warm platter and cover with foil to keep warm.

3. Add remaining olive oil to skillet. Add mushrooms and cook, stirring occasionally, until tender and lightly browned, about 5 minutes. Add vermouth to skillet and stir over heat for a few seconds. Pour mushrooms and any liquid in pan over chicken and garnish with parsley.

110 CLAY POT CHICKEN

Prep: 10 minutes   Cook: 1¼ hours   Serves: 4
Calories per serving: 269

Cooking in a clay pot seals in moisture and flavor, with no extra fat needed.

1 2½-pound chicken
½ teaspoon thyme
½ teaspoon salt
¼ teaspoon pepper
2 medium tomatoes (6 ounces
    each), quartered
4 medium shallots (4 ounces
    total), halved

½ pound mushrooms, sliced
2 garlic cloves, minced
¼ cup chopped fresh basil or
    parsley
½ cup dry red wine

1. Soak a clay pot roaster in water to cover 10 to 15 minutes. Drain.

2. Season chicken inside and out with thyme, salt, and pepper. Place in pot. Scatter tomatoes, shallots, mushrooms, and garlic around chicken. Sprinkle basil over chicken and vegetables. Pour wine into casserole.

3. Cover clay pot and place in a cold oven. Turn temperature to 450°. Bake 1 hour 15 minutes. Carefully remove cover, spoon juice over chicken, and serve from pot.

111 LEMON-PEPPER BROILED CHICKEN BREASTS

Prep: 5 minutes   Marinate: 30 minutes   Cook: 20 to 25 minutes
Serves: 4   Calories per serving: 218

2 tablespoons fresh lemon juice
½ teaspoon grated lemon zest
2 tablespoons extra-virgin olive oil
½ teaspoon salt

1 teaspoon coarsely cracked pepper
½ teaspoon sugar
4 7-ounce chicken breast halves, skinned
4 lemon wedges

1. In medium bowl, combine lemon juice, lemon zest, olive oil, salt, pepper, and sugar. Add chicken breasts and turn to coat. Marinate at room temperature, turning once or twice, 30 to 60 minutes.

2. Preheat broiler. Set chicken, bone side up, about 6 inches from heat. Broil 10 minutes. Turn, baste with any marinade remaining in bowl, and broil 10 to 15 minutes longer, until chicken is white throughout but still moist. Serve with lemon wedges.

112 SPICY THAI CHICKEN LEGS

Prep: 10 minutes   Marinate: 30 minutes   Cook: 35 minutes
Serves: 4   Calories per serving: 188

This flavorful dish is so low in calories it leaves room for boiled rice tossed with scallions and snow peas as accompaniments.

1 cup plain low-fat yogurt
2 tablespoons lime juice
2 garlic cloves, crushed
1 teaspoon minced fresh ginger, or ¼ teaspoon powdered

1 teaspoon ground coriander
¼ to ½ teaspoon cayenne
4 chicken legs with thighs (6 ounces each), skinned

1. In a medium bowl, combine yogurt, lime juice, garlic, ginger, coriander, and cayenne. Pierce chicken legs all over with a fork and place in bowl. Turn to coat and marinate at room temperature, turning occasionally, 30 to 60 minutes.

2. Preheat oven to 350°. Remove chicken from marinade and place in a shallow baking dish. Reserve marinade. Bake chicken 15 minutes; remove from oven.

3. Spoon reserved marinade over chicken. Return to oven and bake 20 minutes longer, or until cooked through to bone.

113 STIR-FRIED CHICKEN WITH ZUCCHINI AND SWEET PEPPER

Prep: 15 minutes   Cook: 5 to 7 minutes   Serves: 4
Calories per serving: 186

Serve this colorful dish with ½ cup cooked white rice and it will cost only 100 calories extra.

3 4½-ounce skinless, boneless
   chicken breast halves
1 medium zucchini
1 medium red bell pepper
2 scallions
1 teaspoon cornstarch

¼ cup chicken broth or water
1 tablespoon soy sauce
1 tablespoon dry sherry
1 tablespoon vegetable oil
1 teaspoon grated fresh ginger
½ teaspoon salt

1. Cut chicken crosswise on a diagonal into very thin slices. Cut zucchini lengthwise in half; then cut crosswise into thin slices. Cut red pepper into thin 1½-inch strips. Slice scallions.

2. In a small bowl, dissolve cornstarch in cold chicken broth. Stir in soy sauce and sherry. Set sauce aside.

3. Heat a wok or large nonstick skillet until hot. Add oil and heat until almost smoking. Add chicken and stir-fry, separating slices, 2 minutes. Add zucchini, red pepper, scallions, ginger, and salt. Cook over high heat, tossing constantly, until chicken is white throughout and vegetables are crisp-tender, 2 to 3 minutes.

4. Stir reserved sauce and add to pan. Cook, stirring, until sauce thickens and coats chicken and vegetables, 1 to 2 minutes. Serve at once.

114 RED-HOT CHICKEN STRIPS

Prep: 15 minutes   Cook: 10 to 12 minutes   Serves: 4
Calories per serving: 229

Serve these fiery chicken strips with a tossed salad for a light supper or with Light Blue Cheese Dressing (page 142) for dipping as an appetizer.

4 4½-ounce skinless, boneless
   chicken breast halves
2 tablespoons butter or
   margarine

2 to 3 tablespoons hot pepper
   sauce

1. Cut chicken into finger-size strips. In a large skillet, melt butter with 1 tablespoon hot sauce over medium heat. Add chicken and toss to coat. Cook, tossing occasionally, until chicken is golden outside and white throughout but still moist, 8 to 10 minutes.

2. Sprinkle remaining 1 to 2 tablespoons hot sauce over chicken, toss, and increase heat to medium-high. Cook, tossing, for 2 minutes, or until chicken is glazed. Serve at once.

115   ORANGE HONEY-GLAZED GAME HENS

Prep: 3 minutes   Cook: 40 minutes   Serves: 4
Calories per serving: 279

Yes, you can plan a dinner party without diet disaster! Accompany these tasty birds with stir-fried asparagus and mushrooms for an elegant, low-calorie meal.

2 1¼-pound Cornish game hens, halved	1 tablespoon white wine vinegar
¼ cup orange juice	1 teaspoon honey
2 tablespoons soy sauce	Dash of powdered ginger

1. Preheat oven to 400°. Place hens, skin side up, in a roasting pan. Roast for 30 minutes.

2. Meanwhile, in a small bowl, combine orange juice, soy sauce, vinegar, honey, and ginger. Blend well.

3. Brush orange juice mixture over hens and roast 10 minutes longer, or until skin is browned and meat is cooked through with no trace of pink near bone.

116   CURRIED CHICKEN PAILLARD

Prep: 20 minutes   Cook: 18 to 20 minutes   Serves: 4
Calories per serving: 226

4 4½-ounce skinless, boneless chicken breast halves	½ teaspoon grated fresh ginger, or ¼ teaspoon powdered
Salt and pepper	
1 tablespoon vegetable oil	½ tart apple, cored, peeled, and finely chopped
1 small onion, finely chopped	
1 garlic clove, minced	1 tablespoon chopped parsley
1 tablespoon curry powder	1 cup chicken broth

1. Pound chicken breasts between 2 sheets of wax paper until an even ¼ to ⅜ inch thick. Season with salt and pepper. Heat oil in a large nonstick skillet over medium-high heat. Add chicken, in 2 batches if necessary, and cook, turning once, until lightly browned and almost cooked through, 3 to 4 minutes. Remove to a plate.

2. Add onion to skillet and cook until softened and translucent, 2 to 3 minutes. Add garlic and cook 1 minute longer. Stir in curry powder, ginger, apple, and parsley. Add chicken broth and bring to a boil. Reduce heat to a simmer and cook until sauce has thickened slightly, about 10 minutes.

3. Return chicken to pan and simmer until just cooked through, 2 to 3 minutes.

117 ROSEMARY CHICKEN BAKED IN FOIL

Prep: 15 minutes   Cook: 50 to 60 minutes   Serves: 4
Calories per serving: 272

1 2½-pound chicken
   Salt and pepper
1 teaspoon rosemary
3 garlic cloves, smashed
1½ teaspoons extra-virgin olive
   oil
1 small onion, sliced

2 carrots, peeled and thinly
   sliced
2 celery ribs, sliced
4 small red potatoes, scrubbed
   and quartered
3 tablespoons water

1. Preheat oven to 450°. Season inside of chicken liberally with salt and pepper. Sprinkle ½ teaspoon rosemary inside cavity and add 2 garlic cloves. Tie chicken legs together.

2. Place chicken on a doubled sheet of heavy-duty aluminum foil 24 inches long. Rub skin with remaining garlic. Brush olive oil all over outside of chicken. Season with salt and pepper and remaining rosemary. Scatter vegetables around chicken. Season vegetables with salt and pepper and sprinkle with water.

3. Bring 2 long sides of foil together over chicken. Fold over twice and pinch to seal. Fold and pinch 2 short ends, leaving package as tented as possible.

4. Place in oven and bake 50 to 60 minutes, or until juices near thigh joint run clear when pricked with a fork. Serve chicken with vegetables and pan juices.

118 POACHED CHICKEN BREASTS WITH TARRAGON

Prep: 10 minutes   Cook: 25 to 30 minutes   Serves: 4
Calories per serving: 225

1½ cups chicken broth or water
½ cup dry white wine
2 teaspoons tarragon
1 medium onion, thinly sliced
2 medium carrots, thinly
   sliced
2 medium celery ribs, thinly
   sliced

½ teaspoon salt
⅛ teaspoon pepper
4 4½-ounce skinless, boneless
   chicken breast halves
1 teaspoon Dijon mustard
   (optional)
1 tablespoon chopped parsley

1. In a large heavy saucepan, combine broth, wine, tarragon, onion, carrots, celery, salt, and pepper. Simmer 10 minutes. Add chicken and simmer 15 to 20 minutes, or until chicken is just white throughout but still moist.

2. With a slotted spoon, transfer chicken and vegetables to a serving casserole. Whisk mustard into sauce, if desired, and ladle over chicken and vegetables. Garnish with parsley.

119 MICROWAVE CHICKEN ALLA DIAVOLO
Prep: 10 minutes   Cook: 12 minutes   Serves: 4
Calories per serving: 224

1 onion, finely chopped
1 garlic clove, minced
1 teaspoon vegetable oil
1 cup tomato sauce (8-ounce can)
2 tablespoons white wine vinegar or cider vinegar
1 tablespoon dark brown sugar

¼ to ½ teaspoon hot pepper sauce
¼ teaspoon dry mustard
¼ teaspoon salt
½ teaspoon pepper
4 4½-ounce skinless, boneless chicken breast halves

1. In a microwavable dish large enough to hold chicken in a single layer, combine onion, garlic, and oil. Cover with microwave-safe plastic wrap and cook on high 1 minute. Stir in tomato sauce, vinegar, brown sugar, hot sauce, mustard, salt, and pepper. Cover and microwave on medium-high 1 minute. Remove dish from microwave and stir.

2. Add chicken to sauce and turn to coat. Spoon sauce over chicken. Cover again and cook on high 5 minutes. Rotate pan 180 degrees and baste chicken with sauce. Cook on high 5 minutes longer.

120 ORANGE CHICKEN MARRAKESH
Prep: 10 minutes   Cook: 45 minutes   Serves: 4
Calories per serving: 257

1 2½-pound chicken, quartered and skinned
1 navel orange, peeled and sliced
1 tablespoon flour
½ teaspoon ground coriander

½ teaspoon cinnamon
½ teaspoon salt
⅛ to ¼ teaspoon cayenne
½ cup orange juice
½ cup chicken broth

1. Preheat oven to 375°. Trim any visible fat from chicken. Place pieces in a 12 x 8½ x 2-inch baking dish. Tuck orange slices around chicken.

2. Combine flour, coriander, cinnamon, salt, and cayenne. Sprinkle over chicken pieces. Pour orange juice and chicken broth into dish.

3. Bake, basting chicken with pan juices occasionally, until chicken is tender with no trace of pink near bone, about 45 minutes. Serve chicken with pan juices.

121 TEQUILA CHICKEN

Prep: 5 minutes   Marinate: 30 minutes   Cook: 25 minutes
Serves: 4   Calories per serving: 239

1 2½-pound chicken, skinned and cut into serving pieces	1 tablespoon vegetable oil
	1 tablespoon minced cilantro or parsley
¼ cup tequila	½ teaspoon salt
2 tablespoons lime juice	¼ teaspoon pepper

1. Rinse pieces and pat dry. Prick all over with a fork.

2. In a medium bowl, combine tequila, lime juice, oil, cilantro, salt, and pepper. Add chicken and turn to coat. Marinate at room temperature, turning several times, 30 to 60 minutes.

3. Prepare a hot fire in a grill or preheat broiler. Set chicken about 6 inches from heat and grill or broil, turning occasionally, until cooked through with no trace of pink near bone, about 25 minutes.

122 TURKEY SCALLOPINI MARSALA WITH MUSHROOMS

Prep: 5 minutes   Cook: 16 to 18 minutes   Serves: 4
Calories per serving: 231

Here's a surprise scallopini made with turkey instead of veal. Even with its rich flavor, it still comes in at under 250 calories, leaving plenty of room for a serving of rice or noodles and a vegetable or salad.

1 pound thinly sliced raw turkey breast	½ pound mushrooms, sliced
Salt and pepper	¼ cup Marsala wine
2 teaspoons olive oil	1½ teaspoons lemon juice
1 tablespoon butter or margarine	

1. Season turkey slices with salt and pepper. In a large nonstick skillet, heat olive oil over medium heat. Add turkey and cook, turning once, until lightly browned outside and tender and just cooked through but still moist, 8 to 10 minutes. Remove and set aside.

2. Add butter to skillet and increase heat to medium-high. As soon as foam subsides, add mushrooms and cook, stirring occasionally, until tender and lightly browned, about 5 minutes. Season with salt and pepper.

3. Add Marsala and lemon juice to skillet and boil for 1 minute. Return turkey to pan and spoon mushrooms and sauce on top. Simmer for 2 minutes before serving.

123 TURKEY ROLLS STUFFED WITH VEGETABLES

Prep: 10 minutes   Cook: 16 to 18 minutes   Serves: 4
Calories per serving: 176

Here's a truly light recipe that leaves room for a baked potato, or even dessert. If asparagus is out of season, substitute 1 small zucchini, cut into thick strips.

4 **skinless, boneless turkey breast slices, about 3 ounces each**	4 **asparagus spears**
2 **tablespoons lemon juice**	1 **carrot**
½ **teaspoon tarragon**	1 **celery rib**
½ **teaspoon salt**	1 **tablespoon vegetable oil**
⅛ **teaspoon pepper**	¼ **cup dry white wine or sherry**

1. Pound turkey slices between 2 sheets of wax paper until flattened evenly to about ⅜ inch. Brush with lemon juice and season with tarragon, ¼ teaspoon salt, and the pepper.

2. Cut off 4 inches of asparagus tops. Reserve remaining stalks for another use. Cut carrot and celery into 4-inch strips.

3. In a small saucepan, bring 1 cup water to a boil. Add asparagus tips, carrot, celery, and remaining salt. Cook 3 minutes. Drain, reserving ¼ cup cooking liquid.

4. Divide vegetables into 4 equal portions and place at one end of each turkey slice. Roll up. In a large nonstick skillet, heat oil over medium heat. Add turkey rolls, seam side down, and cook, turning, until browned outside and tender throughout, 10 to 12 minutes. Remove from pan.

5. Add reserved cooking liquid and wine to skillet. Boil until reduced by half, about 3 minutes. Pour over turkey rolls and serve.

124 TURKEY MEATBALLS ITALIAN-STYLE

Prep: 10 minutes   Cook: 15 to 20 minutes   Serves: 4
Calories per serving: 257

1 **slice firm-textured white bread, crust removed**	1 **garlic clove, crushed**
2 **tablespoons chicken broth or skim milk**	2 **tablespoons grated Parmesan cheese**
1 **pound lean ground turkey**	¾ **teaspoon salt**
⅓ **cup minced onion**	¼ **teaspoon pepper**
3 **tablespoons finely diced green bell pepper**	1 **tablespoon flour**
	1 **tablespoon olive oil**

1. In a medium bowl, soak bread in broth until softened. Mash to a paste. Add turkey, onion, bell pepper, garlic, Parmesan, salt, and pepper. Mix with your hands to blend well. Form turkey mixture into 8 meatballs.

2. On a plate, season flour with additional salt and pepper. Roll turkey meatballs in seasoned flour to coat lightly.

3. Heat oil in a large nonstick skillet. Add meatballs and cook over medium heat, turning until browned and crusty outside and cooked through to the center, 15 to 20 minutes.

---

125   TURKEY ROLLS FLORENTINE
Prep: 15 minutes   Cook: 17 to 22 minutes   Serves: 4
Calories per serving: 204

4 **skinless, boneless turkey cutlets (about 3 ounces each)**
   Salt and pepper
1 **tablespoon olive oil**
½ **cup finely chopped onion**
1 **garlic clove, minced**
½ **cup finely chopped mushrooms**
½ **cup grated carrot**

½ **10-ounce package frozen chopped spinach, thawed and squeezed dry (½ cup)**
1 **tablespoon chopped parsley**
¼ **teaspoon thyme**
⅛ **teaspoon nutmeg**
1 **tablespoon butter or magarine**
½ **cup chicken broth**

1. Pound turkey slices between 2 sheets of wax paper until evenly flattened to about ⅜ inch. Season with salt and pepper.

2. Heat oil in a large nonstick skillet. Add onion and cook over medium-high heat until onion is softened but not browned, about 2 minutes. Add garlic and mushrooms and cook until tender, 3 to 5 minutes longer. Add carrot, spinach, parsley, thyme, nutmeg, ¼ teaspoon salt, and ⅛ teaspoon pepper. Blend well and remove from heat.

3. Spread one fourth of spinach mixture over each turkey slice. Roll up and fasten with wooden toothpicks.

4. Wipe out skillet. Add butter and melt over medium-high heat. Add turkey rolls and cook, turning, until lightly browned all over, about 3 minutes. Reduce heat to medium and cook, turning occasionally, until turkey is tender and filling is hot, 8 to 10 minutes longer.

5. Remove turkey rolls from pan. Add chicken broth to pan and bring to a boil, scraping up browned bits from bottom of pan. Boil for 1 to 2 minutes to reduce and thicken slightly. Pour sauce over turkey rolls and serve.

126 ROAST TURKEY BREAST

Prep: 5 minutes   Cook: 50 minutes   Serves: 4
Calories per serving: 207

Here's a great low-calorie meat that can be eaten as a main course or incorporated into salads or sandwiches.

1 2½-pound turkey breast, skinned	1 tablespoon paprika
1 tablespoon butter or margarine, softened	½ teaspoon thyme
2 tablespoons lemon juice	½ teaspoon salt
	¼ teaspoon pepper

1. Preheat oven to 350°. Place turkey breast in a small roasting pan. Rub butter over turkey. Sprinkle with lemon juice and season with paprika, thyme, salt, and pepper.

2. Roast turkey breast, uncovered, until tender and white to the bone but still moist, about 50 minutes

Chapter 4

Seafood for Slimming

You catch more protein at fewer calories in fish than in poultry or meat. And you haul in a great variety of flavors as well in the recipes that follow.

Since fish is high in moisture, it cooks extremely well in the microwave, and you will find a number of quickly prepared microwave dishes here.

Whether you grill, stew, bake, broil, braise, stir-fry, or microwave, you'll find that fish meals leave you feeling satisfied but not overstuffed. Notice we didn't say fry; why load a good food with needless fat-traps?

The fat in fish itself is good for you. There is evidence that it helps reduce serum cholesterol levels, if you eat enough fish.

Fish is a dieter's best friend. A 3½-ounce broiled or microwaved portion of lean fish without added fat has about half the calories of chicken breast meat and 18 to 19 grams of protein.

Lean fish include: flounder, sole, snapper, haddock. Low-calorie shellfish include lobster and shrimp.

You will also find a salmon recipe. Even though salmon is a relatively fatty fish, and higher in calories than leaner types, recent tests indicate that dieters who ate substantial portions of salmon each day lost weight (and reduced their cholesterol levels) as compared with dieters who ate comparable meat meals.

The tastes of the dishes that follow provide the best reasons to enjoy fish often.

127   BOUILLABAISSE U.S.A.
Prep: 12 minutes   Cook: 17 to 18 minutes   Serves: 4
Calories per serving: 267

This quick and tasty fish stew includes a catch available coast to coast. There's not a bone in the bowl, and calories are low enough to make the traditional slice of toasted French bread affordable.

1½ tablespoons olive oil
1 medium onion, coarsely chopped
1 garlic clove, crushed
¼ cup diced carrots
¼ cup diced celery
1 16-ounce can stewed tomatoes, with their juice
2 cups water
1 teaspoon salt

¼ teaspoon pepper
¼ teaspoon thyme
¼ teaspoon saffron or paprika
1 pound fish fillets, cut into 1-inch chunks
½ pound sea scallops, halved
4 slices toasted French bread, cut ½ inch thick
2 tablespoons chopped parsley

1. In a large flameproof casserole, heat oil, tilting to cover bottom. Add onion, garlic, carrots, and celery. Cook over medium-high heat, stirring occasionally, until onions are softened and translucent, about 3 minutes.

2. Add tomatoes with their juice, water, salt, pepper, thyme, and saffron or paprika. Mix well. Cover, reduce heat to medium-low, and simmer 10 minutes. Add fish and cook for 3 minutes. Add scallops and simmer 1 to 2 minutes longer, until fish and scallops are just opaque throughout.

3. Place a slice of toasted French bread in each of 4 large soup bowls. Ladle fish and broth into bowls. Top with parsley.

128   BAKED SNAPPER CHINOISE
Prep: 5 minutes   Cook: 10 minutes   Serves: 4
Calories per serving: 96

Soy, garlic, and ginger flavor this quick dish of red snapper—a bundle of flavor at under 100 calories a portion. If you choose, this can be microwaved instead of baked. Allow about 5 minutes, covered with microwave-safe plastic wrap, on high. Serve with boiled rice and stir-fried vegetables.

1 tablespoon light soy sauce
½ garlic clove, finely chopped
1 teaspoon finely chopped fresh ginger

½ cup vegetable broth
1 teaspoon sugar
4 red snapper fillets, about 3 ounces each

1. Preheat oven to 450°. Combine soy sauce, garlic, ginger, broth, and sugar in a shallow casserole. Arrange snapper fillets in casserole in a single layer.

2. Bake 10 minutes, basting twice with the sauce, until fish is just opaque throughout.

129 BROILED SOLE WITH LEMON

Prep: 5 minutes   Cook: 5 minutes   Serves: 4
Calories per serving: 114

1 lemon, peeled and cut into 8
    thin slices
4 sole or other white fish
    fillets, about 1 pound

2 tablespoons reduced-calorie
    mayonnaise
1 tablespoon Dijon mustard

1. In a flameproof baking dish, arrange 4 groups of 2 lemon slices each.

2. Place 1 sole fillet on each pair of lemon slices. Combine mayonnaise and mustard; mix to blend well. Spread a generous 2 teaspoons over each fish fillet.

3. Preheat broiler. Broil fish 4 to 6 inches from heat 5 minutes, or until topping is bubbly and brown and fish is opaque throughout.

130 CHILLED MUSSELS IN DIJON MUSTARD SAUCE

Prep: 10 minutes   Cook: 5 minutes   Serves: 4
Calories per serving: 122

Prepare this dish on its own, or make extra mussels one day and top the leftovers with mustard-mayonnaise mixture and scallions for a cool dinner.

2 pounds mussels
½ cup dry white wine
¼ cup water
⅓ cup minced onion
1 bay leaf, broken in half

2 teaspoons reduced-calorie
    mayonnaise
2 teaspoons Dijon mustard
2 tablespoons minced scallion
    greens

1. Scrub mussels well. With a small sharp knife, cut off hairy brownish "beards."

2. In a large nonreactive kettle, bring wine, water, onion, and bay leaf to a boil over high heat. Add mussels and cook, covered, for 5 minutes, until all mussels are open. Stir occasionally to bring those on bottom to the top.

3. Remove mussels with a slotted spoon. Discard any that do not open. Strain liquid through a fine sieve lined with cheesecloth. Measure out and reserve ½ cup clear broth.

4. In a small bowl, whisk together mayonnaise and mustard. Gradually whisk in reserved broth.

5. Place mussels on a serving dish and spoon sauce over them. Garnish with minced scallions.

131 BAKED FLOUNDER FILLETS WITH SCALLIONS AND CHOPPED TOMATO

Prep: 5 minutes   Cook: 10 minutes   Serves: 4
Calories per serving: 121

Lemon, scallion, and tomato add flavor and color at few calories. If you choose, prepare fish fillets in a microwavable dish, cover with plastic, and zap for 5 minutes

4 flounder fillets, about 1 pound total	⅛ teaspoon basil
½ lemon	Salt and pepper
2 scallions, thinly sliced	1 tablespoon butter or margarine
1 medium tomato, coarsely chopped	

1. Preheat oven to 375°. Arrange fish fillets in an ovenproof casserole in a single layer.

2. Squeeze juice from lemon over flounder, then top with scallions and tomato. Season with basil, salt, and pepper.

3. Dot fish fillets with butter or margarine. Bake for 10 minutes, until just opaque throughout.

132 BAKED TURBANS OF SOLE

Prep: 10 minutes   Cook: 18 minutes   Serves: 4
Calories per serving: 143

Sole (or more economical flounder) rolled and baked in a savory wine sauce is a natural to serve over rice or, for a change of pace, on plain angel hair noodles.

1 teaspoon butter or margarine	1 cup tomato sauce
½ cup finely chopped onion	½ cup dry white wine
4 sole or flounder fillets, about 1 pound	¼ cup bottled clam juice
	Salt and pepper
	1 teaspoon chopped parsley

1. Heat oven to 400°. Spread butter or margarine over bottom of a shallow ovenproof baking dish. Sprinkle chopped onion over butter or margarine. Roll up fish fillets, secure with toothpicks, and stand them open-end down on onions.

2. In a small nonreactive saucepan, combine tomato sauce, wine, and clam juice. Heat to boiling. Pour over fish.

3. Bake 15 minutes, or until just opaque throughout. Season with salt and pepper. Garnish with parsley before serving.

133   CAJUN-STYLE FISH FILLETS
Prep: 5 minutes   Cook: 6 to 8 minutes   Serves: 4
Calories per serving: 154

A hot pan that virtually scorches the seasonings onto the fish is the secret of distinctive Cajun flavor. Serve with Spanish rice, for a colorful main course.

¾ **teaspoon basil**	½ **teaspoon black pepper**
½ **teaspoon thyme**	⅛ **teaspoon cayenne**
½ **teaspoon paprika**	4 **catfish fillets, ¼ pound each**
¼ **teaspoon salt**	1 **tablespoon vegetable oil**

1. In a small bowl, combine basil, thyme, paprika, salt, black pepper, and cayenne. Mix well. Pat seasoning mixture into fish fillets with heel of hand.

2. In a large heavy skillet, preferably cast-iron, heat oil; tilt pan to coat bottom. Add fish fillets and cook, over medium heat, turning once, until brown on both sides, 6 to 8 minutes.

134   FISH STRIPS STIR-FRY
Prep: 15 minutes   Cook: 7 to 8 minutes   Serves: 4
Calories per serving: 190

You can make this dish with any fairly firm fish cut into strips. Monkfish has a flavor reminiscent of lobster and is particularly delicious; shrimp are also excellent.

1 **pound monkfish or cod fillets**	1 **teaspoon minced fresh ginger, or ¼ teaspoon powdered**
1 **teaspoon cornstarch**	
1 **tablespoon dry sherry**	1 **large green bell pepper, cut into large dice**
1 **tablespoon light soy sauce**	
2 **tablespoons vegetable oil**	1 **medium onion, thinly sliced**
1 **garlic clove, finely minced**	1 **tablespoon chopped parsley**

1. Cut fish into strips about 2x½ inch. In a medium bowl, combine monkfish, cornstarch, sherry, and soy sauce. Toss to coat fish.

2. Heat 1 tablespoon oil in a wok or large nonstick skillet. Add garlic and stir-fry 30 seconds, until fragrant. Add fish and ginger. Stir-fry over high heat until fish is browned outside and just opaque throughout, about 3 minutes. Remove fish and set aside.

3. Heat remaining 1 tablespoon oil. Add pepper and onion; stir-fry until vegetables are softened but pepper is still bright green, 3 to 4 minutes.

4. Return fish to pan and toss gently with vegetables over low heat until reheated. Sprinkle with parsley and serve at once.

135   LETTUCE-WRAPPED FISH FILLETS

Prep: 10 minutes   Cook: 15 minutes   Serves: 4
Calories per serving: 105

Fish wrapped and steamed is unusually succulent and sweet, an elegant presentation for a simple meal. Slice three medium potatoes and steam them along with the fish packets, to round out a meal at about 200 calories.

1 cup bottled clam juice	2 celery ribs, cut into thin
1 bay leaf	slices
¼ teaspoon thyme	4 sole or ocean perch fillets,
4 large Boston lettuce leaves	about 4 ounces each
1 carrot, cut into thin slices	Salt and pepper

1. In a small saucepan, bring clam juice, bay leaf, and thyme to a boil over medium heat. Add lettuce leaves and boil 1 minute, or until wilted and bright green. Remove lettuce and spread on paper towel to drain.

2. Add carrots and celery to hot broth. Cook until almost tender, about 5 minutes. Remove vegetables with a slotted spoon. Reserve broth.

3. Place a fish fillet on each lettuce leaf. Divide carrots and celery slices evenly among fillets. Season with salt and pepper. Fold over sides of each lettuce leaf and turn ends up to enclose fish completely. Put fish packages, seam side down, in a medium saucepan. Pour broth over fish.

4. Cover saucepan, bring to a simmer, and cook 7 minutes, or until fish is opaque throughout.

136   CREOLE SHRIMP

Prep: 10 minutes   Cook: 15 minutes   Serves: 4
Calories per serving: 133

Oregano and tomatoes season a quick shrimp dish you will want to repeat often. This is a natural with boiled rice.

½ cup finely chopped onion	¼ teaspoon oregano
½ cup finely chopped green	¼ teaspoon salt
bell pepper	⅛ teaspoon pepper
4 medium mushrooms,	¾ pound shrimp, shelled and
coarsely chopped (½ cup)	deveined
1 cup canned tomatoes	

1. In a large saucepan, combine onion, green pepper, mushrooms, tomatoes, oregano, salt, and pepper. Cook over medium heat 10 minutes.

2. Add shrimp. Bring to a simmer and cook 5 minutes longer.

137   FLOUNDER FLORENTINE
Prep: 10 minutes   Cook: 17 minutes   Serves: 4
Calories per serving: 102

Flounder or turbot fillets with spinach stuffing take to an accent of nutmeg. A tasty fish dinner, excellent with couscous for a change of pace.

½ **pound fresh spinach leaves**
½ **cup finely chopped onion**
2 **tablespoons low-fat cottage cheese**
¼ **teaspoon salt**

⅛ **teaspoon pepper**
⅛ **teaspoon nutmeg**
4 **flounder fillets, 3½ ounces each**
¼ **cup tomato juice**

1. Preheat oven to 350°. Rinse spinach well. Place in saucepan, cover, and cook in water clinging to leaves 2 minutes. Drain well and place on a chopping board. Chop spinach coarsely. Combine with onion, cottage cheese, salt, pepper, and nutmeg.

2. Divide spinach mixture, placing one quarter on wide end of each flounder fillet. Roll up.

3. Place fillets in baking dish, narrow end down. Pour tomato juice over fish and bake for 15 minutes, or until fish is opaque throughout.

138   GRILLED FISH STEAKS
Prep: 4 minutes   Cook: 6 to 8 minutes   Serves: 4
Calories per serving: 136

Great cooked over coals, this is also excellent as an oven-broiled dish. Fish steaks, cooked with bone intact, hold in flavor and make satisfying eating. Serve with a salad tossed with a little cold leftover rice or pasta, for a quick meal.

4 **small scrod or halibut steaks, about 5 ounces each**
1 **tablespoon butter or margarine, melted**

Juice of 1 lime
¼ **teaspoon basil**
¼ **teaspoon salt**
¼ **teaspoon pepper**

1. Light grill or preheat broiler. Brush fish steaks with melted butter or margarine. Sprinkle with lime juice and season with basil, salt, and pepper.

2. Grill or broil fish 4 to 6 inches from heat 3 to 4 minutes on each side, until just opaque throughout.

139 MICROWAVE CATFISH IN TOMATO SAUCE

Prep: 5 minutes   Cook: 7 minutes   Serves: 4
Calories per serving: 184

Catfish, tomato, garlic, and oregano make a flavor combo worthy of a southern jazz festival. Prepare this in a microwave-to-table dish and save on clean-up as well.

1 **tablespoon vegetable oil**	⅛ **teaspoon oregano**
1 **medium tomato, chopped**	**Dash of pepper**
1 **garlic clove, finely minced**	1 **pound catfish fillets**
1 **cup tomato sauce**	

1. Place oil in a microwavable dish and tilt dish to coat bottom. Add tomato and garlic. Cover with microwave-safe plastic wrap and microwave on high for 2 minutes. Uncover; stir in tomato sauce, oregano, and pepper.

2. Place catfish in dish. Spoon some sauce over fillets. Cover tightly with plastic wrap. Microwave on high 5 minutes. Loosen plastic to release steam. Uncover, baste with sauce, and serve.

140 MICROWAVE SOLE PROVENÇALE

Prep: 12 minutes   Cook: 7 to 8 minutes   Serves: 4
Calories per serving: 167

Fish fillets microwaved with a topping of colorful and flavorful vegetables may make an interesting new addition to your dinner repertoire.

1 **carrot, coarsely grated**	1½ **teaspoons herbes de Provence***
1 **celery rib, thinly sliced**	½ **teaspoon salt**
1 **small onion, coarsely chopped**	**Dash of pepper**
1 **garlic clove, coarsely chopped**	1½ **tablespoons lemon juice**
2 **pitted black olives, coarsely chopped**	2 **tablespoons olive oil**
	4 **grey sole or other white fish fillets, about 1 pound**

1. In a microwavable dish just large enough to hold fish, combine carrot, celery, onion, garlic, olives, herbes de Provence, salt, pepper, and lemon juice. Stir until salt dissolves. Stir in oil.

2. Cover with microwave-safe plastic wrap and cook on high 2 minutes. Uncover, push vegetables to side of dish, and arrange fish in dish. Spoon vegetable mixture over fish. Replace plastic wrap.

3. Microwave on high 4 to 5 minutes, until fish is opaque throughout. Let stand 1 minute, then uncover, and serve.

* *Herbes de Provence is a blend available in specialty food shops and many general spice lines. If unavailable, substitute ½ teaspoon basil, ½ teaspoon thyme, ¼ teaspoon marjoram, ¼ teaspoon rosemary, and ⅛ teaspoon fennel seed.*

141 MICROWAVE FISH FILLETS WITH HERBS AND TOMATO

Prep: 8 minutes   Cook: 5 minutes   Serves: 4
Calories per serving: 125

When you want a 5-minute meal, turn your fish fillets onto a microwavable dish, add seasonings, and a little later, tomato. A colorful low-calorie meal, ready in jig time.

2 tablespoons lemon juice
½ teaspoon thyme
½ teaspoon basil
1 tablespoon chopped parsley
1 garlic clove, minced
¼ teaspoon salt

⅛ teaspoon pepper
4 ocean perch fillets, about 4 ounces each
1 medium tomato, cut into thin wedges

1. Combine lemon juice, thyme, basil, parsley, garlic, salt, and pepper. Mix well.

2. Place fish fillets in microwavable dish. Spoon seasoning mixture over fillets and cover with microwave-safe plastic wrap. Cook on high 2 minutes.

3. Add tomato wedges and cook 3 minutes longer, until tomato is heated and softened.

142 MICROWAVE FISH FILLETS WITH PEPPER STRIPS

Prep: 7 minutes   Cook: 10 minutes   Serves: 4
Calories per serving: 137

Here the vegetables are precooked in the microwave, then your choice of fish fillets added, to micro-finish in about 5 minutes.

½ large green bell pepper, cut into ½-inch strips
½ large red bell pepper, cut into ½-inch strips
1 medium onion, sliced
2 tablespoons water

2 tablespoons lemon juice
¼ teaspoon salt
⅛ teaspoon pepper
4 snapper fillets, about 4 ounces each

1. Combine green and red peppers, onion, water, lemon juice, salt, and pepper in a microwavable dish. Cover with microwave-safe plastic wrap and cook on high 5 minutes, or until vegetables are tender.

2. Move vegetables to side of dish. Add fish and spoon vegetable mixture over fillets. Cover again with plastic wrap.

3. Microwave on high 4 to 5 minutes, until fish is just opaque throughout.

143 MICROWAVE HALIBUT WITH MUSHROOMS

Prep: 5 minutes   Cook: 10 minutes   Serves: 4
Calories per serving: 171

The high water content of fish makes it an ideal candidate for microwave cooking. In this and the recipes that follow, vegetables, lemon, and other seasonings add appealing flavors and low calories to finished dishes.

1 tablespoon vegetable oil
1 medium onion, finely chopped
1 garlic clove, finely minced
2 cups mushrooms, finely chopped (½ pound)
¼ teaspoon black pepper

Dash of cayenne
2 teaspoons lemon juice
4 halibut fillets, about 4 ounces each
2 teaspoons chopped parsley
1 teaspoon grated lemon zest

1. In a microwavable dish, place 1 teaspoon of the oil and tilt dish to coat bottom. Add onion, garlic, mushrooms, black pepper, and cayenne. Cover with microwave-safe plastic wrap. Cook on high 5 minutes.

2. Sprinkle lemon juice over fish fillets. Place fillets on vegetable mixture. Cover with plastic wrap. Cook on high for 4 to 5 minutes, until fish is opaque throughout.

3. Remove plastic wrap, combine parsley and lemon zest and sprinkle over fish. Serve at once.

144 SCALLOPS SEVICHE

Prep: 10 minutes   Marinate: 12 hours   Cook: none   Serves: 4
Calories per serving: 113

Plan on this a day ahead when you see scallops fresh in the market. The fish "cooks" in the lime juice, with no heat applied. Serve with lettuce and cooked asparagus for a cool low-calorie meal.

1 pound sea scallops
¾ cup fresh lime juice (from about 5 limes)
1 large tomato, peeled and chopped
1 medium white onion, finely chopped

1 teaspoon chopped fresh mint leaves or parsley
¼ teaspoon salt
⅛ teaspoon pepper

1. Put scallops in a glass or ceramic bowl. Pour lime juice over scallops. Cover and refrigerate, tossing occasionally, at least 12 hours, or overnight.

2. Add tomato, onion, and mint or parsley. Season with salt and pepper.

145 SCALLOPS IN GREEN SAUCE
Prep: 12 minutes   Cook: 7 to 11 minutes   Serves: 4
Calories per serving: 75

Scallops are a busy dieter's best friend—they need no fussy preparation or cleaning, cook quickly, and are low in calories. Watercress and ginger make a snappy green sauce for the cooking; parsley and chives may substitute for the cress.

1 bunch watercress (2 ounces)	½ medium green bell pepper, finely chopped (½ cup)
2 tablespoons bottled clam juice or chicken broth	⅛ teaspoon salt
1 medium onion, finely chopped	¾ pound bay scallops
1 teaspoon minced fresh ginger	

1. Wash watercress. Pat dry and chop.

2. In a small saucepan, combine clam juice, onion, ginger, and green pepper. Cook over medium heat, until onion is softened, 3 to 5 minutes. Add watercress and salt. Cook, stirring occasionally, until watercress wilts, 1 to 2 minutes.

3. Stir in scallops. Cook, stirring frequently, 3 to 4 minutes, until scallops are opaque.

146 MUSSELS STEAMED IN WHITE WINE
Prep: 10 minutes   Cook: 5 minutes   Serves: 4
Calories per serving: 157

Sit down to a big bowl of glossy-shelled mussels and dig into the delicate meat for a satisfying eating experience that makes dieting a pleasure.

3 pounds mussels	⅛ teaspoon pepper
½ cup coarsely chopped onion	1 cup dry white wine
¼ cup chopped parsley	½ cup water
¼ teaspoon thyme	

1. Scrub mussels well. With a small sharp knife, cut off hairy brownish "beards."

2. Place mussels in a large kettle. Add onion, 2 tablespoons parsley, thyme, pepper, wine, and water.

3. Cover and bring to a boil over high heat. Cook, covered, 5 minutes, until mussels open. Stir once to bring those on the bottom to the top.

4. Remove mussels with a slotted spoon. Discard any that do not open. Strain juices through a fine sieve lined with cheesecloth. Divide mussels among 4 large soup bowls. Pour hot broth over mussels. Top with remaining parsley.

147 VEGETABLE–SEA BASS BAKE

Prep: 10 minutes   Cook: 30 minutes   Serves: 4
Calories per serving: 86

If you are a fish-lover who appreciates the succulence and the form of a whole fish, baked with head and tail intact, this savory sea bass, on a bed of vegetables, is for you. The vegetables will emerge still lightly crunchy, the fish tender and juicy. A covered ceramic fish cooker is ideal for this bake—or simply cover a roasting pan with foil.

1 **1½-pound whole sea bass** **Salt and pepper**	1 **medium onion, thinly sliced**
2 **medium celery ribs cut into** **¼-inch dice**	¼ **teaspoon tarragon**
1 **medium carrot, peeled, and** **cut into ¼-inch dice**	¼ **teaspoon thyme** ½ **cup bottled clam juice**

1. Preheat oven to 350°. Leave head and tail on fish. Rinse fish under cold running water and pat dry. Season inside and out with salt and pepper.

2. Scatter celery, carrot, and onion over bottom of an ovenproof baking dish large enough to hold fish. Sprinkle tarragon and thyme over vegetables. Set fish on vegetables and pour clam juice over fish.

3. Cover with lid or foil and bake 30 minutes, or until fish is opaque next to bone.

4. Transfer fish to serving platter. Garnish with vegetables and moisten fish and vegetables with pan juices.

148 GRILLED TROUT

Prep: 5 minutes   Cook: 10 minutes   Serves: 4
Calories per serving: 85

4 **small trout, about 8 ounces** **each**	2 **onion slices, cut in half**
2 **teaspoons grated fresh** **ginger**	4 **parsley sprigs** 1 **teaspoon light soy sauce**

1. Light grill or preheat broiler. Lightly rub each trout with ginger.

2. Tuck ½ onion slice and a sprig of parsley into each fish cavity. Sprinkle ¼ teaspoon soy sauce over each trout.

3. Grill or broil fish 4 to 6 inches from heat about 5 minutes on each side, until skin is nicely browned and fish is opaque near bone.

149   SHRIMP IN WHITE WINE SAUCE

Prep: 10 minutes   Cook: 5 to 7 minutes   Serves: 4
Calories per serving: 138

1 tablespoon vegetable oil
1 medium shallot or 2
    scallions, chopped
1 garlic clove, minced
1 pound medium shrimp,
    shelled and deveined

½ cup dry white wine
¼ teaspoon salt
⅛ teaspoon pepper
2 teaspoons lemon juice
½ teaspoon thyme
1½ teaspoons chopped parsley

1. Heat oil in a large skillet and tilt pan to coat bottom. Add shallot and garlic and cook over medium heat 2 minutes, until softened but not browned.

2. Add shrimp and cook, stirring just until pink and loosely curled, about 2 minutes.

3. Stir in wine, salt, pepper, lemon juice, thyme, and parsley. Cook 1 to 2 minutes, stirring to coat shrimp, until sauce is heated through.

150   POACHED SALMON STEAKS

Prep: 6 minutes   Cook: 8 to 10 minutes   Serves: 4
Calories per serving: 170

Salmon is a fatty fish, so calories run higher than for most seafood dishes, but the oils in the fish are good for you. It makes a great meal, served with a salad of greens, tomatoes, and cucumber, and a sauce of a little Low-Fat Dressing (page 144) thinned with the cooking liquid and seasoned with dill.

2 cups water
3 lemon slices
½ teaspoon salt
1 medium celery rib, cut into 4
    pieces
1 medium carrot, cut into 4
    pieces

½ medium onion, sliced
1 teaspoon mixed pickling
    spices
4 salmon steaks, about 5
    ounces each

1. Place water, lemon, salt, celery, carrot, onion, and pickling spices in a large deep skillet or flameproof casserole with a cover. Simmer for 10 minutes over medium heat. Reduce heat to medium-low.

2. Place salmon steaks in poaching mixture in a single layer, cover pan, and simmer slowly for 8 to 10 minutes, or until just opaque throughout. Serve hot, or cool in broth if serving chilled.

151   STEAMED LOBSTER

Prep: 3 minutes   Cook: 10 to 12 minutes   Serves: 4
Calories per serving: 114

4 1-pound live lobsters, or 4
   frozen lobster tails
2 tablespoons whipped butter
   or margarine, melted

4 tablespoons lemon juice

Fill a large kettle with water and bring to a boil over high heat. Plunge in lobsters head first, cover kettle, and cook 10 to 12 minutes. Serve with melted butter or margarine combined with lemon juice for dipping.

152   GRATIN OF SCALLOPS AND MUSHROOMS

Prep: 10 minutes   Cook: 7 to 9 minutes   Serves: 4
Calories per serving: 134

Team scallops with mushrooms and white wine for a low-calorie dish finished off with a crumb topping, browned in scallop shells. No shells? Skip the crumbs and Parmesan and serve with rice, at just a few more calories.

1 pound bay scallops
¼ cup dry white wine
¾ cup bottled clam juice
1½ cups very coarsely chopped
   mushrooms (6 ounces)
¼ teaspoon salt
   Dash of cayenne
½ teaspoon dried dill weed

½ cup finely minced onion
2 tablespoons lemon juice
2 tablespoons low-fat sour
   cream
1 tablespoon grated Parmesan
   cheese
1 tablespoon seasoned bread
   crumbs

1. Place scallops, wine, clam juice, mushrooms, salt, cayenne, dill, onion, and lemon juice in a heavy nonreactive saucepan.

2. Bring to a boil, cover, reduce heat to moderately low, and simmer 3 to 4 minutes.

3. Preheat oven to 450°. Add sour cream to scallop mixture. Spoon mixture into 4 individual scallop shells or shallow individual gratin dishes. Combine cheese and bread crumbs. Sprinkle over scallops.

4. Bake for 4 to 5 minutes, until golden and hot.

153 SHRIMP-VEGETABLE TERIYAKI

Prep: 10 minutes   Marinate: 15 minutes   Cook: 8 to 10 minutes   Serves: 4   Calories per serving: 130

Whether you call these teriyaki or kebabs, shrimp and vegetables with teriyaki seasoning make a colorful, quick, and tasty broiled dish.

¼ cup teriyaki sauce	8 cherry tomatoes
1 garlic clove, minced	12 ½-inch thick slices small
⅛ teaspoon dry mustard	onion
2 tablespoons dry sherry	12 1-inch squares green bell
2 tablespoons unsweetened pineapple juice	pepper
16 large shrimp, shelled and deveined	

1. Combine teriyaki sauce, garlic, mustard, sherry, and pineapple juice in a bowl large enough to hold shrimp. Place shrimp in marinade and turn to coat well. Let stand, tossing several times, 15 to 20 minutes at room temperature, or 2 hours refrigerated.

2. Preheat broiler. On each of 4 skewers, place a tomato, then a shrimp, a slice of onion skewered crosswise, a square of green pepper. Repeat shrimp, onion, and pepper 2 times, then end with a shrimp and a tomato.

3. Broil about 4 inches from heat, turning and basting frequently with marinade, until shrimp are pink and vegetables slightly tender and charred, 8 to 10 minutes.

Chapter 5

Have Your Meat and Eat It, Too

Yes, you can enjoy steak and kebabs or stroganoff, pork goulash and veal dishes, without breaking your diet pattern. But you must be a careful meat shopper to do this.

For many years, U.S.D.A. meat standards were designed so that the highest fat, most larded meat had the highest test grade; and half-pound steaks were deemed an ample portion.

Things have changed. Both beef and pork are now being sold in lean versions. While calories are higher than for fish and chicken, if you trim off all external fat, prepare the meat without high-fat additions, such as oil, bacon, or butter, and choose a low-fat cut, such as round, a 3½-ounce portion of cooked lean meat has only 196 calories. Because leaner meats have less fat, it is important to keep them juicy. Check cooking time carefully; do not overcook.

We've used vegetables with meat in many of these dishes, both to lower the total calorie count and to round out their nutritional profile. And we've speeded preparation times. Even a meat loaf can be cooked in 25 minutes with an easy skillet method.

---

154 VEAL PICCATA
Prep: 2 minutes   Cook: 3 to 4 minutes   Serves: 4
Calories per serving: 235

1 **pound veal scallopini** **Salt and pepper** 1 **tablespoon olive oil** 3 **tablespoons lemon juice**	1 **tablespoon butter or** **margarine** 1 **tablespoon minced parsley**

1. Pound veal between 2 sheets of wax paper to flatten evenly; pat dry. Season with salt and pepper.

2. In a large heavy skillet, heat olive oil. Add veal and sauté over medium-high heat, turning once, until browned outside and just cooked through, 3 to 4 minutes. Remove veal to a platter.

3. Add lemon juice to skillet and scrape up browned bits from bottom of pan. Remove from heat and add butter. Swirl until melted. Pour over veal and garnish with minced parsley.

155 VEAL BURGERS

Prep: 10 minutes   Cook: 10 to 12 minutes   Serves: 4
Calories per serving: 156

1 pound ground veal	2 tablespoons minced parsley
2 tablespoons water	½ teaspoon salt
2 tablespoons minced onion	¼ teaspoon pepper
2 tablespoons minced green	2 teaspoons olive oil
bell pepper	Lemon wedges
1 tablespoon chopped fresh	
tarragon, or ¾ teaspoon	
dried	

1. In a medium bowl, gently blend veal, water, onion, green pepper, tarragon, parsley, salt, and pepper. Lightly form into 4 patties about ¾ inch thick.

2. In a large nonstick skillet, heat oil, tilting pan to cover bottom. Add patties and cook over medium-high heat, turning once, until browned outside and cooked through but still juicy, 5 to 6 minutes per side. Serve with lemon wedges to squeeze over burgers.

156 VEAL PARMESAN

Prep: 10 minutes   Cook: 10 minutes   Serves: 4
Calories per serving: 297

4 boneless veal cutlets	⅛ teaspoon pepper
(1 pound)	1 egg white
⅓ cup seasoned bread crumbs	1 tablespoon olive oil
2 tablespoons grated	1 cup tomato sauce
Parmesan cheese	¼ cup shredded low-fat
¼ teaspoon oregano	mozzarella cheese
¼ teaspoon salt	

1. Pound veal between 2 sheets of wax paper to flatten evenly. On another sheet of wax paper or a plate, combine bread crumbs, Parmesan cheese, oregano, salt, and pepper.

2. In a wide shallow bowl, beat egg white with 2 tablespoons water. Dip each veal cutlet first in egg white and then in bread crumb mixture to coat both sides lightly.

3. In a large nonstick skillet, heat olive oil over medium heat. Add veal and cook, turning once, until browned outside and just cooked through, about 10 minutes. Transfer to a serving plate.

4. Add tomato sauce to skillet and bring to a boil. Pour over veal. Immediately sprinkle mozzarella cheese on top.

157 VEAL SCALLOPINI WITH SHIITAKE MUSHROOMS

Prep: 10 minutes   Cook: 8 to 11 minutes   Serves: 4
Calories per serving: 235

Here's an elegant dish you can whip up in minutes. If fresh shiitakes are not available in your market, simply increase the fresh white mushrooms to ½ pound.

1 **pound veal scallopini**	¼ **pound fresh shiitake**
2 **tablespoons flour**	**mushrooms, stemmed,**
½ **teaspoon salt**	**caps sliced**
¼ **teaspoon pepper**	1 **teaspoon lemon juice**
¼ **teaspoon thyme**	**Dash of cayenne**
1 **tablespoon olive oil**	
¼ **pound fresh white**	
mushrooms, sliced	

1. If veal slices are uneven, pound between 2 sheets of wax paper to flatten. Combine flour, ¼ teaspoon salt, ⅛ teaspoon pepper, and thyme. Sprinkle over both sids of veal to coat lightly.

2. In a large nonstick skillet, heat olive oil. Add veal and sauté over medium-high heat, turning once, until lightly browned and just cooked through, 3 to 4 minutes. Remove veal to a platter and cover with foil to keep warm.

3. Add white mushrooms and shiitakes to pan. Sauté, tossing frequently, until lightly browned and tender, 5 to 7 minutes. Sprinkle lemon juice over mushrooms and season with cayenne and remaining salt and pepper. Cover veal with sautéed mushroom slices and serve.

158 VEAL MARSALA

Prep: 5 minutes   Cook: 5 to 6 minutes   Serves: 4
Calories per serving: 245

1 **pound veal scallopini**	¼ **cup beef broth**
½ **teaspoon salt**	1 **teaspoon lemon juice**
¼ **teaspoon pepper**	1 **tablespoon minced parsley**
1 **tablespoon olive oil**	1 **tablespoon butter**
¼ **cup Marsala wine**	

1. Season veal with salt and pepper. In a large skillet, heat olive oil over medium-high heat. Add veal and cook, turning once, until lightly browned and just cooked through, about 2 minutes per side. Remove veal from pan.

2. Add Marsala to skillet and boil, scraping up browned bits from bottom of pan, until wine is reduced by half, 1 to 2 minutes. Add beef broth, lemon juice, and parsley and bring to a boil. Remove from heat, add butter, and swirl until melted. Return veal to pan and turn to reheat in hot sauce. Serve at once.

159 BEEF FAJITAS WITH FRESH TOMATO SALSA

Prep: 10 minutes   Marinate: 15 minutes   Cook: 8 to 12 minutes
Serves: 4   Calories per serving: 259

Lime-marinated beef, quickly grilled and wrapped in warm tortillas, captures the zesty flavors of Mexico.

1 **pound skirt or flank steak**	¼ **cup plain low-fat yogurt**
1½ **tablespoons fresh lime juice**	4 **flour tortillas**
½ **teaspoon cumin**	¾ **cup shredded iceberg lettuce**
½ **teaspoon salt**	¼ **cup red or green salsa**
⅛ **teaspoon cayenne**	

1. Trim off any fat or silvery membrane from steak. About 15 minutes before cooking, rub steak with lime juice, cumin, salt, and cayenne.

2. Prepare a hot fire in a grill or preheat broiler. Set steak about 4 inches from heat and grill or broil, turning once, until browned outside but still pink and juicy inside, 4 to 6 minutes per side for rare, or longer if desired.

3. Let meat rest for 5 minutes before carving across grain on the diagonal into thin slices. Spread 1 tablespoon yogurt over each tortilla. Arrange one fourth of steak slices in center of each tortilla, top each with 3 tablespoons lettuce and 1 tablespoon salsa. Roll up and enjoy.

160 BEEF SUKIYAKI

Prep: 20 minutes   Cook: 10 minutes   Serves: 4
Calories per serving: 209

Freeze the meat for about 30 minutes to make it easier to cut, or ask your butcher to slice it for you. Serve this lean dish with ½ cup steamed white rice at an extra 100 calories and still come in at about 300.

1 **pound fillet of beef, cut into paper-thin slices**	1 **garlic clove, minced**
¾ **cup beef broth**	4 **large mushrooms, sliced**
¼ **cup soy sauce**	1 **cup fresh bean sprouts or 2 celery ribs, cut diagonally into ½-inch slices**
2 **tablespoons apple juice or water**	4 **scallions, cut into 3-inch lengths**
1 **large sweet onion, sliced paper-thin**	¼ **pound spinach leaves**
1 **teaspoon grated fresh ginger, or ½ teaspoon powdered**	1 **5-ounce can sliced water chestnuts, drained**

1. Be sure beef is trimmed of all excess fat. In a large skillet, bring beef broth, soy sauce, and apple juice to a simmer. Add onion, ginger, and garlic and simmer 5 minutes.

2. Add mushrooms and bean sprouts or celery and simmer 3 minutes longer.

3. Add scallions, spinach, and water chestnuts. Simmer 2 minutes. Add beef and swirl in hot liquid until it just loses its redness, about 10 seconds. Serve immediately in soup plates, with some meat and each vegetable and some broth in each bowl.

---

161 CHUCKWAGON BEEF STEW
Prep: 20 minutes   Cook: 56 to 64 minutes   Serves: 4
Calories per serving: 283

1 **pound beef round, cut into**	½ **teaspoon marjoram**
¾-inch cubes	1 **bay leaf**
Salt and pepper	1 **pound red potatoes, cut into**
1 **tablespoon vegetable oil**	**1-inch chunks**
1 **large onion, coarsely**	2 **large carrots, thickly sliced**
chopped	¼ **pound green beans, cut into**
1 **garlic clove, minced**	**1-inch lengths**

1. Season beef lightly with salt and pepper. In a large flameproof casserole, heat oil over medium-high heat. Add beef and cook, stirring occasionally, until browned, 5 to 7 minutes. Remove with a slotted spoon and set aside.

2. Add onion to pan and cook until beginning to brown, 5 to 7 minutes longer. Add garlic and cook 1 minute. Return meat to pan. Add marjoram, bay leaf, and enough water to barely cover. Cover casserole and simmer 30 minutes.

3. Add potatoes and carrots. Simmer, covered, stirring once or twice, 10 minutes. Add green beans and simmer until meat and vegetables are tender, 5 to 10 minutes longer.

4. Remove ½ cup potatoes and carrots and ½ cup liquid from stew and puree in a food processor or blender. Stir puree back into stew to thicken liquid slightly. If necessary, boil uncovered for a few minutes to thicken further. Season with salt and pepper.

162 BEEF TACOS
Prep: 10 minutes   Cook: 15 minutes   Serves: 4
Calories per serving: 260

¾ **pound ground round**
¼ **cup chopped onion**
1 **garlic clove, minced**
1 **tablespoon chili powder**
1 **teaspoon cumin**
½ **teaspoon oregano**
½ **teaspoon salt**

¼ **teaspoon pepper**
1 **cup tomato sauce**
4 **taco shells**
1 **medium tomato, chopped**
1 **cup shredded iceberg lettuce**
¼ **cup shredded cheddar**
cheese

1. In a medium bowl, blend together beef, onion, garlic, chili powder, cumin, oregano, salt, and pepper.

2. In a large nonstick skillet, cook meat mixture over medium-high heat, stirring to break up lumps, until browned, about 5 minutes. Add tomato sauce and bring to a boil. Reduce heat and simmer, stirring occasionally, until mixture is thickened, about 10 minutes.

3. To assemble tacos, fill each shell with one quarter of meat mixture. Top each with 2 tablespoons chopped tomato, ¼ cup shredded lettuce, and 1 tablespoon cheese.

163 CHILI CON CARNE WITH VEGETABLES
Prep: 15 minutes   Cook: 35 minutes   Serves: 4
Calories per serving: 289

1 **tablespoon vegetable oil**
1 **medium onion, chopped**
1 **medium green bell pepper,**
chopped
1 **garlic clove, minced**
½ **pound lean ground beef**
2½ **tablespoons chili powder**
1 **teaspoon cumin**

½ **teaspoon cinnamon**
1 **16-ounce can red beans,**
rinsed and drained
1 **14-ounce can Italian-style**
peeled tomatoes,
crushed, with their liquid
1 **teaspoon salt**
1 **large zucchini, diced**

1. In a large flameproof casserole, heat oil. Add onion and cook over medium-high heat until softened but not browned, about 3 minutes. Add green pepper and garlic and cook 2 minutes longer.

2. Add ground beef, chili powder, cumin, and cinnamon and cook, stirring to break up lumps, until beef is browned, about 5 minutes.

3. Add beans, tomatoes and their juice, and salt. Simmer, stirring occasionally, 15 minutes. Add zucchini and cook 10 minutes longer, or until zucchini is tender.

164 QUICK BEEF STROGANOFF
Prep: 7 minutes   Cook: 16 minutes   Serves: 4
Calories per serving: 188

1 **pound lean round steak**
   Salt, pepper, and paprika
2 **teaspoons vegetable oil**
1 **medium onion, thinly sliced**

½ **pound fresh mushrooms,**
   sliced
¾ **cup beef broth**
2 **tablespoons low-fat sour**
   cream

1. Cut beef across grain on the diagonal into thin strips. Season with salt, pepper, and paprika. Heat oil in a large nonstick skillet. Add beef and sauté over high heat, turning, until browned, about 3 minutes. Quickly remove beef with tongs.

2. Add onion to skillet, reduce heat to medium-high, and cook, stirring frequently, 2 minutes. Add mushrooms to skillet and sauté, stirring occasionally, until lightly browned and tender, about 5 minutes.

3. Add beef broth to skillet. Simmer 5 minutes. Stir in sour cream. Return beef to pan and cook just until heated through, but do not let sauce boil, about 1 minute.

165 STIR-FRIED BEEF AND BROCCOLI
Prep: 10 minutes   Cook: 6 minutes   Serves: 4
Calories per serving: 180

Fresh ginger adds piquancy to this dish. To keep fresh ginger on hand, seal it in a plastic bag and store it in the freezer. To use, grate the amount needed while still frozen and return the unused portion to the freezer.

¾ **pound flank steak**
2 **tablespoons soy sauce**
½ **teaspoon sugar**
1 **garlic clove, minced**
1 **teaspoon grated fresh ginger**

1 **teaspoon cornstarch**
½ **cup beef broth**
1 **tablespoon vegetable oil**
1 **large onion, thinly sliced**
1 **cup steamed broccoli florets**

1. Cut beef crosswise against grain into thin strips. Place in a medium bowl. Add soy sauce, sugar, garlic, and ginger. Toss to coat. Dissolve cornstarch in beef broth and set aside.

2. Heat oil in a wok or large heavy skillet over high heat; tilt pan to coat bottom. Add onion and stir-fry for 2 minutes. Add beef strips and stir-fry for 2 minutes longer, or until medium-rare.

3. Add broccoli to pan and toss. Stir cornstarch-broth mixture and add to pan. Cook, tossing gently, until broccoli is hot and sauce thickens, about 2 minutes. Serve at once.

166 GRILLED MARINATED FLANK STEAK

Prep: 5 minutes   Marinate: 30 minutes
Cook: 10 to 14 minutes   Serves: 4   Calories per serving: 168

Leftovers of this savory steak make great sandwiches and salads. Be sure to cook the meat only until rare or at most medium-rare to keep it tender.

1 **pound flank steak**	2 **teaspoons red wine vinegar**
2 **tablespoons dry red wine**	½ **teaspoon oregano**
2 **tablespoons water**	1 **garlic clove, minced**
2 **teaspoons soy sauce**	1 **small onion, chopped**

1. Trim all excess fat from steak. Place in a shallow nonreactive pan and prick with a fork. Add remaining ingredients and turn steak to coat. Let marinate at room temperature 30 to 60 minutes, turning once or twice.

2. Prepare a hot fire in a grill or preheat broiler. Remove steak from marinade and pat dry. Grill or broil 4 to 6 inches from heat, turning once, until rare to medium-rare, 10 to 14 minutes. Let stand for 5 minutes before carving against grain on a diagonal into thin slices.

167 JUICY HAMBURGERS DIJONNAISE

Prep: 3 minutes   Cook: 8 to 10 minutes   Serves: 4
Calories per serving: 196

Tasty burgers complete with their own tangy mustard sauce make a satisfying supper. Serve with half a roll, in a pita bread, or with Fluffy Mashed Potatoes (page 104) and still end up below 275 calories.

1 **pound ground round**	¼ **teaspoon pepper**
3 **tablespoons ice water**	¼ **cup chopped parsley**
2 **tablespoons minced onion**	¼ **cup beef broth**
½ **teaspoon salt**	1 **tablespoon Dijon mustard**

1. As lightly as possible, mix ground beef with ice water, onion, salt, pepper, and parsley. Quickly and gently form into 4 patties ½ to ¾ inch thick.

2. Heat a large nonstick skillet until hot over medium-high heat. Add patties and cook, turning once, until lightly browned outside, about 2 minutes per side. Reduce heat to medium and continue to cook, turning once more, until hamburgers are brown outside but still pink and juicy inside, 4 to 6 minutes longer.

3. Remove burgers from skillet. Pour off any fat. Add beef broth and mustard and cook, whisking to blend, until sauce boils. Pour over burgers and serve hot.

168 QUICK SKILLET MEAT LOAF

Prep: 10 minutes   Cook: 20 to 25 minutes   Serves: 4
Calories per serving: 268

1 pound lean ground beef
½ cup soft bread crumbs
1 teaspoon Worcestershire
   sauce
½ teaspoon garlic powder
½ teaspoon thyme
½ teaspoon salt
¼ teaspoon pepper

1 small onion, finely chopped
   (½ cup)
½ cup chopped celery
¼ cup chopped green bell
   pepper
1 cup tomato sauce
1 tablespoon vegetable oil

1. In a medium bowl, combine beef, bread crumbs, Worcestershire sauce, garlic powder, thyme, salt, pepper, onion, celery, green pepper, and ¼ cup tomato sauce. Mix well.

2. In a heavy medium-size skillet, preferably cast iron, heat oil. Add meat mixture and press to distribute evenly. Cover and cook over medium heat 20 to 25 minutes, until meat loaf is cooked through.

3. Invert meat loaf onto a platter. Add remaining tomato sauce to skillet and bring to a boil. Pour over meat loaf.

169 THAI BEEF SALAD

Prep: 15 minutes   Cook: none   Serves: 4
Calories per serving: 221

If your supermarket doesn't have fresh ginger, just leave it out. The salad will still be sparkling and delicious.

10 ounces cooked flank steak or
   deli roast beef, trimmed
   of excess fat
2 tablespoons fresh lime juice
1 tablespoon soy sauce
1 tablespoon water
1 teaspoon grated fresh ginger
1 garlic clove, crushed
¼ to ½ teaspoon crushed hot
   pepper flakes

3 scallions, sliced
1 cucumber, peeled, seeded,
   and sliced
1 red bell pepper, thinly
   sliced
½ head iceberg lettuce,
   shredded (about 4 cups)
¼ cup dry-roasted peanuts,
   chopped

1. Cut beef into thin strips and place in a medium bowl. Add lime juice, soy sauce, water, ginger, garlic, and hot pepper. Toss to mix. Add scallions, cucumber, and red pepper. Toss again. Cover and refrigerate until serving time.

2. Arrange lettuce in a salad bowl. Pour beef, vegetables, and any liquid in bowl over lettuce. Sprinkle peanuts on top. Toss at table just before serving.

170   SHERRY-MARINATED STEAK KEBABS

Prep: 15 minutes   Cook: 8 to 10 minutes   Serves: 4
Calories per serving: 221

Colorful skewers of beef, onion, and tomatoes make a lean meal that is quick and satisfying. Bulgur pilaf would provide a hearty accompaniment at 100 calories a ½-cup serving.

1 **pound lean sirloin steak**	1 **tablespoon sherry wine**
1 **tablespoon olive oil**	**vinegar or red wine**
1 **bay leaf**	**vinegar**
½ **teaspoon oregano**	2 **tablespoons beef broth or**
½ **teaspoon salt**	**water**
¼ **teaspoon pepper**	2 **medium onions, cut into 8**
1 **tablespoon medium-dry**	**wedges each**
sherry	2 **medium tomatoes, cut into 8**
	wedges each

1. Trim all excess fat from steak. Cut meat into 1-inch cubes.

2. Prepare a hot fire in a grill or preheat broiler. In a medium bowl, combine olive oil, bay leaf, oregano, salt, pepper, sherry, vinegar, and beef broth. Add beef cubes and tumble about until well coated. Let stand while grill is heating.

3. Thread steak, onions, and tomatoes onto 4 long metal skewers, alternating ingredients. Grill or broil, turning and basting with marinade several times, until beef is browned outside but still pink and juicy inside, 8 to 10 minutes for rare to medium-rare, or longer if desired.

171   STUFFED CABBAGE IN TOMATO SAUCE

Prep: 20 minutes   Cook: 50 to 60 minutes   Serves: 4
Calories per serving: 273

10 **large cabbage leaves**	1 **teaspoon salt**
¾ **pound lean ground beef**	¼ **teaspoon pepper**
¾ **cup cooked rice**	1 **tablespoon vegetable oil**
2 **tablespoons finely chopped**	1 **medium onion, thinly sliced**
green bell pepper	1 **16-ounce can tomatoes**
2 **tablespoons minced onion**	2 **tablespoons cider vinegar**
1 **garlic clove, minced**	⅓ **cup apple juice**
½ **teaspoon caraway seeds**	

1. Shred 2 cabbage leaves and set aside. In a large pot of boiling water, cook remaining 8 leaves until slightly wilted, about 3 minutes; drain. As soon as they are cool enough to handle, trim off thick part of ridge on back of each leaf.

2. In a medium bowl, combine beef, rice, green pepper, minced onion, garlic, caraway seeds, ½ teaspoon salt, and ⅛ teaspoon pepper. Mix well. Mound about ¼ cup stuffing at the broad end of each cabbage leaf. Fold the sides in and roll up to close.

3. In a large flameproof casserole, heat oil over medium-high heat. Add sliced onion and cook, stirring frequently, until lightly browned, about 5 minutes. Add shredded cabbage and cook, stirring, 2 minutes longer.

4. Add tomatoes with their liquid. Crush tomatoes with a large spoon to break them up. Add vinegar and apple juice. Bring to a boil. Place cabbage rolls, seam side down, in sauce. Reduce heat and simmer, covered, until cabbage is tender and meat is cooked through, 40 to 50 minutes.

---

172   SPAGHETTI SQUASH AND MEATBALLS
Prep: 10 minutes   Cook: 35 or 50 minutes   Serves: 4
Calories per serving: 292

These light meatballs borrow an Italian family trick: they are cooked directly in the sauce rather than browned first in fat.

1 **1-pound spaghetti squash**	1 **medium onion, finely**
1 **slice white bread, crust**	**chopped (¾ cup)**
removed	1 **teaspoon oregano**
2 **tablespoons dry red wine**	1 **teaspoon salt**
1 **28-ounce can Italian-style**	½ **teaspoon pepper**
crushed tomatoes	1 **teaspoon olive oil**
1 **pound lean ground round**	1 **medium carrot, shredded**
2 **garlic cloves, minced**	

1. Boil spaghetti squash in a large pot of water to cover 30 minutes, or microwave on high 15 minutes, turning once, until tender.

2. Meanwhile, in a medium bowl, soften bread in wine and ¼ cup crushed tomatoes; mash to a paste. Add beef, half the garlic, half the onion, ½ teaspoon oregano, ½ teaspoon salt, and ¼ teaspoon pepper.

3. In a large nonreactive saucepan, heat olive oil. Add remaining onion and cook over medium-high heat until softened, about 3 minutes. Add carrot and remaining garlic and cook 1 minute longer. Add remaining crushed tomatoes, oregano, salt, and pepper. Bring to a boil, then reduce heat to a simmer.

4. With moistened hands, form beef mixture into 8 meatballs. Add to tomato sauce, cover, and cook 15 minutes. To serve, cut open spaghetti squash and separate strands with 2 forks. Arrange squash on a platter and pour meatballs and tomato sauce on top.

173   MINUTE STEAK DIANE
Prep: 2 minutes   Cook: 6 to 8 minutes   Serves: 4
Calories per serving: 197

Here's a classic that's due for a comeback. Since your steak is under 200 calories, you can add a baked potato and vegetable and still have an allowance for dessert.

1 tablespoon olive oil	2 teaspoons Worcestershire
4 thin minute steaks, 4 ounces	sauce
each	2 tablespoons chopped
1½ tablespoons fresh lemon	parsley
juice	1 tablespoon unsalted butter

1. In a large skillet, heat olive oil over medium-high heat. Add steaks and cook, turning once, 3 to 4 minutes per side, or until medium rare. Remove from pan.

2. Add lemon juice, Worcestershire sauce, and parsley to pan. Scrape up browned bits from bottom of pan. Remove from heat and swirl in butter until just melted. Pour over steaks and serve.

174   STEAK PIZZAIOLA
Prep: 5 minutes   Cook: 12 minutes   Serves: 4
Calories per serving: 181

1 14-ounce can tomatoes	1 tablespoon olive oil
4 thin minute steaks, 4 ounces	2 garlic cloves, minced
each	½ teaspoon basil
Salt and pepper	½ teaspoon oregano

1. Drain tomatoes and chop coarsely. Set aside.

2. Season steaks lightly with salt and pepper. In a large nonstick skillet, heat olive oil. Add steaks and sauté over medium-high heat, turning, until nicely browned, about 4 minutes. Remove steaks from pan.

3. Add garlic, reduce heat to medium, and cook until fragrant and softened but not browned, about 1 minute. Add tomatoes, basil, and oregano. Boil sauce uncovered, stirring occasionally, until thickened slightly, about 5 minutes. Season with salt and pepper.

4. Return steaks to sauce and simmer for 2 minutes. Serve at once.

175 MEDITERRANEAN LAMB KEBABS WITH MUSHROOMS

Prep: 10 minutes   Marinate: 30 minutes
Cook: 12 to 15 minutes   Serves: 4   Calories per serving: 191

Here's a savory shish kebab that's good broiled or grilled.

1 pound boneless leg of lamb, trimmed of excess fat
¼ cup red wine vinegar
1 tablespoon extra-virgin olive oil
¼ cup chicken broth or water
1 garlic clove, crushed
½ teaspoon rosemary
½ teaspoon oregano
½ teaspoon salt
¼ teaspoon pepper
2 medium onions, quartered
8 medium mushrooms
1 green bell pepper, cut into 1½-inch squares

1. Cut lamb into 1-inch cubes and place in a medium bowl. Add vinegar, olive oil, broth, garlic, rosemary, oregano, salt, and pepper. Toss to coat meat with marinade. Let stand, tossing occasionally, 30 to 60 minutes.

2. Preheat broiler or prepare a hot fire in a grill. Thread lamb, onions, mushrooms, and green pepper onto 4 long metal skewers. Broil or grill, turning and basting meat with marinade several times, until meat is browned outside but still pink and juicy inside and vegetables are crisp-tender, about 12 to 15 minutes.

176 HONEY MUSTARD LAMB CHOPS WITH ROSEMARY

Prep: 5 minutes   Marinate: 15 minutes
Cook: 10 minutes   Serves: 4   Calories per serving: 204

Small loin lamb chops have their own portion control built right in. Here mustard and rosemary combine for extra flavor that makes every bite count. If you can't find honey mustard in your supermarket, simply blend equal parts Dijon mustard and honey.

8 loin lamb chops, cut 1 inch thick (4 ounces each)
3 tablespoons honey mustard
1 garlic clove, crushed
1 teaspoon rosemary, crumbled
½ teaspoon salt
¼ teaspoon pepper

1. Remove excess fat from lamb chops. In a small bowl, blend together honey mustard, garlic, rosemary, salt, and pepper. Spread over both sides of lamb chops. Let stand at room temperature for at least 15 minutes before cooking.

2. Prepare a hot fire in a grill or preheat broiler. Set lamb chops 4 to 6 inches from heat and grill or broil, turning once, until browned outside but still pink and juicy inside, about 10 minutes for medium-rare.

177   LAMB CHOPS ITALIENNE

Prep: 10 minutes   Cook: 10½ minutes   Serves: 4
Calories per serving: 162

1 tablespoon olive oil
4 lean shoulder lamb chops,
   trimmed of excess fat
1 garlic clove, crushed
3 tablespoons dry red wine
1 tablespoon red wine vinegar

½ teaspoon basil
¼ teaspoon salt
⅛ teaspoon pepper
¼ cup oil-cured black olives,
   halved and pitted

1. Heat olive oil in a large nonstick skillet. Add lamb chops and cook over medium-high heat, turning once, until browned outside and partially cooked through, about 5 minutes.

2. Reduce heat to medium-low. Add garlic, wine, vinegar, basil, salt, and pepper. Cover and simmer, turning chops once, until medium rare, about 5 minutes. Remove lamb chops to a platter or plates.

3. Add olives to sauce in pan and boil for 30 seconds, scraping up any browned bits from bottom of pan. Pour sauce over chops and serve.

178   PORK GOULASH WITH CABBAGE

Prep: 5 minutes   Cook: 1 hour   Serves: 4
Calories per serving: 200

Here's a flavorful dish complete with cabbage at 200 calories.

¾ pound boneless pork loin,
   trimmed of all excess fat
1 tablespoon flour
½ teaspoon salt
¼ teaspoon pepper
1 tablespoon vegetable oil
2 garlic cloves, minced

2 tablespoons imported sweet
   paprika
¾ cup chicken broth
1 pound cabbage, coarsely
   shredded
¼ cup plain low-fat yogurt

1. Cut pork into ¾-inch cubes. Place on a sheet of wax paper. Sprinkle flour, salt, and pepper over meat and toss to coat lightly.

2. In a large nonstick skillet, heat oil over medium-high heat. Add pork and cook, tossing, until lightly browned, about 5 minutes. Reduce heat to medium, add garlic and paprika and cook, stirring frequently, 1 minute. Add chicken broth, cover, and simmer 45 minutes, or until pork is very tender.

3. Steam cabbage over boiling water until tender but still firm, about 10 minutes; drain.

4. Remove pork goulash from heat. Stir in yogurt and season with additional salt and pepper. Serve goulash over cabbage.

179   THREE-PEPPER PORK
Prep: 10 minutes   Cook: 20 to 24 minutes   Serves: 4
Calories per serving: 207

The red, yellow, and green sweet peppers in this recipe make it as attractive as it is delicious. If colored peppers are out of season, make the dish with all green.

1 **pound boneless pork loin chops, trimmed of all excess fat**
½ **teaspoon salt**
¼ **teaspoon pepper**
1 **tablespoon olive oil**
1 **small onion, thinly sliced**
½ **green bell pepper, cut into thin strips**
½ **red bell pepper, cut into thin strips**
½ **yellow bell pepper, cut into thin strips**
¼ **cup chicken broth**
1 **tablespoon balsamic vinegar**
½ **teaspoon sage**

1. Season pork with salt and pepper. In a large nonstick skillet, heat olive oil over medium-high heat. Add pork chops and cook, turning once, until lightly browned outside, about 3 minutes on each side. Reduce heat to medium, cover skillet, and cook, turning once, until pork is white throughout but still moist, about 6 minutes longer. Remove chops.

2. Add onion to skillet and cook, stirring occasionally, until softened but not browned, 3 to 5 minutes. Add green, red, and yellow peppers and cook, tossing, until just softened but still bright colored, 2 to 3 minutes.

3. Add broth, balsamic vinegar, and sage. Simmer for 2 minutes. Return pork to pan and cook, turning, until just heated through, 1 to 2 minutes.

180   PORK TERIYAKI
Prep: 5 minutes   Marinate: 20 minutes   Cook: 10 to 12 minutes
Serves: 4   Calories per serving: 184

1 **pound boneless pork loin, trimmed of excess fat**
¼ **cup light soy sauce**
2 **tablespoons dry sherry**
2 **garlic cloves, crushed**
½ **teaspoon sugar**
1 **teaspoon grated fresh ginger, or ½ teaspoon powdered**

1. Cut pork into 1-inch cubes. In a medium bowl, combine remaining ingredients. Add pork and toss to coat. Let marinate at room temperature 20 to 30 minutes.

2. Preheat broiler or prepare a hot fire in a grill. Thread pork cubes onto long metal skewers. Set 4 to 6 inches from heat and broil or grill, turning and basting several times with marinade, until browned outside and white throughout but still moist, 10 to 12 minutes.

Chapter 6

Healthy Vegetables and Grains

Enjoy more meals starring vegetables, and you are likely to lose weight faster. According to current nutritional recommendations, you will also reduce your risk of leading life-threatening diseases. Vegetables and grains have no cholesterol. They are rich in dietary fiber, which does not exist in animal foods. And they are relatively low in calories.

You can play artist in designing meals with contrasts of flavor, color, and texture using vegetables. And here's where you can splurge on quantity.

There are differences in the calorie content of vegetables, mostly because of the higher amount of sugar and/or starch in certain varieties. Vegetables low in calories, which you can enjoy in almost unlimited amounts, include:

Artichokes	Cabbage	Mushrooms
Asparagus	Chinese Cabbage	Okra
Bamboo Shoots	Cucumber	Rutabagas
Bean Spouts	Endive	Spinach
Green Beans	Kale	Watercress
Beet Greens	Leeks	Water Chestnuts
Brussels Sprouts	Lettuce	Zucchini

Be moderate with the use of these higher-calorie vegetables:

Beets	Carrots	Peas
Broccoli	Corn	Tomatoes
Green Beans	Potatoes	Winter Squash
	Eggplant	

Most grains and pasta average 100 calories for a one-ounce portion. Rice swells 3 times after cooking: bulgur swells 4 times—and water has no calories—so a one-ounce portion is sufficient.

As in everything else, the additions you add to vegetables and grains can upset the calorie count. Steam vegetables or cook in broth, and spare the butter and cheese sauces. Bake or microwave mushrooms and eggplant rather than frying in oil.

181 STEAMED ASPARAGUS WITH LEMON VINAIGRETTE

Prep: 5 minutes   Cook: 5 minutes   Serves: 4
Calories per serving: 41

1 pound asparagus	2 tablespoons lemon juice
1 teaspoon extra-virgin olive oil	½ teaspoon salt
	¼ teaspoon pepper

1. Snap off tough ends of asparagus. If desired, trim off tiny "scales" on stalks.

2. Stand asparagus upright in a tall narrow pot with 3 inches of boiling water. Cover and steam over high heat about 5 minutes, or until just tender. Or place asparagus in a glass pie plate with a small amount of water, cover tightly with microwave-safe plastic wrap, and microwave on high 5 minutes. Drain.

3. Combine olive oil, lemon juice, salt, and pepper. Pour over asparagus and toss gently to coat. Serve warm or at room temperature.

182 BRAISED CELERY

Prep: 3 minutes   Cook: 20 minutes   Serves: 4
Calories per serving: 20

We often forget that celery can be cooked. Served warm, it makes a lovely accompaniment to most meats and poultry. As a chilled salad, it is particularly nice as a first course. Save the cooking broth for your next soup.

4 celery hearts (¼ pound each)	2 tablespoons marinated
2 cups beef broth	roasted red pepper strips

1. Wash celery well. Cut off tops to leave bunches about 5 inches long.

2. In a saucepan or flameproof casserole large enough to hold all 4 celery hearts, bring broth to a boil over high heat. Add celery, cover, reduce heat to medium, and cook 20 minutes, or until celery is tender.

3. If serving hot, transfer to a platter or plates. If serving chilled, let cool in broth. Garnish each serving with ½ tablespoon marinated pepper strips.

183 BROILED ONION SLICES

Prep: 5 minutes   Cook: 5 minutes   Serves: 4
Calories per serving: 27

2 large onions (¾ pound total), cut into ½-inch-thick slices
¼ teaspoon salt
⅛ teaspoon pepper

2 tablespoons chicken broth or water
2 teaspoons chopped fresh basil, or ½ teaspoon dried
1 tablespoon chopped parsley

1. Preheat broiler. Place onion slices in a shallow flameproof baking pan. Season with salt and pepper.

2. Drizzle chicken broth over onions. Sprinkle basil and parsley evenly over slices. Set about 4 inches from heat and broil 5 minutes, or until onions are tender and lightly browned.

184 OVEN POTATO CRISPS

Prep: 5 minutes   Cook: 14 minutes   Serves: 4
Calories per serving: 70

2 large baking potatoes (½ pound each)
½ teaspoon paprika
½ teaspoon salt

¼ teaspoon pepper
2 tablespoons chicken broth or water

1. Preheat broiler. Scrub potatoes well. Cut into thin slices. Arrange potato slices in a single layer on a large baking sheet. Season with paprika, salt, and pepper. Drizzle chicken broth over potatoes.

2. Set potatoes about 4 inches from heat and broil 14 minutes, turning with tongs about halfway through, until potatoes are browned and crisp.

185 CAULIFLOWER WITH SCALLIONS

Prep: 5 minutes   Cook: 5 to 7 minutes   Serves: 4
Calories per serving: 36

2 cups cauliflower florets
2 teaspoons butter or margarine

3 scallions, sliced
Salt and pepper

1. In a large pot of boiling salted water, cook cauliflower until tender, 3 to 5 minutes. Drain and transfer to a serving dish.

2. In a small skillet, melt butter over medium-low heat. Add scallions and cook 2 minutes. Pour over cauliflower and toss. Season with salt and pepper and serve hot.

186   DILLED CARROTS AND SNOW PEAS

Prep: 10 minutes   Cook: 7 minutes   Serves: 4
Calories per serving: 53

2   **large carrots (about 6 ounces total)**
¼   **pound snow peas**
2   **tablespoons chopped fresh dill, or 1½ teaspoons dried dill weed**

2   **teaspoons butter**
   Salt and pepper

1. Peel carrots and cut into 2-inch matchsticks. Trim stem ends from snow peas and pull off strings. Set aside separately.

2. In a medium saucepan of boiling salted water, cook carrots 5 minutes, until crisp-tender. Add snow peas and cook 1 minute longer. Drain, return vegetables to pan, and toss with butter over medium-high heat until butter is melted and coats vegetables. Season with salt and pepper and serve hot.

187   RED CABBAGE WITH APPLE

Prep: 7 minutes   Cook: 28 to 33 minutes   Serves: 4
Calories per serving: 87

This teaming of red cabbage with apple, accented with apple juice, white wine vinegar, and brown sugar, makes a robust dish that is excellent with pork, turkey, or chicken.

1¼   **pounds red cabbage**
½   **medium McIntosh or other tart-sweet apple**
2   **teaspoons vegetable oil**
1   **medium onion, chopped (½ cup)**
1   **teaspoon salt**

½   **teaspoon pepper**
⅛   **teaspoon ground cloves**
½   **cup apple juice**
½   **cup water**
¼   **cup white wine vinegar or cider vinegar**
1   **teaspoon brown sugar**

1. Coarsely shred red cabbage on large holes of a hand grater or in a food processor. Core and slice apple, but do not peel.

2. In a large nonreactive saucepan or flameproof casserole, heat oil. Add onion and cook over medium heat until softened, about 3 minutes. Add cabbage and apple and tumble about to coat with oil. Add salt, pepper, cloves, apple juice, and water. Cover and cook, stirring occasionally, until cabbage is tender, 15 to 20 minutes.

3. Combine vinegar and brown sugar. Stir into cabbage. Cook, stirring occasionally, 10 minutes. Serve hot.

188   BROILED SCALLOPED TOMATOES

Prep: 4 minutes   Cook: 3 to 5 minutes   Serves: 4
Calories per serving: 50

2 large tomatoes (¾ pound
    total)
2 tablespoons seasoned bread
    crumbs
½ teaspoon basil

¼ teaspoon salt
⅛ teaspoon pepper
2 teaspoons butter or
    margarine

1. Preheat broiler. Core tomatoes and cut into thick slices. Arrange slices in a single layer in a flameproof gratin dish or on a small baking sheet.

2. Combine bread crumbs, basil, salt, and pepper. Sprinkle over tomato slices. Dot with butter.

3. Set tomato slices 4 to 6 inches from heat and broil 3 to 5 minutes, until crumbs are lightly browned and tomatoes are hot.

189   GREEN BEANS PROVENÇALE

Prep: 10 minutes   Cook: 15 to 17 minutes   Serves: 4
Calories per serving: 46

1 pound green beans
1 teaspoon extra-virgin olive
    oil
¼ cup chopped onion
⅓ cup chopped tomato
1 garlic clove, crushed

1 tablespoon minced parsley
½ teaspoon basil
¼ teaspoon thyme
¼ teaspoon fennel seeds
¼ teaspoon salt
⅛ teaspoon pepper

1. In a large saucepan of boiling salted water, cook green beans until just crisp-tender, 3 to 5 minutes. Drain and rinse under cold running water; drain well.

2. In a large nonstick skillet, heat olive oil over medium heat. Add onion and cook until softened, about 2 minutes. Add tomato, garlic, parsley, basil, thyme, fennel seeds, salt, and pepper. Reduce heat to medium-low and simmer 5 minutes.

3. Add green beans and cook 5 minutes longer, tossing frequently. Serve hot or at room temperature.

190   RATATOUILLE

Prep: 10 minutes   Cook: 18 minutes   Serves: 4
Calories per serving: 90

1 medium onion, coarsely chopped (½ cup)	1 medium tomato (6 ounces), cut into 8 wedges
1 garlic clove, minced	1½ tablespoons chopped fresh basil, or ¾ teaspoon dried
½ cup chicken broth	
1 small eggplant (½ pound), cut into ¾-inch cubes	¾ teaspoon salt
1 small zucchini (5 ounces), sliced	¼ teaspoon pepper
	1 tablespoon extra-virgin olive oil
1 medium green bell pepper (6 ounces), cut into thin strips	

1. In a large nonstick skillet or flameproof casserole, combine onion, garlic, and ¼ cup chicken broth. Cook over medium heat, stirring occasionally, until onion is softened and translucent, about 5 minutes.

2. Add another 2 tablespoons chicken broth and the eggplant. Cook, tossing frequently, until eggplant is almost tender, about 5 minutes. Remove to a bowl.

3. Add remaining chicken broth to skillet along with zucchini and green pepper. Cook, stirring occasionally, until slightly softened, about 3 minutes. Add to bowl.

4. Add tomato and basil to pan and cook, stirring, 3 minutes, or until tomato is softened. Return all vegetables to skillet. Season with salt and pepper and toss. Simmer 2 minutes to blend flavors. Stir in olive oil and serve warm, at room temperature, or slightly chilled.

191   FLUFFY MASHED POTATOES

Prep: 5 minutes   Cook: 15 minutes   Serves: 4
Calories per serving: 95

2 large baking potatoes (1 pound total)	¼ cup buttermilk or skim milk
1½ cups chicken broth	½ teaspoon salt
1 tablespoon butter or margarine	¼ teaspoon pepper
	Pinch of nutmeg

1. Peel potatoes and cut into thin slices. Place potatoes and chicken broth in a medium saucepan and bring to a boil. Cover over medium heat 15 minutes, or until potatoes are soft. (Do not drain.)

2. Mash potatoes with any broth remaining in pan. Add butter and buttermilk and mix well. Season with salt, pepper, and nutmeg.

192   OVEN-ROASTED GARLIC POTATOES

Prep: 3 minutes   Cook: 45 to 50 minutes   Serves: 4
Calories per serving: 93

1 **pound large red potatoes, scrubbed and quartered**	1 **garlic clove, minced**
2 **teaspoons extra-virgin olive oil**	½ **teaspoon salt** ¼ **teaspoon pepper**

1. Preheat oven to 350°. Place potatoes in a small roasting pan. Drizzle oil over potatoes. Sprinkle with garlic and season with salt and pepper.

2. Bake potatoes for 45 to 50 minutes, until tender and browned.

193   STUFFED EGGPLANT

Prep: 10 minutes   Cook: 28 minutes   Serves: 4
Calories per serving: 74

1 **small eggplant (½ pound)**	1 **tablespoon minced fresh basil, or ½ teaspoon dried**
2 **teaspoons olive oil**	½ **teaspoon salt**
¼ **cup finely chopped onion**	¼ **teaspoon pepper**
¼ **cup chopped celery**	⅛ **teaspoon cinnamon**
2 **garlic cloves, minced**	½ **cup tomato sauce**
1 **medium tomato (6 ounces), coarsely chopped**	1 **tablespoon grated Parmesan cheese**

1. Cut eggplant lengthwise in half. Scoop out pulp with a spoon, leaving a ½-inch shell. Coarsely chop eggplant pulp.

2. In a medium saucepan or small flameproof casserole, heat oil. Add onion, celery, and garlic and cook over medium heat until softened, about 3 minutes. Add chopped eggplant, tomato, basil, salt, pepper, and cinnamon. Tumble about to mix. Cover and cook 15 minutes. Stir in tomato sauce and spoon mixture into eggplant shells. (Recipe can be prepared up to a day ahead to this point. Set aside at room temperature for up to 3 hours, or refrigerate overnight.)

3. Preheat oven to 400°. Sprinkle Parmesan cheese evenly over eggplant. Bake 10 minutes, or until eggplant is hot and cheese is melted.

194 SPEEDY EGGPLANT WITH CHEESY OAT TOPPING

Prep: 7 minutes   Cook: 11 minutes   Serves: 4
Calories per serving: 56

2 small eggplants (1 pound total)
2 tablespoons minced fresh basil or parsley
2 garlic cloves, crushed
2 tablespoons chicken broth
2 tablespoons crisp oat cereal, crumbled
2 tablespoons grated Parmesan cheese
¼ teaspoon salt
⅛ teaspoon pepper

1. Cut eggplants lengthwise in half. Score eggplants about ½ inch deep in a crisscross diamond pattern. Mix together basil or parsley and garlic and tuck into slits. Drizzle chicken broth over eggplants to moisten.

2. Wrap the cut side of each eggplant with a sheet of microwave-safe plastic wrap and set cut sides down in a microwave oven. Cook on high 6 minutes, or until eggplant is soft. Set aside for up to 3 hours, if desired.

3. Shortly before serving, preheat oven to 450°. Remove plastic wrap. Place eggplants, cut sides up, in a small baking dish. Combine oat cereal crumbs, Parmesan cheese, salt, and pepper. Bake about 5 minutes, until topping is crisp and lightly browned.

195 ITALIAN SPAGHETTI SQUASH

Prep: 3 minutes   Cook: 30 minutes   Serves: 4
Calories per serving: 50

From the outside, spaghetti squash looks like a smooth, football-shaped melon. True to its name, though, after cooking and separating with a fork, the strands inside very much resemble spaghetti. It tastes like naturally crisp strands of grated summer squash and takes well to tomato sauce.

1 1-pound spaghetti squash
½ cup tomato sauce, heated
2 tablespoons grated Parmesan cheese
1 tablespoon chopped fresh basil, or 1 teaspoon dried
½ teaspoon salt
⅛ teaspoon pepper

1. Pierce spaghetti squash several times with a fork or the tip of a knife. Place in a large saucepan filled with boiling water and cook over medium-high heat 30 minutes, or until tender. Drain and let cool slightly.

2. As soon as squash is cool enough to handle, cut in half. Scoop out and discard seeds. With a fork, scrape and pull spaghetti-like strands of squash into a bowl. Add tomato sauce, cheese, basil, salt, and pepper and toss to combine.

196 SPINACH SOUFFLE

Prep: 20 minutes Cook: 20 minutes Serves: 4
Calories per serving: 48

1 10-ounce package frozen chopped spinach, thawed	¼ teaspoon nutmeg
2 tablespoons low-fat sour cream	⅛ teaspoon pepper
	4 egg whites
	½ teaspoon salt

1. Preheat oven to 425°. Squeeze spinach to remove as much moisture as possible. Place in a food processor and puree until smooth. Blend with sour cream, nutmeg, and pepper.

2. Beat egg whites with salt until stiff but not dry. Fold one third of egg whites into spinach puree to lighten mixture. Then fold in remaining egg whites until just blended. Don't worry if a few streaks of white remain.

3. Spray a 3-cup soufflé dish with nonstick vegetable cooking spray. Bake for 20 minutes, or until puffed and golden.

197 STEAMED VEGETABLE PLATTER WITH LEMON AND DILL

Prep: 10 minutes Cook: 10 to 15 minutes Serves: 4
Calories per serving: 45

1 cup broccoli florets	3 tablespoons minced onion
2 medium carrots (¼ pound total), thinly sliced	3 tablespoons fresh lemon juice
1 medium zucchini (6 ounces), sliced	2 tablespoons minced fresh dill, or 1 teaspoon dried dill weed
1 small yellow summer squash (¼ pound), sliced	

1. Place a steaming basket or rack in a deep saucepan. Add enough water to come just beneath the bottom of the basket. Place the broccoli, carrots, zucchini, and squash in the basket. Sprinkle the onion on top.

2. Cover the saucepan and bring the water to a boil over high heat. Steam until the vegetables are just tender, 10 to 15 minutes. Remove to a serving dish and sprinkle the lemon juice and dill over the vegetables.

MICROWAVE STEAMED VEGETABLES

Place vegetables in a microwavable dish with 3 tablespoons water. Cover tightly with microwave-safe plastic wrap and steam on high about 7 minutes, until tender. Transfer to a serving dish and sprinkle lemon juice and dill over vegetables.

198 SUMMER SQUASH WITH APPLE

Prep: 7 minutes Cook: 6 to 8 minutes Serves: 4
Calories per serving: 46

2 small yellow summer
  squash (1 pound total)
½ small tart apple
1 cup chicken broth
½ teaspoon salt

⅛ teaspoon pepper
⅛ teaspoon nutmeg
1 tablespoon minced chives or
  parsley

1. Trim ends from squash and cut into thin slices. Core apple and cut into thin slices.

2. In a medium saucepan, combine squash, apple, chicken broth, salt, pepper, and nutmeg. Cook until squash and apple are tender, 6 to 8 minutes. Garnish with chives or parsley before serving.

199 NEW POTATOES WITH DILL

Prep: 2 minutes Cook: 20 minutes Serves: 4
Calories per serving: 80

12 small red potatoes, about 1½
  inches in diameter
2 cups chicken broth

1 tablespoon chopped fresh
  dill, or 1 teaspoon dried
1 tablespoon minced parsley

1. Scrub potatoes and cut in half. Place in a large saucepan and add chicken broth. Bring to a boil and cook 20 minutes, or until potatoes are tender.

2. Transfer potatoes to a serving dish and toss with dill and parsley.

200 EGGPLANT AND TOMATOES PARMESAN

Prep: 10 minutes Cook: 17 to 18 minutes Serves: 4
Calories per serving: 85

1 small eggplant (about 8
  ounces)
Salt and pepper
2 tablespoons chicken broth
2 medium tomatoes (8 ounces
  total)

1 tablespoon seasoned bread
  crumbs
1 tablespoon grated Parmesan
  cheese
¼ teaspoon basil

1. Preheat oven to 425°. Trim eggplant and cut into ⅜- to ½-inch-thick slices. Arrange on a baking sheet in a single layer. Season with salt and pepper and brush with chicken broth. Bake 12 minutes, or until almost tender. Remove from oven but leave oven on.

2. Place a slice of tomato on each eggplant slice. Combine bread crumbs with cheese and basil and sprinkle evenly over tomatoes. Return to oven and bake 5 to 6 minutes, until crumbs are lightly browned.

201 STUFFED MUSHROOMS
Prep: 8 minutes   Cook: 17 minutes   Serves: 4
Calories per serving: 33

Serve as an accompaniment to roast meats or as an hors d'oeuvre.

8 medium mushrooms
1 small garlic clove, crushed
1 large shallot or small onion, minced
2 tablespoons chicken broth
2 tablespoons low-fat cream cheese

1 tablespoon lemon juice
1 teaspoon Worcestershire sauce
¼ teaspoon salt
¼ teaspoon thyme
Dash of cayenne

1. Preheat oven to 425°. Remove mushroom stems and chop fine. Set caps aside.

2. In a heatproof glass bowl, combine chopped mushrooms, garlic, shallot or onion, and chicken broth. Cover with microwave-safe plastic wrap and microwave on high 2 minutes. (Or cook in a small saucepan until softened, 3 to 5 minutes.)

3. Add cream cheese, lemon juice, Worcestershire, salt, thyme, and cayenne. Blend well. Spoon filling into mushroom caps, dividing evenly.

4. Place stuffed mushrooms in a small baking pan. Pour ½ cup water around them and bake 15 minutes. Serve hot.

202 MIXED VEGETABLE TOSS
Prep: 8 minutes   Cook: 10 minutes   Serves: 4
Calories per serving: 40

½ cup chicken broth
1 onion, thinly sliced
1 carrot, thinly sliced
1 cup broccoli florets
1 cup shredded cabbage
½ cup red bell pepper strips (½ medium)

1 tablespoon white wine vinegar
¼ teaspoon salt
¼ teaspoon crushed hot pepper flakes

1. In a wok or large skillet, heat chicken broth over medium heat. Add onion, carrot, and broccoli. Cook, tossing occasionally, 5 minutes.

2. Add cabbage, bell pepper, vinegar, salt, and hot pepper. Cook, tossing frequently, 5 minutes longer.

203   TOASTED BUCKWHEAT

Prep: 2 minutes   Cook: 15 to 17 minutes   Serves: 4
Calories per serving: 94

1   cup medium-cut buckwheat
       groats (kasha)
1   medium egg white, lightly
       beaten

2   cups boiling chicken broth
       or water
       Salt and pepper

1. Place buckwheat in a heavy medium saucepan, preferably nonstick. Add egg white and mix well, until absorbed by grain. Set pan over medium heat and cook, shaking pan constantly, until buckwheat is toasted and golden, 3 to 4 minutes.

2. Add broth or water. Cover, reduce heat to medium-low, and cook 12 minutes, or until buckwheat is tender and liquid is absorbed. Season with salt and a generous grinding of pepper.

204   BROWN RICE MUSHROOM PILAF

Prep: 5 minutes   Cook: 35 minutes   Serves: 4
Calories per serving: 119

2   teaspoons vegetable oil
⅓   cup finely chopped onion
3   ounces fresh mushrooms
       (about 6 medium)

½   cup brown rice
1½   cups beef broth
       Salt and pepper

1. In a small saucepan, heat oil. Add onion and cook over medium heat 2 minutes. Add mushrooms and cook, stirring occasionally, 5 minutes longer. Add rice and cook, stirring, 2 minutes.

2. Add beef broth, cover pan, reduce heat to low, and cook 25 minutes, or as directed on package. Season with salt and pepper if desired.

205   QUICK COUSCOUS

Prep: 2 minutes   Cook: 5 minutes   Serves: 4
Calories per serving: 100

Here's an easy grain that's ideal with just about any meat or vegetable.

1¼   cups water
¼   teaspoon salt
⅛   teaspoon cinnamon

1   teaspoon vegetable oil
¾   cup couscous

1. In a small saucepan, bring water, salt, cinnamon, and oil to a boil.

2. Stir in couscous. Cover, remove from heat, and let stand 5 minutes. Fluff lightly with a fork before serving.

206 BULGUR PILAF

Prep: 3 minutes   Cook: 18 minutes   Serves: 4
Calories per serving: 100

Serve this hearty wheat dish as an accompaniment to meat, especially kebabs of beef or lamb.

1 **teaspoon butter or olive oil**	1½ **cups chicken broth**
1 **small onion, chopped**	½ **teaspoon salt**
(¼ cup)	¼ **teaspoon pepper**
½ **cup bulgur wheat**	

1. In a small saucepan, melt butter or heat oil. Add onion and cook over medium heat until softened, about 3 minutes. Add bulgur and stir to coat with butter. Add broth, salt, and pepper.

2. Bring to a boil, cover, reduce heat to low, and simmer 14 minutes. Let stand, covered, 5 minutes before serving.

207 LEMON RICE PILAF

Prep: 10 minutes   Cook: 20 minutes   Serves: 4
Calories per serving: 100

2 **teaspoons butter or**	⅔ **cup rice**
margarine	1⅓ **cups water**
3 **medium celery ribs, thinly**	1 **teaspoon grated lemon zest**
sliced	**Salt and pepper**
3 **scallions, thinly sliced**	

1. In a large skillet with a cover, melt butter over medium heat. Add celery, scallions, and rice. Cook, stirring occasionally, 5 minutes.

2. Pour water into skillet, bring to a boil, cover, and reduce heat to low. Cook 14 minutes, or until rice is tender and water is absorbed. Stir in lemon zest and season with salt and pepper before serving.

208   POTATO AND CARROT PUREE

Prep: 5 minutes   Cook: 20 minutes   Serves: 4
Calories per serving: 65

¾ pound baking potatoes	1 teaspoon butter or
½ pound carrots	margarine
1 small leek (¼ pound), or 3	½ teaspoon salt
scallions, white part only	¼ teaspoon pepper
2 cups chicken broth or water	Pinch of nutmeg

1. Peel potatoes and carrots and cut both into thin slices. Clean leek well and slice.

2. In a medium saucepan, heat broth to boiling over medium-high heat. Add potatoes, carrots, and leeks. Cook 20 minutes, or until vegetables are very soft. Drain, reserving cooking liquid.

3. In a blender or food processor, puree vegetables with enough of reserved cooking liquid to make a thick puree. Blend in butter and season with salt, pepper, and nutmeg.

209   MINTED ZUCCHINI AND CARROTS

Prep: 5 minutes   Cook: 8 minutes   Serves: 4
Calories per serving: 35

2 large carrots (6 ounces total)	¼ teaspoon salt
½ cup chicken broth	¼ teaspoon pepper
2 small zucchini (½ pound	1 tablespoon chopped fresh
total)	mint, or 1 teaspoon dried

1. Peel carrots and cut into thin strips about 2 inches long. In a small saucepan, heat chicken broth to boiling over medium heat. Add carrot sticks, cover, and cook 4 minutes.

2. Add zucchini and cook until both vegetables are just tender, about 4 minutes longer. Season with salt and pepper and toss with mint.

210   OVEN-ROASTED VEGETABLES

Prep: 10 minutes   Cook: 40 minutes   Serves: 4
Calories per serving: 82

4 small red potatoes (½ pound	1 medium red bell pepper
total), scrubbed	(6 ounces)
4 small carrots (6 ounces total),	½ cup chicken broth
peeled	1 tablespoon coarse salt
4 small zucchini (1 pound	Freshly ground pepper
total)	

1. Preheat oven to 400°. If potatoes are larger than 1½ inches in diameter, cut in half. Cut carrots and zucchini crosswise into 1-inch chunks. Quarter pepper, discarding stem and seeds.

2. Arrange potatoes and carrots on a baking sheet and drizzle on ⅓ cup chicken broth. Season with 2 teaspoons salt and a generous grinding of pepper. Set in oven and roast 20 minutes.

3. Add zucchini and red pepper to baking sheet. Drizzle on remaining chicken broth and season with 1 teaspoon salt and more pepper. Roast until all vegetables are browned and tender, about 20 minutes longer. Serve warm or at room temperature.

---

211 CREAMY SPINACH PUREE
Prep: 8 minutes   Cook: 8 minutes   Serves: 4
Calories per serving: 58

Fresh spinach made creamy with low-fat ricotta cheese makes a tempting accompaniment to any meat or fish.

1 **pound fresh spinach**	2 **tablespoons chicken broth**
1 **teaspoon butter or**	1 **tablespoon soy sauce**
margarine	2 **tablespoons low-fat ricotta**
3 **scallions, sliced**	**cheese**

1. Trim off thick stems from spinach. Rinse well and drain. Coarsely chop spinach leaves.

2. In a medium saucepan, melt butter. Add scallions and cook over medium heat until softened, about 2 minutes. Add spinach, chicken broth, and soy sauce. Cover and cook, stirring several times, until spinach is wilted and tender but still bright green, 3 to 5 minutes.

3. In a food processor or blender, puree spinach with all the liquid remaining in the pan until smooth. Add ricotta and puree again. Before serving, reheat puree in a bowl in microwave or in a pan over low heat.

---

212 SAVORY GREEN BEANS
Prep: 10 minutes   Cook: 4 to 5 minutes   Serves: 4
Calories per serving: 33

1 **pound green beans**	1 **teaspoon winter savory**
1 **teaspoon extra-virgin olive**	¾ **teaspoon salt**
oil	¼ **teaspoon pepper**

1. Trim ends of beans. If desired, snap in half or cut into thirds.

2. Bring a large pot of salted water to a boil. Add beans and cook until just tender, 4 to 5 minutes. Drain, transfer to a serving bowl, and toss with olive oil, savory, salt, and pepper.

213 VEGETABLE AND RICE MEDLEY

Prep: 7 minutes   Cook: 20 minutes   Serves: 4
Calories per serving: 100

Here's a low-calorie version of risotto primavera. Call it what you like, it is delicious by itself with a light dusting of grated Parmesan cheese or as an accompaniment to fish or chicken.

1 teaspoon olive oil	⅓ cup minced green bell
½ cup chopped onion	pepper
1 garlic clove, minced	1½ cups chicken broth
2 celery ribs, sliced	½ cup rice

1. In a small saucepan, heat oil. Add onion, garlic, celery, and green pepper. Cook over medium heat, stirring occasionally, 5 minutes.

2. Add chicken broth and rice and bring to a boil. Reduce heat to low, cover, and cook 15 minutes, or until rice is tender and broth is absorbed.

Chapter 7

Pasta, Pasta, Pasta!

Pasta offers a lot of eating satisfaction and a seemingly endless variety of shapes at sensible calories for the pasta itself. After cooking, an ounce of pasta, which measures a little over a half cup on average, has about 100 calories. Angel hair noodles will be more compact; large bulky shapes occupy more space. Fool yourself, if you'd like, by cooking bulkier varieties. We have allowed 2-ounce portions, or about 2 ¼ cups cooked pasta, for most recipes. Some are made bulkier with the addition of vegetables and other garnitures. Sometimes these are cooked with the pasta to add flavor and to save time—and pot washing.

Taste the pasta itself; it has a wonderful, subtle flavor, which seems to change with the varied shapes and textures. Heighten the flavor by adding an onion slice or a piece of leek to the cooking water. A spoonful of fine olive oil adds flavor, too, and it helps prevent the pasta from sticking together when it is drained.

The sauces in these recipes are far lower in calories than usual. They are made with less oil, little butter, limited amounts of cheese, and generous amounts of other flavorful factors, such as broth, herbs, spices, and vegetables. If you like plenty of sauce, scoop out and reserve a few tablespoons of the cooking liquid to add to the finished dish, extending the sauce.

In cooking pasta, use plenty of water. When it begins to bubble, drop the pasta in gradually. Let the water return to a boil, then cook until the pasta is al dente, tender but slightly resistant to the teeth.

Microwave pasta is an exception to all the above. The recipe for microwave spaghetti with marinara sauce cooks spaghetti and sauce with just enough liquid to give the spaghetti the moisture it needs, in one microwavable bowl. No draining, no rinsing, no extra-sauce making—and an interesting texture for the pasta.

Traditionally, a bowl of Parmesan cheese is passed with the pasta. You can, too. Just remember that each tablespoon adds 23 calories.

214 PASTA BOWS WITH CREAMY GREEN BEAN SAUCE

Prep: 5 minutes   Cook: 10 to 12 minutes   Serves: 4
Calories per serving: 280

8 ounces pasta bows
1 10-ounce package frozen
    French-cut green beans
½ cup plain low-fat yogurt
1 ounce Blue Fine Forme
    cheese or low-fat cream
    cheese, at room
    temperature

1 tablespoon grated Parmesan
    cheese
1 scallion, chopped
1 garlic clove, crushed
½ teaspoon salt
¼ teaspoon pepper
¼ teaspoon oregano
    Dash of cayenne

1. Bring a large pot filled with salted water to a boil. Add pasta bows and cook until tender but still firm, 10 to 12 minutes. Scoop out and reserve 2 tablespoons pasta cooking water. Immediately drain pasta.

2. While pasta is cooking, microwave green beans as directed on package; drain and transfer to a pasta serving bowl.

3. In a small bowl, combine yogurt, Blue Fine Forme or cream cheese, Parmesan, scallion, garlic, salt, pepper, oregano, and cayenne. Mix sauce to blend well.

4. As soon as pasta is drained, add to green beans. Add reserved pasta cooking liquid to sauce. Pour over pasta and green beans, toss, and serve.

215 FETTUCCINE ALMOST ALFREDO

Prep: 2 minutes   Cook: 8 to 10 minutes   Serves: 4
Calories per serving: 280

8 ounces fettuccine
1 tablespoon unsalted butter
    or margarine
¼ cup plain low-fat yogurt
2 tablespoons light cream
3 tablespoons grated
    Parmesan cheese

2 tablespoons grated Romano
    cheese
¼ teaspoon salt
    Coarsely cracked black
    pepper

1. Bring a large pot filled with salted water to a boil. Add fettuccine and cook until tender but still firm, 8 to 10 minutes. Scoop out and reserve ¼ cup pasta cooking liquid. Drain fettuccine immediately and transfer to a pasta serving bowl.

2. Toss fettuccine with butter, reserved cooking liquid, yogurt, cream, Parmesan cheese, Romano cheese, salt, and as much black pepper as you like.

216 HAY AND STRAW NOODLES

Prep: 5 minutes   Cook: 10 to 12 minutes   Serves: 4
Calories per serving: 281

This classical combination of green and white noodles is usually served with peas in the sauce. Frozen artichoke hearts are lower in calories, and they add a lovely subtle flavor to the dish.

4 ounces green noodles
4 ounces white egg noodles
2 teaspoons olive oil
1 medium onion, finely
    chopped (½ cup)
1 garlic clove, minced
4 frozen artichoke hearts,
    thawed and cut into
    slivers

¼ cup Light Crème Fraîche
    (page 143) or plain low-fat
    yogurt
¼ cup chicken broth
2 tablespoons slivered Alpine
    Lace cheese
    Salt and pepper

1. Bring a large pot filled with salted water to a boil. Add noodles slowly so that water continues to boil. Cook until pasta is tender but still firm, 10 to 12 minutes. Drain noodles and rinse briefly under running water. Transfer immediately to a serving bowl.

2. While pasta is cooking, heat oil in a medium skillet. Add onion and cook, stirring occasionally, until golden, about 5 minutes. Add garlic and artichoke hearts and cook 3 minutes longer. Add crème fraîche, chicken broth, and cheese. Cook, stirring, for 1 minute.

3. Pour sauce over hot noodles. Toss lightly to coat. Season with salt and pepper.

217 PASTA WITH TUNA PESTO

Prep: 5 minutes   Cook: 10 to 12 minutes   Serves: 4
Calories per serving: 297

8 ounces shells or other pasta
    of your choice
1 6½-ounce can water-packed
    tuna, drained and flaked

2½ teaspoons chopped walnuts
¼ cup Pesto Sauce (page 128)

1. Bring a large pot filled with salted water to a boil. Add pasta and cook until tender but still firm, 10 to 12 minutes. Scoop out and reserve ¼ cup pasta cooking liquid. Drain pasta immediately.

2. Meanwhile, toss together flaked tuna and walnuts. Add to Pesto Sauce and mix well. Stir in reserved pasta cooking liquid.

3. Place pasta in a serving bowl, add tuna pesto, and toss to coat. Serve warm or at room temperature.

218   PASTA SHELLS FRA DIAVOLO
Prep: 5 minutes   Cook: 12 minutes   Serves: 4
Calories per serving: 293

8 ounces pasta shells
2 teaspoons olive oil
1 medium onion, finely
   chopped (½ cup)
1 garlic clove, minced
3 tablespoons dry red wine
⅛ to ¼ teaspoon crushed hot
   pepper flakes
1 tablespoon chopped parsley

½ teaspoon basil
½ teaspoon oregano
¼ teaspoon salt
⅛ teaspoon pepper
1 cup tomato sauce
¼ pound small shelled
   shrimp, cooked, or frozen
   precooked shelled
   shrimp, thawed

1. Bring a large pot filled with salted water to a boil. Add pasta slowly so that water continues to boil. Cook until pasta is tender but still firm, about 12 minutes. Drain.

2. Meanwhile, in a medium saucepan, heat olive oil. Add onion and garlic and cook over medium heat until softened but not brown, about 3 minutes. Add wine, hot pepper flakes, parsley, basil, oregano, salt, and pepper. Cook 2 minutes.

3. Stir in tomato sauce and simmer 2 minutes longer. Place pasta in a serving dish, add shrimp to sauce, and pour over pasta. Toss gently and serve.

219   SPINACH ZITI
Prep: 3 minutes   Cook: 13 to 14 minutes   Serves: 4
Calories per serving: 269

8 ounces ziti or penne
1 14-ounce can Italian-style
   tomatoes, with their juice
⅛ to ¼ teaspoon crushed hot
   pepper flakes
½ teaspoon salt

¼ pound spinach, rinsed,
   drained, and coarsely
   chopped
2 ounces low-fat cream cheese
¼ teaspoon nutmeg

1. Bring a large pot filled with salted water to a boil. Add ziti and cook until tender but still firm, about 12 minutes.

2. Meanwhile, in a medium nonreactive saucepan, combine tomatoes, hot pepper flakes, and salt. Warm over medium-low heat, breaking up tomatoes with a large spoon, while pasta cooks.

3. Drain pasta and return to hot pan. Add spinach, cream cheese, and nutmeg. Cook, stirring, over low heat until spinach wilts, 1 to 2 minutes. Pour tomato sauce over spinach ziti and stir gently to mix.

220 VEGETABLE LASAGNE
Prep: 15 minutes   Cook: 43 to 46 minutes   Serves: 6
Calories per serving: 258

8 ounces lasagne noodles
1 medium zucchini (about 6 ounces), thinly sliced
1½ teaspoons olive oil
1 medium onion, finely chopped (½ cup)
1 garlic clove, minced
1 10-ounce package frozen chopped broccoli, thawed and well drained

¾ cup low-fat ricotta cheese
2 tablespoons grated Parmesan cheese
1 tablespoon chopped parsley
½ teaspoon salt
¼ teaspoon pepper
1½ cups tomato sauce
2 ounces low-fat mozzarella cheese, coarsely grated

1. Bring a large pot filled with salted water to a boil. Add lasagne noodles and cook until tender but still chewy, 7 to 10 minutes. Drain and rinse under cold running water; drain well.

2. Either blanch zucchini in a large saucepan of boiling water for 2 minutes or place in a microwavable bowl with 3 tablespoons water, cover with microwave-safe plastic wrap, and cook on high 1 minute. Drain zucchini and set aside.

3. In a medium saucepan, heat olive oil. Add onion and cook until softened but not brown, about 3 minutes. Add garlic and cook 1 minute longer. Remove from heat. Add chopped broccoli, ricotta, Parmesan, parsley, salt, and pepper. Blend well. Fold in cooked zucchini.

4. Spread 2 tablespoons tomato sauce over bottom of a 9 x 9 x 2-inch baking dish. Arrange a single layer of lasagne noodles over sauce. Spread half of vegetable filling over noodles and spoon one third of remaining tomato sauce over filling. Make another layer with half of remaining noodles, all of remaining filling, and half of remaining tomato sauce. Top with remaining noodles and sauce. Sprinkle mozzarella cheese evenly over top. (Recipe can be made ahead to this point up to a day in advance. Cover and refrigerate.)

5. Preheat oven to 400°. Bake lasagne uncovered 30 minutes, or slightly longer if chilled, until hot and bubbling.

221 MICROWAVE SPAGHETTI WITH MARINARA SAUCE

Prep: 1 minute   Cook: 8 to 11 minutes   Serves: 1
Calories per serving: 273

This surprising dish does away with boiling water and cooking spaghetti separately. The pasta cooks in the sauce for a cook-and-serve dish. Easy is an understatement! Microwaves vary in power—if yours is a 700-watt unit, 8 minutes will do it; lower power takes longer. Toss with Parmesan cheese, allowing 25 calories per tablespoon.

½ **cup hot water**
½ **cup Marinara Sauce (page 127)**

2 **ounces thin spaghetti**
1 **tablespoon chopped parsley**

1. Combine water and sauce in a 1-quart microwavable casserole; stir to mix well. Break spaghetti strands in half. Add spaghetti to sauce mixture, using a fork to submerge strands. Cover with casserole lid.

2. Microwave on high 4 minutes. Stir to separate spaghetti strands. Rotate casserole one-half turn and cook another 4 to 7 minutes, stirring occasionally, until spaghetti is cooked and sauce is thickened. Add parsley and stir before serving.

222 SHRIMP MARINARA WITH LINGUINE

Prep: 1 minute   Cook: 10 to 12 minutes   Serves: 4
Calories per serving: 272

8 **ounces linguine**
1½ **cups Marinara Sauce (page 127)**
½ **pound medium shrimp, peeled and deveined**

Pinch of crushed hot pepper flakes
1 **tablespoon lemon juice**

1. Bring a large pot filled with salted water to a boil. Add linguine gradually so that water continues to boil. Cook until tender but still firm, 10 to 12 minutes. Drain and place in a serving dish.

2. Meanwhile, in a medium nonreactive saucepan, heat Marinara Sauce. When sauce is hot, add shrimp, hot pepper flakes, and lemon juice. Cook over medium heat 4 minutes. Pour over linguine, toss, and serve.

223   FUSILLI WITH FRESH TOMATO SAUCE

Prep: 7 minutes   Cook: 12 minutes   Serves: 4
Calories per serving: 292

Ideal to serve when fresh ripe tomatoes are plentiful. Set off their rich flavor with plenty of basil.

3 **very ripe medium tomatoes, peeled, seeded, and chopped (1 cup)**
2 **garlic cloves, minced**
2 **teaspoons extra-virgin olive oil**
1 **cup fresh basil leaves, chopped**
1 **teaspoon oregano**
⅛ **teaspoon salt**
¼ **teaspoon pepper**
8 **ounces fusilli or pasta of your choice**

1. In a small nonreactive saucepan, combine tomatoes, garlic, olive oil, basil, oregano, salt, and pepper. Cook over medium-low heat 10 minutes.

2. Meanwhile, bring a large pot filled with salted water to a boil. Add pasta slowly so that water continues to boil. Cook until tender but still firm, about 12 minutes. Drain.

3. Place pasta in a serving dish, pour on tomato sauce, and toss to coat.

224   ROTELLI FLORENTINE

Prep: 8 minutes   Cook: 12 minutes   Serves: 4
Calories per serving: 289

8 **ounces rotelli or fusilli**
1 **tablespoon olive oil**
1 **small onion, finely chopped (¼ cup)**
1 **garlic clove, minced**
½ **pound fresh spinach, washed and chopped**
1 **tablespoon chopped parsley**
1 **tablespoon chopped fresh basil, or ½ teaspoon dried**
⅛ **teaspoon nutmeg**
½ **teaspoon salt**
⅛ **teaspoon pepper**
2 **tablespoons chopped walnuts**

1. Cook rotelli in a large pot filled with boiling salted water until tender but still firm, about 12 minutes. Drain.

2. Meanwhile, heat olive oil in a large nonstick skillet. Add onion and garlic and cook over medium heat until softened but not brown, about 3 minutes. Add spinach, parsley, basil, nutmeg, salt, and pepper. Cook for 3 minutes, stirring occasionally.

3. Place rotelli in a serving dish, toss with spinach mixture, and top with nuts.

225 ZUCCHINI MACARONI AND CHEESE

Prep: 5 minutes   Cook: 12 to 15 minutes   Serves: 4
Calories per serving: 257

This version of the all-time favorite is lower in calories but equally good in taste.

6 ounces elbow macaroni	½ cup skim milk
2 medium zucchini	Dash of cayenne
(10 ounces total), coarsely	¾ teaspoon salt
shredded	¼ teaspoon pepper
¼ pound low-fat cheddar	½ teaspoon paprika
cheese	

1. Cook macaroni in a large saucepan of boiling salted water until tender but still firm, 7 to 10 minutes. Stir in shredded zucchini during last minute. Scoop out and reserve ¼ cup cooking liquid. Drain macaroni and zucchini.

2. Place macaroni-zucchini mixture in a 1½-quart microwavable serving casserole. Add cheddar cheese, milk, and cayenne; season with salt and pepper. Stir to combine.

3. Place casserole in microwave and cook on high 4 minutes; stir. Sprinkle top with paprika and return to microwave for 1 minute longer. Or bake in a 375°-oven 20 minutes, until hot and bubbly.

226 ANGEL HAIR NOODLES WITH SMOKED SALMON

Prep: 5 minutes   Cook: 2 to 3 minutes   Serves: 4
Calories per serving: 274

The slimmest and most delicate of all the pastas, these noodles cook in just a few minutes.

2 ounces smoked salmon, cut	Freshly ground pepper
into small dice	8 ounces angel hair noodles
3 scallions, sliced	1 teaspoon olive oil
¼ cup Light Crème Fraîche	
(page 143)	

1. In a small bowl, combine salmon with scallions, crème fraîche, and a generous grinding of pepper.

2. Heat a large pot filled with salted water to a boil. Add noodles slowly so that water continues to boil. Add oil to prevent sticking. Cook noodles until just tender, 2 to 3 minutes. Drain.

3. Immediately transfer noodles to a serving dish. Pour smoked salmon mixture over noodles and toss to combine.

227 PASTA PRIMAVERA

Prep: 10 minutes   Cook: 10 to 12 minutes   Serves: 4
Calories per serving: 273

Vary the vegetables for this dish according to what you find in the market. Keep variety of color, texture, and flavor in mind.

½ **pound linguine**
¼ **pound slender green beans,**
cut in half
1 **cup broccoli florets**
1 **cup thin zucchini slices**
1 **tablespoon butter or**
margarine
1 **small onion, finely chopped**
(¼ cup)

1 **garlic clove, minced**
⅛ **to ¼ teaspoon crushed hot**
pepper flakes
Salt and pepper
½ **roasted red pepper (recipe**
follows), cut into strips

1. Bring a large pot filled with salted water to a boil. Add linguine and cook until tender but still firm, 10 to 12 minutes. Drain.

2. Meanwhile, in another large saucepan of boiling salted water, cook green beans, broccoli, and zucchini slices for 3 to 4 minutes, until just tender. Scoop out and reserve ¼ cup cooking liquid. Drain vegetables immediately.

3. Heat butter or margarine in a deep skillet. Add onion and garlic and cook until softened but not brown, about 3 minutes. Add cooked green beans, broccoli, and zucchini slices and tumble about to coat. Add reserved cooking liquid and hot pepper flakes.

4. Add linguine to vegetables and toss to mix. Season with salt and pepper. Transfer to a serving dish. Garnish with roasted red pepper strips.

ROASTED RED PEPPER

1 **medium red bell pepper**
(6 ounces)

1. Preheat broiler. Cut pepper in half and remove seeds. Broil pepper halves, skin side up, as close to heat as possible until skin is blistered and black, about 5 minutes. Remove from broiler.

2. Cool pepper halves under cold running water. Slip off darkened skin, and use pepper as recipe directs.

228 SPAGHETTI WITH SHRIMP IN WHITE WINE

Prep: 10 minutes   Cook: 10 minutes   Serves: 4
Calories per serving: 299

8 ounces spaghetti	½ cup dry white wine
¾ pound medium shrimp, peeled and deveined	½ teaspoon basil
	½ teaspoon thyme
2 garlic cloves, minced	½ teaspoon salt
2 teaspoons olive oil	¼ teaspoon pepper

1. Bring a large pot filled with salted water to a boil. Add spaghetti slowly so that water continues to boil. Cook until tender but still firm, about 10 minutes. Drain pasta. Scoop out and reserve ¼ cup pasta cooking liquid.

2. Meanwhile, in a large nonstick skillet, cook shrimp and garlic in oil over medium-high heat, turning often, until shrimp are pink, 2 to 3 minutes.

3. Add wine, basil, thyme, salt, pepper, and reserved pasta cooking liquid. Cover, reduce heat to medium-low, and cook 2 minutes longer.

4. Place pasta in a serving dish, pour shrimp sauce over pasta, and toss.

229 VEGETABLE-PASTA GRATIN

Prep: 14 minutes   Cook: 25 to 30 minutes   Serves: 4
Calories per serving: 286

A healthful meatless meal you'll want to serve often.

8 ounces penne or other small tubular pasta	1 small zucchini, shredded (½ cup)
2 teaspoons olive oil	1 medium green bell pepper, diced (½ cup)
1 medium onion, finely chopped (½ cup)	1 medium tomato, peeled and coarsely chopped (⅓ cup)
2 garlic cloves, sliced	¼ cup grated Parmesan cheese
1 medium carrot, shredded (⅓ cup)	

1. Bring a large pot of salted water to a boil. Add pasta slowly so that water continues to boil. Cook pasta until tender but still firm, 10 to 12 minutes. Drain.

2. Meanwhile, heat olive oil in a large nonstick skillet. Add onion and garlic and cook 3 minutes. Add carrot, zucchini, bell pepper, and tomato and tumble about to mix well. Cook 3 minutes longer.

3. Preheat oven to 350°. In an 8-inch square baking dish, combine vegetables, 2½ tablespoons cheese, and pasta. Toss to mix well. Sprinkle remaining cheese over top. Bake for 15 minutes. Cut into squares to serve.

PASTA SAUCES

Here are eight pasta sauces that you can toss with two ounces per person of any pasta you choose and still come in at under 300 calories per serving.

---

230 WHITE CLAM SAUCE
Prep: 5 minutes   Cook: 4 to 5 minutes   Serves: 4
Calories per serving: 57

1   teaspoon extra-virgin
       olive oil
2   garlic cloves, minced
1½ cups bottled clam juice
½   teaspoon thyme leaves

⅛   teaspoon pepper
1   8-ounce can minced clams,
       liquid reserved
2   tablespoons chopped
       parsley

1. In a small saucepan, heat the oil. Add garlic and cook over medium heat until softened and fragrant, 1 to 2 minutes.

2. Add clam juice, thyme, and pepper. Bring to a boil. Add clams, reduce heat, simmer 3 minutes. Stir in parsley just before serving.

---

231 TOMATO-CLAM SAUCE
Prep: 10 minutes   Cook: 15 minutes   Serves: 4
Calories per serving: 54

1   cup coarsely chopped
       tomato (1 large)
½   medium green bell pepper,
       finely diced (½ cup)
¼   cup finely chopped onion
1   garlic clove, minced

½   teaspoon oregano
1   8-ounce can minced clams,
       liquid reserved
⅛   teaspoon pepper
    Salt
1   tablespoon chopped parsley

1. In a medium saucepan, combine tomato, green pepper, onion, garlic, and oregano. Cover and cook over medium heat 10 minutes, or until onion is softened.

2. Add clams with their liquid. Taste and season with pepper and salt. Simmer 5 minutes longer. Stir in chopped parsley.

232   MUSHROOM SAUCE

Prep: 8 minutes   Cook: 18 minutes   Serves: 4
Calories per serving: 56

This is an elegant sauce that can be tossed with pasta or with strips of chicken and sun-dried tomato for a quick dinner.

1 tablespoon extra-virgin olive oil
⅓ cup finely chopped onion
1 garlic clove, minced
½ pound mushrooms, coarsely chopped

½ cup chicken broth
1½ teaspoons lemon juice
¼ teaspoon thyme
½ teaspoon salt
¼ teaspoon pepper

1. In a large nonstick skillet, heat olive oil over medium heat. Add onion and garlic and cook until soft and translucent, about 3 minutes.

2. Add mushrooms and cook, stirring occasionally, 10 minutes. Add chicken broth, lemon juice, thyme, salt, and pepper. Reduce heat to medium-low and simmer 5 minutes.

233   SWEET RED PEPPER SAUCE

Prep: 15 minutes   Cook: 25 minutes   Serves: 4
Calories per serving: 98

1 tablespoon extra-virgin olive oil
⅓ cup chopped onion
1 pound red bell peppers (2 large), chopped
1 fresh red chili pepper, seeded and chopped, or ½ teaspoon crushed hot pepper flakes

2 garlic cloves, chopped
1 teaspoon paprika
½ cup dry white wine
1½ cups water
¾ teaspoon salt
¼ teaspoon pepper

1. In a medium nonreactive saucepan or small flameproof casserole, heat oil. Add onion and cook over medium heat until golden, about 5 minutes.

2. Add bell peppers, chili pepper, garlic, and paprika. Reduce heat to medium-low and cook, stirring occasionally, until softened, about 5 minutes.

3. Add wine, water, salt, and pepper. Cover partially and simmer 15 minutes. Remove from heat and let cool slightly.

4. In a blender or food processor, puree pepper sauce until smooth. Return to saucepan and reheat before serving.

234 MEAT SAUCE
Prep: 5 minutes   Cook: 20 minutes   Serves: 4
Calories per serving: 88

Round is a lean cut of beef. Look for a package of ground round that is labeled "Extra Lean," which means there is no more than 15 percent fat. For even fewer calories, buy a package of round steak and trim off all the external fat before you grind it. The resulting ground round will contain only about 5 percent fat.

¼ **pound ground round**
1 **medium onion, chopped**
  (½ cup)
1 **garlic clove, minced**
1 **14-ounce can Italian-style**
  tomatoes, coarsely
  chopped, juice reserved

½ **teaspoon basil**
¼ **teaspoon nutmeg**
½ **teaspoon salt**
¼ **teaspoon pepper**
2 **tablespoons grated**
  Parmesan cheese

1. In a medium nonstick flameproof casserole or saucepan, cook ground round over medium heat, stirring to break up lumps, until no longer pink, about 3 minutes. Push meat to side of pan.

2. Add onion and garlic and cook 2 minutes. Mix with beef and continue to cook 3 minutes longer.

3. Add tomatoes with their juice, basil, nutmeg, salt, and pepper. Bring to a boil, reduce heat to medium-low, and simmer, stirring occasionally, 10 minutes. Stir in Parmesan cheese and simmer 2 minutes longer.

235 MARINARA SAUCE
Prep: 6 minutes   Cook: 26 minutes   Serves: 6
Calories per serving: 62

1 **tablespoon olive oil**
1 **large Spanish onion,**
  chopped (1¼ cups)
2 **large garlic cloves, minced**
1 **28-ounce can Italian-style**
  tomatoes in puree
1 **tablespoon chopped fresh**
  basil, or 1 teaspoon dried

½ **teaspoon oregano**
½ **teaspoon salt**
¼ **teaspoon pepper**
⅛ **teaspoon crushed hot**
  pepper flakes

1. In a large nonreactive saucepan or flameproof casserole, heat olive oil over medium heat. Add onion and cook, stirring often, until softened and translucent, about 5 minutes. Add garlic and cook 1 minute longer.

2. Add tomatoes with puree, basil, oregano, salt, pepper, and hot pepper flakes. Bring to a boil, breaking up tomatoes with a large spoon. Reduce heat to a simmer, cover, and cook 20 minutes.

236   HERBED TOMATO SAUCE

Prep: 7 minutes   Cook: 10 minutes   Serves: 4
Calories per serving: 57

1 16-ounce can tomatoes, with
    their juice
2 garlic cloves, crushed
⅓ cup chopped onion
2 tablespoons chopped fresh
    basil, or 2 teaspoons dried
1 tablespoon chopped parsley

½ teaspoon oregano
½ teaspoon thyme
¼ teaspoon salt
⅛ teaspoon pepper
2 teaspoons extra-virgin
    olive oil

1. Place all ingredients in a food processor or blender and puree until smooth.

2. Transfer to a nonreactive saucepan and simmer over medium-low heat 10 minutes.

237   PESTO SAUCE

Prep: 5 minutes   Cook: none   Serves: 8
Calories per ¼-cup serving: 59

This easy-to-make sauce will brighten pasta of all shapes and sizes.

2 cups fresh basil leaves
4 garlic cloves
½ cup Italian parsley leaves
2 tablespoons extra-virgin
    olive oil

6 tablespoons chicken broth
¼ cup grated Parmesan cheese
¼ teaspoon salt
¼ teaspoon pepper

1. In a food processor or blender, combine basil, garlic, and parsley; whirl to chop. Add olive oil, chicken broth, Parmesan cheese, salt, and pepper. Process until fairly smooth.

2. Use pesto at once, refrigerate for up to 2 days, or pack into clean 4- to 8-ounce jars, cover tightly with lids, and freeze to use as needed.

Chapter 8

Salads and Salad Dressings

Here is a range of salads for all seasons and meal-time moods, and all avoiding the high-calorie booby traps. Enjoy a chef's salad with turkey breast instead of beef and one thin slice of prosciutto for keen flavor impact. Make a main dish of Oriental Beef and Rice Salad and enjoy a fruit salad instead of dessert. Skip fat-trap croutons.

Salad dressings are normally the biggest culprit in adding calories. Ours, however, reverse the classic injunction about the ratio of oil to vinegar—be a miser with oil (even though salad oils are cholesterol-free), and a spendthrift with flavorful vinegars, herbs, and seasonings. In some dressings, tofu at about 8 calories per tablespoon substitutes for oil at 125 calories a tablespoon—with satisfying smooth texture.

Chicken broth and vegetable juice are used to extend some dressings. To take advantage of the minimum amount of oil used, think about the specific flavor that will add most to the salad you are preparing. Extra-virgin olive oil in small quantity adds large flavor; in some salads, you may want the nutty richness of walnut oil, the distinctive flavor of sesame, the pinch of balsamic, or a very light peanut oil. Some oils now appear in light versions, too. Note that these are generally light in flavor, not calorie reduced.

While vinegar is low in calories, you may want to temper its "bite" by adding wine or juice or broth. Choose your vinegar in keeping with the style of the meal, too.

It pays to make up those dressings by the bottle or carafe, to keep refrigerated and use as needed, for cooking as well as for snacks and salads. Light French Dressing and Light Italian Dressing also make excellent marinades for meat, fish, and poultry. The Light Vinaigrette is great for vegetables, as well as fish.

Note that our Low-Fat Dressing is far lower in calories than the calorie-reduced or light mayonnaise on store shelves. Mayonnaise is a product, with a standard for the minimum of oil that can be used, so in order to call their product mayonnaise, manufacturers are bound to use the oil required—higher in calories than our dressing at only 18 calories per tablespoon.

With this range of recipes, you can match your salad to the characteristics of the meal. For example, an Oriental salad dressing sets off a stir-fry, or Italian dressing, a spaghetti meal.

238   CARROT-RAISIN SALAD

Prep: 5 minutes   Cook: none   Serves: 4
Calories per serving: 73

4 **large carrots (½ pound)**
2 **tablespoons raisins**
3 **tablespoons minced onion**
2 **tablespoons lemon juice**
2 **tablespoons apple juice**

2 **tablespoons reduced-calorie mayonnaise**
¼ **teaspoon salt**
⅛ **teaspoon pepper**
Salad bowl lettuce leaves

Peel and grate carrots. Place in a bowl. Add raisins, onion, lemon juice, apple juice, mayonnaise, salt, and pepper. Toss to mix well. Serve on lettuce leaves.

239   CAESAR SALAD

Prep: 15 minutes   Cook: 5 minutes   Serves: 4
Calories per serving: 107

1 **medium head romaine lettuce (about 1 pound)**
1 **½-ounce slice French bread**
1 **garlic clove, minced**
1 **tablespoon grated Parmesan cheese**
2 **tablespoons extra-virgin olive oil**

2 **tablespoons water**
2 **tablespoons fresh lemon juice**
½ **teaspoon mustard**
Salt and pepper

1. Cut stem from base of lettuce. Separate leaves, wash, wrap in towel, and chill in refrigerator.

2. Cut bread into cubes, spread in a baking dish, sprinkle with garlic, and toast 5 minutes, until golden.

3. Arrange lettuce leaves in a salad bowl. Sprinkle with croutons and Parmesan cheese. Combine olive oil, water, lemon juice, and mustard. Pour over lettuce and toss to coat. Season with salt and pepper.

240   CHEF'S SALAD

Prep: 12 minutes   Cook: none   Serves: 4
Calories per serving: 161

This main-dish salad makes a satisfying lunch or light supper. Great with a thin slice of dark bread.

½ head Boston lettuce (about ¼ pound)
½ head romaine lettuce (about ½ pound)
½ medium cucumber, peeled and sliced
2 plum tomatoes, cut into 4 wedges each
2 celery ribs, sliced
4 thin slices roast turkey breast (about ¼ pound), cut into slivers
1 thin slice (½ ounce) prosciutto or Black Forest ham, cut into slivers
3 ounces Alpine Lace or other low-fat cheese, cut into strips
⅓ cup Light Blue Cheese Dressing (page 142) or Light French Dressing (page 140)

Wash and dry lettuces. Break into pieces in a salad bowl. Arrange cucumber slices, tomatoes, celery, turkey, prosciutto, and cheese on top of lettuce. Serve with your choice of dressing.

241   CHICKEN AND ORANGE SALAD

Prep: 10 minutes   Cook: none   Serves: 4
Calories per serving: 196

Chicken chunks and orange sections set off with crisp celery and scallions make a refreshing salad meal. A pinch of curry in the dressing adds flavor.

1½ cups cooked chicken breast, cut into ½-inch cubes
2 navel oranges, peeled and sectioned
2 celery ribs, diced
2 scallions, sliced
⅓ cup reduced-calorie mayonnaise
¼ teaspoon salt
⅛ teaspoon pepper

Combine all ingredients in a bowl. Tumble about gently to combine. Serve on lettuce or watercress.

242   CONFETTI COLESLAW
Prep: 10 minutes   Cook: none   Serves: 4
Calories per serving: 83

Red cabbage and green cabbage combine to make a colorful low-calorie coleslaw.

1 **cup shredded green cabbage**
1 **cup shredded red cabbage**
2 **scallions, thinly sliced**
1 **carrot, peeled and grated**
¼ **cup Low-Fat Dressing (page 144) or reduced-calorie mayonnaise**

2 **tablespoons cider vinegar**
1 **teaspoon sugar**
1 **teaspoon caraway seeds**
½ **teaspoon salt**
¼ **teaspoon pepper**

1. In a bowl, combine green and red cabbage, scallions, and carrot.

2. Mix dressing with vinegar, sugar, and caraway seeds. Pour over vegetables. Toss to combine. Season with salt and pepper.

243   CURRIED TURKEY AND RICE SALAD WITH GREEN GRAPES
Prep: 3 minutes   Cook: none   Serves: 4
Calories per serving: 232

Curry-accented turkey with refreshing grapes and satisfying rice makes a sensible-calorie main dish salad. Distinctive to serve even for company.

1¾ **cups diced cooked turkey breast**
¼ **cup seedless green grapes**
1 **cup cooked rice**
1 **tablespoon balsamic or white wine vinegar**

⅓ **cup reduced-calorie mayonnaise**
1 **teaspoon curry powder**
¼ **teaspoon salt**
⅛ **teaspoon pepper**

1. Combine turkey cubes, grapes, and rice in a bowl. Add vinegar and toss to mix.

2. Combine mayonnaise, curry powder, salt, and pepper. Pour over turkey and grapes. Tumble about until coated.

244 GERMAN POTATO SALAD
Prep: 6 minutes   Cook: 20 to 25 minutes   Serves: 4
Calories per serving: 95

Hot German potato salad sets off a simple grilled chop, or a burger, in zesty style.

4 medium potatoes (1¼ pounds)	**1 teaspoon Dijon mustard**
2 teaspoons extra-virgin olive oil	**½ teaspoon salt**
	Freshly ground pepper
2 tablespoons white wine vinegar	**1 tablespoon minced chives**
	2 tablespoons chopped parsley

1. Place potatoes in a medium saucepan. Add enough water to cover by at least 1 inch. Bring to a boil and cook until tender, 20 to 25 minutes. As soon as potatoes are cool enough to handle, peel off skins. Cut potatoes into large cubes.

2. Combine olive oil, vinegar, and mustard. Pour vinegar mixture over hot potatoes and tumble about to coat.

3. Season with salt and pepper and sprinkle with chives and parsley. Serve potato salad warm or at room temperature.

245 CREAMY DILLED CUCUMBER SALAD
Prep: 4 minutes   Chill: 2 to 3 hours   Cook: none   Serves: 4
Calories per serving: 31

Cucumbers with low-calorie crème fraîche, dill accent, and a touch of sharp-sweet flavor make a superb salad with a fish meal.

2 medium cucumbers	**1 teaspoon sugar**
2 tablespoons rice wine vinegar or cider vinegar	**1 tablespoon chopped fresh dill**
3 tablespoons Light Crème Fraîche (recipe follows) or plain low-fat yogurt	**¼ to ½ teaspoon coarse salt**
	⅛ teaspoon pepper

Trim off ends of cucumbers. Cut cucumbers into thin slices and place in a bowl. Add remaining ingredients and toss to mix. Chill for 2 to 3 hours.

246 GREEN BEAN AND TOMATO SALAD WITH BASIL

Prep: 15 minutes   Cook: 3 to 5 minutes   Serves: 4
Calories per serving: 56

This colorful and refreshing salad serves equally well as a first course or as a side dish, instead of a vegetable. If you have leftover cooked green beans, by all means use them and begin with step 2.

5 ounces green beans	1 tablespoon extra-virgin olive
3 ripe tomatoes	oil
1 garlic clove, minced	3 tablespoons chicken broth
3 tablespoons chopped basil	or vegetable juice
leaves, or 1 teaspoon	³⁄₈ teaspoon salt
dried	¹⁄₈ teaspoon pepper

1. Trim ends from green beans and cut into 1- to 1½-inch lengths. Cook in a medium saucepan of boiling salted water until just tender, 3 to 5 minutes. Add tomatoes to pan during last 10 to 20 seconds of cooking to loosen skins.

2. Peel, seed, and dice tomatoes. In a medium bowl, combine green beans and tomatoes with garlic, basil, olive oil, and chicken broth. Season with salt and pepper.

3. Toss gently. Serve at room temperature or slightly chilled.

247 MARINATED MUSHROOMS

Prep: 3 minutes   Cook: none   Serves: 4
Calories per serving: 49

Just two ingredients make a memorable mushroom salad. It pays to keep a jar of your own pre-mixed Italian dressing in the refrigerator for occasions like this.

½ pound medium mushrooms	¼ pound iceberg lettuce,
¼ cup Light Italian Dressing	shredded
(page 141)	

1. Cut stem ends from the mushrooms and discard. Wipe caps and stems with a damp paper towel and slice.

2. Toss mushrooms with Italian dressing. Chill and serve on lettuce.

248 MINTY FRUIT SALAD
Prep: 8 minutes   Cook: none   Serves: 4
Calories per serving: 80

A refreshing salad to follow a soup meal, or enjoy anytime.

1   **navel orange**
1   **cup strawberries**
1   **ripe pear**
¼   **cup Minted Citrus Dressing
    (page 146)**

1   **small head Boston lettuce
    Mint leaves, for garnish
    (optional)**

1. Peel and dice orange, hull and cut strawberries in half, and core and dice pear.

2. Combine fruit in a bowl with Minted Citrus Dressing; chill. Serve on lettuce, garnished with mint leaves.

249 MEDITERRANEAN RICE SALAD
Prep: 8 minutes   Cook: none   Serves: 4
Calories per serving: 158

A refreshing salad to serve with fish or chicken. Particularly good with a zesty main dish. To make a complete meal salad, add tuna or cold diced chicken to the rice mixture.

1½   **cups cold cooked rice**
¼   **cup Light Italian Dressing
    (page 141)**
2   **teaspoons chopped parsley**
½   **teaspoon salt**
¼   **teaspoon pepper**
¼   **cup finely chopped green
    bell pepper**

4   **pitted small black olives,
    sliced**
2   **sun-dried tomato halves,
    slivered**
2   **cups shredded lettuce**

1. In a small bowl, combine rice with Italian dressing, parsley, salt, and pepper. Toss to coat thoroughly.

2. Add green pepper and olives and mix gently.

3. Garnish with sun-dried tomatoes. Serve on a bed of shredded lettuce.

250   SEAFOOD COCKTAIL SALAD
Prep: 5 minutes   Cook: none   Serves: 4
Calories per serving: 98

Fish or seafood salad accented with salsa makes it worth cooking an extra amount of fish. Or, steam ¾ pound cod to make this dish. Allow about 6 minutes to steam through.

1½ **cups cooked shrimp,**
     scallops, and/or crab
  2 **scallions, sliced**
  2 **celery ribs, diced**

  ¼ **cup bottled salsa**
  2 **tablespoons reduced-calorie**
     mayonnaise

Place all ingredients in a bowl, tossing to combine.

251   SHRIMP AND ARTICHOKE SALAD
Prep: 18 minutes   Cook: 8 to 9 minutes   Serves: 4
Calories per serving: 83

This superlative shrimp salad takes on added flavor from a fumet made with shells flavored with soy sauce and ginger. Total cooking is just 9 minutes—and there is a shortcut below.

  ¾ **pound raw shrimp**
  1 **slice onion**
  1 **tablespoon light soy sauce**
  1 **slice fresh ginger**
  ½ **cup water**
  ½ **cup Light French Dressing**
     (page 140)

  ¼ **cup canned water chestnuts,**
     sliced
  4 **canned artichoke bottoms,**
     quartered
  2 **scallions, sliced**
     Salt and pepper

1. Shell and devein shrimp. Save the shells.

2. Cook shrimp shells, onion, soy sauce, and ginger in the water for 5 minutes. Strain liquid into another saucepan. Discard solids. Cook shrimp in the savory liquid for 3 to 4 minutes. Let cool in liquid, then drain, reserving liquid.

3. In a bowl, add 2 tablespoons of shrimp liquid to French dressing. Add shrimp, water chestnuts, artichoke bottoms, scallions, salt, and pepper. Toss to combine.

EASY SHRIMP SALAD

Instead of first 5 ingredients, use 12 ounces cooked shrimp. Omit water chestnuts; add 1 tablespoon capers to French dressing. Add artichokes and scallions. Toss to combine.

252   ORIENTAL BEEF AND RICE SALAD
Prep: 8 minutes   Cook: none   Serves: 4
Calories per serving: 120

Rice, beef, and vegetables toss up a new salad combination, with oriental dressing.

1   cup cooked rice
¼   pound cooked lean beef, cut into strips
2   scallions, sliced
1   red or green bell pepper, cut into strips

1   medium tomato, cut into chunks
¼   cup Oriental Dressing (page 145)
1½   cups shredded lettuce or Chinese cabbage

1. Combine rice, beef, and vegetables in a bowl. Add Oriental Dressing and toss to combine.

2. Serve on a bed of shredded lettuce or cabbage.

253   SPINACH MUSHROOM SALAD
Prep: 11 minutes   Cook: none   Serves: 4
Calories per serving: 67

Spinach, mushrooms, and a zesty dressing add up to a satisfying yet low-calorie salad. To serve as a main dish, add chopped hard-cooked eggs and/or chicken strips. Remember to count the extra calories.

½   pound fresh spinach
8   large mushrooms
2   scallions, sliced
4   radishes, sliced

½   cup Lemon Mustard Dressing (page 140)
1   tablespoon light soy sauce
Salt and pepper

1. Wash spinach well. Remove stems and discard or save for soup. Shake spinach dry and refrigerate while preparing mushrooms.

2. Cut off stem ends of mushrooms and discard. Slice mushrooms.

3. Place spinach leaves and mushrooms in a bowl. Add scallions and radishes. Combine Lemon Mustard Dressing with soy sauce and pour over salad. Season with salt and pepper.

254   WALDORF SALAD
Prep: 7 minutes   Cook: none   Serves: 4
Calories per serving: 121

4 **celery ribs, sliced**
2 **medium tart apples, diced**
1 **tablespoon coarsely**
    chopped walnuts
¼ **cup reduced-calorie**
    mayonnaise

2 **tablespoons lemon juice**
2 **tablespoons apple juice**
¼ **teaspoon tarragon**
4 **Boston lettuce leaves**

1. In a medium bowl, combine celery, apples, and chopped walnuts. Toss to mix.

2. In a small bowl, combine mayonnaise, lemon juice, apple juice, and tarragon. Pour over celery and apple mixture and toss until coated.

3. To serve, spoon salad onto lettuce leaves.

255   MIXED VEGETABLE SALAD
Prep: 8 minutes   Cook: none   Serves: 4
Calories per serving: 38

1 **cup broccoli florets**
1 **medium zucchini**
    (6 ounces), scrubbed and
    shredded
1 **large carrot, peeled and**
    shredded

1 **scallion, sliced**
⅓ **cup Light French Dressing**
    (page 140)
½ **teaspoon salt**
    Freshly ground pepper

In a salad bowl, combine broccoli, zucchini, carrot, and scallion. Add Light French Dressing and salt and toss. Season generously with pepper.

256   TROPICAL FRUIT SALAD
Prep: 7 minutes   Cook: none   Serves: 4
Calories per serving: 152

This combination of tropical fruits is so juicy and delicious, it needs no dressing. If you don't find mango and papaya at the same time, substitute banana, orange, ripe pear, berries, or melon.

1 **ripe mango**
1 **1-pound papaya**

1 **kiwi**
2 **tablespoons lime juice**

1. Peel mango and cut into lengthwise slices. (A serrated knife is easiest for this; angle knife against seed in slicing.) Place mango slices in a medium bowl.

2. Peel papaya. Cut in half and scoop out seeds. Cut each half crosswise into slices. Add to bowl.

3. Peel and slice kiwi into bowl. Add lime juice and toss gently.

4. Arrange fruit on flat plates. Serve with a knife and fork.

---

257   SMOKED TURKEY SALAD WITH SESAME SEEDS AND SPROUTS

Prep: 5 minutes   Cook: none   Serves: 4
Calories per serving: 126

1½ **cups diced smoked turkey (8 ounces)**
1½ **cups bean sprouts**
2 **scallions, sliced**
1 **tablespoon rice wine vinegar or white wine vinegar**

2 **tablespoons chicken broth or water**
1 **teaspoon soy sauce**
½ **teaspoon sugar**
1 **tablespoon sesame seeds**

1. In a medium bowl, combine smoked turkey, bean sprouts, and scallions.

2. In a small bowl, combine vinegar, chicken broth, soy sauce, and sugar. Stir to dissolve sugar.

3. Pour dressing over salad and toss to coat. Sprinkle sesame seeds over top.

---

258   TUNA-MUSHROOM SALAD

Prep: 5 minutes   Cook: none   Serves: 4
Calories per serving: 174

Sliced mushrooms and low-fat cheddar cheese add extra flavor and appetite appeal to tuna salad—at under 175 calories a portion.

1 **7-ounce can water-packed tuna**
4 **large mushrooms**
2 **celery ribs, diced**
1 **onion, finely chopped**
2 **ounces low-fat cheddar cheese, grated**

¼ **cup reduced-calorie mayonnaise**
1 **tablespoon lemon juice**
¼ **teaspoon salt**
⅛ **teaspoon pepper**
1 **head Boston lettuce leaves, washed and dried**

1. Drain tuna and break up with a fork.

2. Cut off stem ends of mushrooms and discard. Wipe off caps and stems with a damp paper towel and slice; add to tuna. Add celery, onion, cheese, mayonnaise, and lemon juice. Season with salt and pepper.

3. Serve in lettuce cups.

259 LIGHT FRENCH DRESSING
Prep: 4 minutes   Cook: none   Makes: 1 cup
Calories per tablespoon: 6

Vegetable juice instead of oil is the low-calorie secret of this dressing. This zesty combination will dress your salad to everyone's taste, and it makes a versatile base for other flavor combinations. Try it as a marinade, too.

¾ **cup vegetable juice**
2 **tablespoons red wine vinegar**
2 **tablespoons lemon juice**
2 **teaspoons olive oil**

1 **garlic clove, crushed through a press**
2 **teaspoons Dijon mustard Salt and pepper**

Combine all ingredients in a lidded jar. Shake well. Season with salt and pepper. Refrigerate. Shake to combine before each use.

260 CREOLE DRESSING
Prep: 2 minutes   Cook: none   Makes: 1 cup
Calories per tablespoon: 7

¾ **cup Light French Dressing (see recipe above)**
4 **tablespoons lemon juice**

4 **tablespoons low-calorie ketchup**
½ **teaspoon Worcestershire sauce**

Combine all ingredients in a bowl and mix well. Refrigerate until ready to serve.

261 LEMON MUSTARD DRESSING
Prep: 3 minutes   Cook: none   Makes: 1 cup
Calories per tablespoon: 6

Wonderful sweet-tart flavor is the appeal of this dressing. Good contrast for chicken salad, turkey, or sprouted greens.

¾ **cup Light French Dressing (see recipe above)**
2 **tablespoons lemon juice**

1 **tablespoon honey mustard**
½ **teaspoon grated lemon zest**

Combine all ingredients. Mix well and serve.

262   GARLIC DRESSING
Prep: 2 minutes   Cook: none   Makes: 1 cup
Calories per tablespoon: 6

For garlic lovers, this packs a zesty punch.

1 cup Light French Dressing
    (page 140)

1 garlic clove, crushed
    through a press
1 scallion, finely minced

Combine French dressing, garlic, and scallion in a jar or cruet with tight closure. Let stand in the refrigerator for an hour or two before using to marry the flavors.

263   LIGHT ITALIAN DRESSING
Prep: 6 minutes   Cook: none   Makes: 1 cup
Calories per tablespoon: 6

Add oregano and a garlic clove to French dressing for extra seasoning and serve up a dressing to go with pasta or any Italian-accent meals.

1 cup Light French Dressing
    (page 140)
1 garlic clove
1 scallion, minced

½ teaspoon oregano
    Dash of crushed hot pepper
    flakes

Combine all ingredients in a jar with lid. Refrigerate. Shake to combine before using.

264   CHIFFONADE DRESSING
Prep: 5 minutes   Cook: none   Makes: 1 cup
Calories per tablespoon: 7

This color-specked dressing adds flavor to a cold vegetable salad, to tomatoes, or to greens.

½ cup Light French Dressing
    (page 140)
1 medium hard-cooked
    egg white, chopped
¼ cup coarsely chopped onion
2 tablespoons coarsely
    chopped red bell pepper

2 tablespoons chopped
    parsley
2 tablespoons lemon juice
    Salt and pepper

Combine all ingredients in a blender, adding salt and pepper to taste. Blend just until coarsely chopped. Store in refrigerator.

265   LORENZO DRESSING
Prep: 2 minutes   Cook: none   Makes: 1 cup
Calories per tablespoon: 9

A French dressing to wake up your appetite and lend character to any simple green salad.

1   **cup watercress sprigs**   ¼   **cup chili sauce**
¾   **Light French Dressing**
     (page 140)

1. Wash watercress and chop fine.

2. Combine with French dressing and chili sauce. Mix well.

266   OIL-FREE DRESSING
Prep: 4 minutes   Cook: none   Makes: 1 cup
Calories per tablespoon: 3

¾   **cup tomato juice**   1   **thin slice of onion**
2   **tablespoons diced green**   ½   **teaspoon paprika**
     pepper   ¼   **teaspoon pepper**
1   **tablespoon chopped parsley**   ⅛   **teaspoon powdered mustard**

Place all ingredients in a blender and blend until smooth. Pour into a jar with lid. Store in refrigerator. Shake before using.

267   LIGHT BLUE CHEESE DRESSING
Prep: 4 minutes   Cook: none   Makes: 1 cup
Calories per tablespoon: 15

Creamy and tangy, this blue cheese dressing adds character to a simple salad.

6   **ounces tofu, mashed, or**   ¼   **cup crumbled blue cheese**
     ½ cup plain low-fat   **(1 ounce)**
     yogurt   ¼   **teaspoon salt**
1   **tablespoon white wine**   ¼   **teaspoon pepper**
     vinegar   **Dash of cayenne**
1   **tablespoon lemon juice**

Combine tofu, vinegar, and lemon juice in a blender. Remove to lidded jar and stir in crumbled blue cheese. Season with salt, pepper, and cayenne. Store in refrigerator.

268 LIGHT CREME FRAICHE
Prep: 5 minutes   Cook: none   Standing time: 4 hours
Makes: 1¼ cups   Calories per tablespoon: 22

Make crème fraîche, refrigerate, and use as wanted.

½ **cup low-fat yogurt**   ¼ **cup heavy sweet cream**
½ **cup low-fat sour cream**

1. Combine yogurt, sour cream, and sweet cream. Stir until smooth. Cover loosely and let stand at room temperature 4 to 6 hours.

2. Cover tightly and refrigerate for up to 10 days.

269 CREAMY CUCUMBER DRESSING
Prep: 3 minutes   Cook: none   Makes: 6 tablespoons
Calories per tablespoon: 5

Delicious on sliced tomatoes, on tuna or other fish, or any cold cooked vegetable salad.

3½ **tablespoons plain low-fat**   1 **tablespoon chopped fresh**
     yogurt   **dill, or 1 teaspoon dried**
1½ **tablespoons white wine**   **dill weed**
     vinegar   **Salt and pepper**
  2 **tablespoons chopped,**
     peeled, and seeded
     cucumber

1. In a bowl, combine yogurt and vinegar. Mix until smooth.

2. Add cucumber and dill. Season with salt and pepper. Store in refrigerator.

270 CREAMY HERB DRESSING
Prep: 5 minutes   Cook: none   Makes: 1 cup
Calories per tablespoon: 7

Try this creamy herbed dressing in tuna salad, on cucumbers as a dip, or as a sauce for fish or potatoes.

  5 **ounces plain low-fat yogurt**   1 **teaspoon chopped chives**
  1 **tablespoon whipped light**   1 **teaspoon chopped basil, or**
     cream cheese   ½ **teaspoon dried**
1½ **tablespoons cider vinegar**   ½ **teaspoon celery seed**
  1 **tablespoon chopped parsley**   **Salt and pepper**

Combine all ingredients in a lidded jar, adding salt and pepper to taste. Store in refrigerator.

271   LOW-FAT DRESSING
Prep: 3 minutes   Cook: none   Makes: 1⅓ cups
Calories per tablespoon: 18

This versatile spread has less than one-fifth the calories of mayonnaise, and holds up well in salads and for many recipe uses. Accent to your taste with chili or curry powder, chopped chives or parsley. You can substitute it for reduced-calorie mayonnaise in any recipe in this book and slash the calorie count by 32 per tablespoon.

1 cup low-fat cottage cheese
1 medium egg
1 tablespoon olive oil
1 teaspoon white wine vinegar

¼ teaspoon powdered mustard
½ teaspoon garlic salt
   Dash of cayenne
1 tablespoon lemon juice

Combine all ingredients in a food processor or blender and beat until very smooth. Spoon into a lidded jar and store in refrigerator. Keeps about 2 weeks.

272   HERB MAYONNAISE
Prep: 4 minutes   Cook: none   Makes: 1 cup
Calories per tablespoon: 39

¾ cup Low-Fat Dressing (see recipe above)
2 tablespoons chopped parsley

1 tablespoon minced chives
½ teaspoon tarragon
½ teaspoon thyme
   Salt and pepper

In a small bowl, combine dressing, parsley, chives, tarragon, and thyme. Blend well. Season with salt and pepper. Cover and refrigerate for up to 2 weeks before serving.

273   GREEN GODDESS DRESSING
Prep: 10 minutes   Cook: none   Makes: 1 cup
Calories per tablespoon: 37

¾ cup Low-Fat Dressing (see recipe above)
2 scallions, thinly sliced
4 spinach leaves, finely chopped

½ green pepper, finely diced
6 parsley sprigs, finely chopped
2 tablespoons lemon juice
   Salt and pepper

1. Place dressing, scallions, spinach, green pepper, parsley, and lemon juice in the blender.

2. Blend until very finely chopped and pale green in color. Scrape into a jar and season with salt and pepper. Cover and refrigerate until ready to use.

274 ORIENTAL DRESSING
Prep: 5 minutes   Cook: none   Makes: 1 cup
Calories per tablespoon: 3

No one will ever guess the ingredients of this Oriental dressing, ideal to serve with the salad accompanying a compatible main dish.

⅓ cup chicken broth	½ teaspoon grated fresh
¼ cup unsweetened	ginger, or a pinch of
applesauce	powdered ginger
3 tablespoons rice wine	¼ teaspoon grated lemon zest
vinegar	¼ teaspoon sesame oil
2 tablespoons light soy sauce	

Combine all ingredients in a lidded jar, stir until smooth, and store in refrigerator.

275 SNAPPY TOMATO DRESSING
Prep: 4 minutes   Cook: none   Makes: ½ cup
Calories per tablespoon: 8

Stir up this flavorful dressing for a seafood salad, chef's salad—or to wake up a plain green salad.

⅓ cup tomato juice	½ teaspoon minced garlic
1 tablespoon red wine vinegar	1 teaspoon white horseradish
1 tablespoon lemon juice	Salt and pepper
1 teaspoon olive oil	

Combine all ingredients in a lidded jar, adding salt and pepper to taste. Shake well and refrigerate.

276 LIGHT VINAIGRETTE
Prep: 2 minutes   Cook: none   Makes: 1 cup
Calories per tablespoon: 7

Great for marinating vegetables such as green beans, asparagus, or potatoes, or as dressing for vegetable salads, greens, or chef's salad.

1¾ cups chicken broth	1 garlic clove, minced
¼ cup white wine vinegar or	2 teaspoons Dijon mustard
cider vinegar	½ teaspoon tarragon
2 teaspoons olive oil	Salt and pepper

Combine all ingredients, adding salt and pepper to taste. Store in refrigerator. Shake well before serving.

263   MINTED CITRUS DRESSING

Prep: 4 minutes   Cook: none   Makes: 1 cup
Calories per tablespoon: 12

A flavorful tangy dressing for fruit salads, fish, or chicken salad.

¾ **cup orange juice**
2 **tablespoons lemon juice**
2 **tablespoons red wine**
     vinegar
2 **teaspoons olive oil**

1 **teaspoon Dijon mustard**
1 **teaspoon chopped fresh**
     mint leaves, or ¼
     teaspoon dried
Salt and pepper

Combine all ingredients, adding salt and pepper to taste, in a lidded jar or cruet. Store in refrigerator.

Chapter 9

Breakfast and Late Night

Breakfast, brunch, and late-night meals have a lot in common. All occur at a time of day when you have refreshing food that is fairly quick to prepare, light and easy to eat.

For many families, breakfast is now the meal most often eaten together. This makes the morning meal, or a late evening get-together, important for emotional as well as nutritional support. Since breakfast comes before major energy expenditures of the day, breakfast calories tend to get used up in activities. Keep late-night meals on the light-calorie side. king eggs offers some interesting gamesmanship for a dieter. Large eggs have more calories and are higher in cholesterol than medium eggs. We have used medium eggs throughout. The white of a medium egg has 15 calories and no cholesterol. The yolk has 52 calories and a high cholesterol load. We have made lower-calorie and lower-cholesterol egg dishes using more whites than yolks. If you have a cholesterol restriction, you might want to use all white. More whites also make for light and high-rising soufflés and omelets.

Breads include some quickies you can bake; some you slice thin to cut the calories per portion. Here are cereals and refreshing fruits, microwave quickies and some dishes to star at that fast-growing favorite way to entertain—the weekend brunch. Your guests will bless you for the calorie savings, too.

278   CHEESE SOUFFLE
Prep: 7 minutes   Cook: 28 to 34 minutes   Serves: 4
Calories per serving: 150

Here's a soufflé that's quick to mix and to bake, with elegant cheese flavor, great height and lightness. The low-calorie secrets? No panade of butter and flour, just 2 egg yolks to 5 whites. For an even more spectacular presentation, bake this soufflé in a 5-cup soufflé dish with a collar wrapped around it.

1 cup skim milk	⅛ teaspoon pepper
1 tablespoon cornstarch	¼ teaspoon dry mustard
⅔ cup grated low-fat cheddar	Pinch of cayenne
or Monterey jack cheese	2 medium egg yolks
with jalapeño	5 medium egg whites
1 tablespoon grated Parmesan	¼ teaspoon salt
cheese	

1. Stir milk and cornstarch until well combined; heat mixture in a small saucepan, stirring until thickened, 1 to 2 minutes. Off heat, add cheeses and seasonings and stir until cheese is melted.

2. Beat egg yolks with a fork. Add a little of hot cheese mixture to yolks, then add yolks to remaining cheese mixture. Cook, stirring, over low heat 2 minutes.

3. Preheat oven to 400°. Beat 5 egg whites with salt until stiff but not dry. Fold about one third of egg whites into cheese mixture very thoroughly to lighten. Fold in remaining egg whites very gently until just barely blended.

4. Pour into an ungreased 6-cup soufflé dish and bake for 25 to 30 minutes, until puffed and golden. Serve at once.

279   HOLLANDAISE-LESS SAUCE
Prep: 4 minutes   Cook: 4 minutes   Makes: ½ cup
Calories per tablespoon: 24

Another fooler, this tasty sauce at fewer than half the calories of the real thing is ideal to top eggs or asparagus.

1 medium egg	1 tablespoon unsalted butter
1 tablespoon apple cider	Pinch of salt
vinegar	Pinch of dry mustard
3 tablespoons chicken broth	Pinch of cayenne
1 teaspoon lemon juice	

Place all ingredients in a small double boiler or in a bowl. Beat with a whisk, place over simmering water, and continue beating until thick and creamy, about 4 minutes.

280   HERB-SCRAMBLED EGGS

Prep: 3 minutes   Cook: 3 minutes   Serves: 4
Calories per serving: 80

Extra egg white lowers the calories for an herb-seasoned scramble—a good quick dish for four.

2 **whole medium eggs**	2 **teaspoons chopped parsley**
4 **medium egg whites**	2 **teaspoons minced chives**
¼ **cup skim milk**	2 **teaspoons butter or**
⅛ **teaspoon salt**	**margarine**
Pinch of pepper	

1. Break whole eggs and egg whites into a bowl. Add milk, salt, pepper, parsley, and chives and beat together with a fork.

2. Melt butter or margarine in a large nonstick skillet over medium heat.

3. When fat is sizzling, add eggs and stir with a fork, shaking the pan until eggs are no longer runny but not dry, about 3 minutes.

281   EGGS BENEDICT ARNOLD

Prep: 8 minutes   Cook: 2 minutes   Serves: 4
Calories per serving: 113

A traitor to fat and calorie overload, this fool-the-eye creation is fun for any brunch.

3 **medium egg whites**	**Pinch of powdered saffron**
¼ **teaspoon salt**	4 **round brown rice cakes**
¼ **cup low-fat cottage cheese**	2 **teaspoons yellow mustard**
1 **teaspoon grated Parmesan**	**Hollandaise-Less Sauce**
cheese	**(recipe follows)**
2 **tablespoons reduced-calorie**	
mayonnaise	

1. Beat egg whites with salt until softly thickened and fluffy. Spray 4 wells of an egg poacher with nonstick vegetable spray and drop one fourth of egg whites in each; make an indentation with the back of a tablespoon at the center of each. Cover and poach in simmering water 2 minutes, or until set; if necessary, to maintain indentation, press with tablespoon again.

2. Meanwhile, in a food processor or in a bowl, whip together cottage cheese, Parmesan cheese, mayonnaise, and saffron, until well blended.

3. Spread each rice cake with ½ teaspoon mustard. Place poached egg white on each and fill hollow with beaten cheese mixture. Top each with 1 tablespoon Hollandaise-Less Sauce. Pass remaining sauce on the side, allowing 24 extra calories for each additional tablespoon of sauce.

282   VEGETABLE FRITTATA

Prep: 15 minutes   Cook: 8 to 9 minutes   Serves: 4
Calories per serving: 142

This tasty Italian egg dish, cousin to both omelet and quiche, sets on top of the range, then finishes quickly under the broiler.

3 **whole medium eggs**
3 **medium egg whites**
1 **tablespoon olive oil**
½ **cup chopped onion**
   (1 medium)
3 **tablespoons diced red or**
   green bell pepper
1 **small zucchini, thinly sliced**
   (¾ cup)

1 **tablespoon chopped fresh**
   basil, or 1 teaspoon dried
¼ **cup skim milk**
2 **tablespoons grated**
   Parmesan cheese
½ **teaspoon salt**
¼ **teaspoon pepper**
1 **small tomato (4 ounces),**
   cut into 8 wedges

1. Break 3 whole eggs plus 3 egg whites into a medium bowl and let stand.

2. Heat oil in a 9-inch ovenproof nonstick skillet. Cook onion, diced pepper, zucchini, and basil until zucchini is crisp-tender, about 3 minutes.

3. Preheat broiler. Add milk to eggs and beat until light and bubbly; beat in 1 tablespoon cheese, salt, and pepper. Pour over vegetables in skillet and cook over medium heat, stirring gently with a plastic spatula, until eggs begin to set, about 2 minutes. Continue cooking without stirring until almost set, about 2 minutes longer.

4. Arrange tomato wedges on top of frittata. Sprinkle with remaining cheese. Place skillet under preheated broiler 4 to 6 inches from heat until top sets and cheese melts, 1 to 2 minutes. Serve cut into wedges.

NOTE: *If the handle of your skillet is not heatproof, wrap with aluminum foil.*

283   HUEVOS RANCHEROS

Prep: 1 minute   Cook: 6 minutes   Serves: 1
Calories per serving: 84

A breakfast with a Mexican accent—complete the meal with a steamed tortilla for a morning holiday mood.

2 **tablespoons bottled salsa**
2 **tablespoons water**

1 **medium egg**

1. Place salsa and water in a small skillet. Bring to a boil.

2. Break egg into the salsa, reduce heat, and cook 3 to 4 minutes to desired doneness.

284 EGGS CREOLE

Prep: 5 minutes   Cook: 10 to 13 minutes   Serves: 4
Calories per serving: 134

Colorful and tasty eggs Creole make a satisfying brunch dish.

1 medium green bell pepper, diced	1 cup tomato sauce
1 medium onion, finely chopped	¼ teaspoon tarragon
	¼ teaspoon salt
2 teaspoons butter or margarine	⅛ teaspoon pepper
	Dash of hot pepper sauce
	4 medium eggs

1. Combine green pepper, onion, and butter in a large nonstick skillet. Cook over medium heat until vegetables are softened slightly, about 3 minutes.

2. Add tomato sauce, tarragon, salt, pepper, and hot sauce. Cook 2 minutes longer.

3. With a spoon, make 4 nests in the sauce. Drop eggs, one at a time into nests. Simmer 5 to 8 minutes longer, or until eggs are set to desired doneness. Serve eggs with Creole sauce.

285 QUICK COFFEECAKE WITH OATMEAL-WALNUT TOPPING

Prep: 10 minutes   Cook: 35 minutes   Makes: 16 squares
Calories per square: 112

Classic ingredients used in moderate amounts make this satisfying nibble —cut into brownie-size portions for calorie control. Great to share with friends after a meeting.

1½ cups flour	1 tablespoon uncooked oatmeal
2½ teaspoons baking powder	1 teaspoon cinnamon
¼ teaspoon salt	1 tablespoon dark brown sugar
5 tablespoons butter or margarine	1 tablespoon chopped walnuts
½ cup sugar	
1 medium egg, beaten	
¾ cup skim milk	

1. Preheat oven to 375°. Grease an 8 x 8 x 2-inch baking pan. Combine flour, baking powder, and salt. Set aside.

2. Cream 4 tablespoons butter or margarine. Add sugar and beat until light and smooth. Add egg and blend well. Add flour mixture, alternating with milk and ending with flour. Pour into baking pan.

3. Combine remaining ingredients, including 1 tablespoon butter. Sprinkle over the batter and bake for 35 minutes, until brown.

286   GINGERED BROCCOLI FRITTATA

Prep: 10 minutes   Cook: 10 to 12 minutes   Serves: 4
Calories per serving: 139

3 whole medium eggs	1 cup steamed broccoli florets
3 medium egg whites	3 tablespoons coarsely
¼ cup skim milk	shredded red bell pepper
½ teaspoon salt	1 teaspoon grated fresh ginger
¼ teaspoon pepper	2 tablespoons grated
1 tablespoon olive oil	Parmesan cheese
½ cup chopped onion (1 medium)	

1. Break whole eggs and egg whites into a medium bowl. Add milk and beat until light and fluffy. Beat in salt and pepper.

2. Heat oil in a 9-inch ovenproof nonstick skillet. Add onion and cook over medium heat until softened and translucent, about 3 minutes. Add broccoli, red pepper, and ginger. Cook, tossing broccoli frequently, until heated through, 2 to 3 minutes longer.

3. Preheat broiler. Beat 1 tablespoon grated cheese into eggs and pour over vegetables in skillet. Cook, stirring gently with a plastic spatula, until eggs begin to set, about 2 minutes. Continue cooking without stirring until almost set, about 2 minutes longer.

4. Sprinkle remaining 1 tablespoon cheese over frittata. Transfer skillet to preheated broiler and cook 4 to 6 inches from heat until top sets and cheese melts, 1 to 2 minutes. Serve cut into wedges.

287   BREAKFAST POPOVERS

Prep: 3 minutes   Cook: 40 minutes   Makes: 10 popovers
Calories per popover: 74

Light and puffed popovers, a big treat at modest calories.

1 cup all-purpose flour	2 medium eggs
¼ teaspoon salt	1 cup skim milk
2 teaspoons vegetable oil	

1. Preheat oven to 450°. Grease a heavy cast-iron popover pan or a muffin pan. Preheat pan.

2. Place flour and salt in a mixing bowl. Add oil, eggs, and milk and beat for about 2 minutes until smooth, or whirl in a blender for 45 seconds.

3. Fill 10 popover or muffin cups half-full. Bake for 40 minutes. Serve hot.

288   HERB OMELET

Prep: 2 minutes   Cook: 1 to 2 minutes   Serves: 1
Calories per serving: 116

Herbs add flavor and color to a one-egg omelet—at negligible calorie cost.

1 **medium egg**	1 **teaspoon minced chives**
Pinch of salt	½ **teaspoon chopped fresh**
Dash of pepper	**basil or ¼ teaspoon dried**
1 **tablespoon skim milk**	½ **teaspoon butter or**
1 **teaspoon chopped parsley**	**margarine**

1. Separate the yolk from the white of the egg, putting the white in a soup bowl and reserving the yolk.

2. Add salt and pepper to the white and beat it with a fork until foamy. Beat in the yolk, skim milk, and herbs.

3. Heat butter or margarine in a small nonstick skillet over medium heat. Add beaten egg mixture. Shake pan so that mixture is evenly distributed.

4. Cook 1 to 2 minutes to set the egg, then roll out onto a serving plate.

289   MICROWAVE OMELET

Prep: 2 minutes   Cook: under 1 minute   Serves: 1
Calories per serving: 80

A quick, effortless omelet, lower in calories than you would think possible.

1 **whole medium egg**	2 **grinds of pepper**
1 **medium egg white**	1 **teaspoon chopped parsley**
2 **tablespoons skim milk**	1 **teaspoon minced chives**
⅛ **teaspoon salt**	

1. Rinse shallow microwavable soup bowl with water. Break egg into bowl; add egg white, milk, salt, pepper, parsley, and chives. Beat with fork until well combined and light.

2. Cover bowl tightly with microwave-safe plastic wrap. Microwave on high 50 seconds, or until puffy and set. Let stand covered for 10 seconds. Remove plastic carefully and serve.

NOTE: *Before beating, add 1 tablespoon grated Parmesan cheese for a cheese omelet —23 added calories. For a mushroom omelet, add ¼ cup sliced mushrooms and increase cook time to 1 minute—10 added calories.*

290　BREAKFAST RICE CAKE "RIZZAS"

Prep: 2 minutes　Cook: 3 minutes　Serves: 1
Calories per serving: 53

A rice cake makes the base for this pizza-like treat.

1　**whole-grain rice cake**	2　**teaspoons grated low-fat**
1　**slice tomato**	**mozzarella cheese**
	Pinch of basil

1. Place rice cake on an ovenproof dish. Place tomato slice on rice cake. Sprinkle cheese over the tomato slice and sprinkle basil over the cheese.

2. Broil 4 to 6 inches from heat for 3 minutes until cheese is melted.

291　FRUIT-FILLED CLOUD PANCAKES

Prep: 5 minutes　Cook: 10 minutes　Serves: 6
Calories per serving: 128

These reduced-calorie griddlecakes are smooth, light, and fluffy and have no cholesterol—no egg or butter.

1　**cup all-purpose flour**	1　**medium egg white**
1　**tablespoon baking powder**	¾　**cup blueberries or sliced**
¼　**teaspoon salt**	**strawberries**
1¼　**cups skim milk**	2　**tablespoons blueberry or**
1　**tablespoon vegetable oil**	**strawberry fruit spread**

1. Heat a nonstick griddle or skillet. In a small bowl, combine flour, baking powder, and salt. Add milk and oil to flour mixture and beat just to combine. Beat egg white until stiff but not dry. Fold in egg white.

2. Pour about 2½ tablespoons batter for each pancake onto hot skillet and bake until underside is brown. Turn and brown top side. Slide out and keep warm.

3. Combine berries and preserves. Place a spoonful of berries with preserves on one side of each pancake and roll up. Allow 2 pancakes per serving.

292   HONEY–RAISIN BRAN MUFFINS
Prep: 4 minutes   Cook: 15 minutes   Makes: 18 muffins
Calories per muffin: 79

A wholesome and tasty muffin, at affordable calories. If you prefer a less grainy muffin, sutstitute unbleached all-purpose flour for the whole wheat.

1½ **cups whole-wheat flour**	1 **cup plain low-fat yogurt**
½ **cup oat bran or bran cereal**	¼ **cup vegetable oil**
2½ **teaspoons baking powder**	¼ **cup honey**
1 **teaspoon baking soda**	2 **tablespoons raisins**
⅛ **teaspoon salt**	

1. Preheat oven to 375°. Spray 18 muffin cups with nonstick cooking oil.

2. Combine dry ingredients in a mixing bowl. Add yogurt, oil, and honey and mix until just moistened; the batter should not be smooth. Fold in raisins.

3. Spoon into muffin cups until half-filled and bake 15 minutes, or until brown.

293   SPINACH AND WALNUT FRITTATA
Prep: 10 minutes   Cook: 13 to 14 minutes   Serves: 4
Calories per serving: 160

3 **whole medium eggs**	2 **tablespoons coarsely**
3 **medium egg whites**	**chopped walnuts**
¼ **cup skim milk**	¼ **teaspoon grated nutmeg**
1 **tablespoon olive oil**	2 **tablespoons grated**
½ **cup chopped onion**	**Parmesan cheese**
¼ **pound spinach, well rinsed,**	½ **teaspoon salt**
drained, and chopped	¼ **teaspoon pepper**

1. Break 3 whole eggs plus 3 egg whites into a medium bowl. Add milk and beat with a fork until light and bubbly. Set aside.

2. Heat oil in a 9-inch ovenproof nonstick skillet. Add onion and cook over medium heat until softened, about 3 minutes. Add spinach, walnuts, and nutmeg and cook, stirring frequently, until spinach wilts but is still bright green and excess liquid evaporates, about 5 minutes.

3. Preheat broiler. Beat 1 tablespoon cheese into eggs. Season with salt and pepper. Pour over spinach mixture and cook, stirring gently with a plastic spatula, until eggs begin to set, about 2 minutes. Continue to cook without stirring until almost set, about 2 minutes longer.

4. Sprinkle remaining cheese over frittata. Transfer to broiler and cook 4 to 6 inches from heat until top sets and cheese melts, 1 to 2 minutes. Serve cut into wedges.

294   SKINNY BAGEL BREAKFAST

Prep: 5 minutes   Cook: 1 minute   Serves: 2
Calories per serving: 119

Split a bagel to enjoy a breakfast with good nutritional points as well as eating pleasure.

1 whole wheat or pumpernickel bagel	**4 teaspoons fruit spread of choice**
¼ cup low-fat cottage cheese	

1. Preheat broiler. Cut bagel crosswise into 4 slices. Toast slices in toaster.

2. Spread each slice with 1 tablespoon cottage cheese and top with 1 teaspoon fruit spread. Allow 2 slices per serving.

295   THREE-GRAIN BRAN CRISPS

Prep: 6 minutes   Cook: 5 to 6 minutes   Serves: 4
Calories per serving: 109

A surprisingly crisp breakfast cake: quick to brown, warm, and crunchy. A good cereal, fruit, and milk breakfast.

1 cup crisp bran cereal, crushed	**½ cup nonfat dry milk**
½ cup oat bran	**2 medium egg whites**
2 tablespoons cornmeal	**½ cup orange juice**
	1 teaspoon grated orange zest

1. Pour bran cereal, oat bran, and cornmeal into a food processor, blender, or plastic bag and blend or coarsely crush. Transfer to a medium bowl.

2. Add nonfat milk, egg whites, orange juice, and orange zest. Mix to blend well. Let stand 10 minutes, or refrigerate until ready to use.

3. Preheat griddle; spray with nonstick vegetable coating. Scoop up rounded tablespoonfuls of bran mixture. Place on griddle and flatten with back of spoon. Cook over medium heat until brown on one side, about 3 minutes. Flip over with spatula and cook second side until browned, 2 to 3 minutes longer.

296   HOT OAT BRAN WITH APRICOTS
Prep: 3 minutes   Cook: 5 minutes   Serves: 1
Calories per serving: 177

1 cup hot oat bran cereal

22 dried apricot halves, cut into small pieces

1. Prepare oat bran cereal with water according to directions on the package.

2. Add cut apricots and stir to combine. Eat as is or with ½ cup skim milk, and add 44 calories.

297   APPLE-RAISIN OATMEAL
Prep: 3 minutes   Cook: 5 minutes   Serves: 1
Calories per serving: 163

⅓ cup oatmeal
½ red apple, cored and grated but not peeled

2 teaspoons raisins
Dash of cinnamon

1. Prepare oatmeal with water as directed on package. Add grated apple, raisins, and cinnamon.

2. Enjoy as is or with ½ cup skim milk, and add 44 calories.

298   CHEESE-ORANGE BREAKFAST-ON-THE-GO
Prep: 1 minute   Cook: none   Serves: 1
Calories per serving: 143

1 orange, unpeeled

1 1-ounce slice low-fat American cheese

1. Cut orange down, but not through, into 4 sections.

2. Cut slice of cheese into 4 pieces and tuck one between each orange section.

3. Wrap in plastic wrap or foil and take with you.

299   MUESLI

Prep: 5 minutes   Cook: none   Standing time: 10 minutes   Serves: 1
Calories per serving: 183

¼ cup uncooked oatmeal
½ cup skim milk
1 tablespoon fresh lemon
   juice

½ apple, grated
1 teaspoon brown sugar
1 teaspoon raisins

Place all ingredients in a cereal bowl. Stir to combine. Let stand for 10 minutes before eating.

300   BRUNCH PEACH PARFAIT

Prep: 5 minutes   Cook: 1 minute   Serves: 2
Calories per serving: 181

2 ripe medium peaches or
   nectarines
1 teaspoon lemon juice
1 teaspoon honey

¼ teaspoon vanilla extract
1 cup plain low-fat yogurt
2 graham crackers
   Pinch of cinnamon

1. Bring a large saucepan of water to a boil. Add peaches and cook 30 to 60 seconds, until skins loosen. Drain and rinse under cold running water. Peel peaches, halve, and remove pits. Cut peaches into ½-inch dice. Place in a bowl and put lemon juice and honey over. Stir to combine.

2. Stir vanilla into yogurt.

3. Into 2 parfait glasses place half the fruit, then half the yogurt; repeat with other half fruit and end with yogurt.

4. Crumble graham crackers and combine with cinnamon. Sprinkle over yogurt.

301   SUMMER MIXED BERRY SALAD

Prep: 2 minutes   Cook: none   Serves: 2
Calories per serving: 49

⅓ cup quartered strawberries
⅓ cup raspberries
⅓ cup blueberries

2 tablespoons orange juice
½ teaspoon grated orange zest

1. In a small bowl, combine strawberries, raspberries, and blueberries.

2. Add orange juice and orange zest. Toss gently to mix. Spoon berries into 2 glass dishes, dividing evenly. Serve at room temperature or slightly chilled.

302   STRAWBERRY-YOGURT TOPPING
Prep: 2 minutes   Cook: none   Serves: 2
Calories per serving: 50

Serve this berry-good topping over cold cereal, a pancake, or a slice of toast.

½ **cup halved strawberries,**   ¼ **cup plain low-fat yogurt**
   washed and hulled
1 **tablespoon confectioners'**
   sugar

Place strawberries and confectioners' sugar in a bowl. Mash well with a fork. Add yogurt and stir.

303   WINTER FRUIT COMPOTE
Prep: 3 minutes   Cook: 10 minutes   Serves: 2
Calories per serving: 125

1 **ounce pitted prunes**   ¼ **cup water**
1 **ounce dried apricots**   1 **navel orange**
2 **lemon slices**

1. In a small saucepan, combine prunes, apricots, lemon slices, and water. Simmer 10 minutes. Set aside and let fruit cool in liquid.

2. Peel orange and divide into sections. Add orange sections to compote. Cover and refrigerate until chilled.

304   GLAZED GRAPEFRUIT
Prep: 2 minutes   Cook: 3 to 4 minutes   Serves: 1
Calories per serving: 113

You will warm up to this new flavor for grapefruit on a cold winter morning. It's good for dessert, too.

1 **medium grapefruit**   ¼ **teaspoon cinnamon**
   (1 pound)
2 **teaspoons orange**
   marmalade

1. Preheat broiler. Cut grapefruit in half. Combine orange marmalade and cinnamon and spread over grapefruit.

2. Set grapefruit 4 to 6 inches from heat and broil 3 to 4 minutes, until caramelized and nicely glazed. Serve warm.

305   MICROWAVE APPLE MELT
Prep: 1 minute   Cook: 3 minutes   Serves: 1
Calories per serving: 160

The soft and crunchy texture of this dish makes it fun to eat early in the morning or late at night.

1 **apple**	2 **tablespoons crunchy cereal**
1 **1-ounce slice low-fat**	**with fruits and nuts,**
muenster cheese	**crushed**
Pinch of cinnamon	

1. Cut apple into 8 wedges, cut out core, and place close together, skin side down, on a microwavable plate. Microwave 2 minutes, or until apple wedges soften but are not mushy.

2. Place cheese over wedges, sprinkle with cinnamon, and top with crushed cereal. Microwave 30 seconds to 1 minute, or until cheese melts. Serve warm.

306   FALL FRUIT COMPOTE
Prep: 2 minutes   Cook: none   Serves: 2
Calories per serving: 82

½ **medium red apple**	½ **cup unsweetened pineapple**
½ **medium firm, ripe pear**	**chunks, drained**
	3 **tablespoons apple juice**

1. Core apple half, but do not peel. Cut into ½-inch dice. Core pear and cut into ½-inch dice.

2. In a small bowl, combine apple, pear, and pineapple chunks. Add apple juice and toss gently. Spoon into 2 glass dishes, dividing evenly. Cover and refrigerate until chilled.

307   CRISPY BREAKFAST AMBROSIA
Prep: 2 minutes   Cook: none   Serves: 2
Calories per serving: 94

1 **small banana**	½ **cup crispy rice cereal**
1 **small navel orange**	

Peel banana and cut into chunks. Place on a shallow plate. Peel and section orange, letting any juice fall onto the banana chunks. Arrange orange slices around banana. Sprinkle lightly with cereal. Serve as breakfast fruit.

308   APPLE-BUTTERED RYE TOAST
Prep: 30 seconds   Toast: 45 seconds   Serves: 1
Calories per serving: 99

Rediscover apple butter, an American spread about one third lower in calories than most fruit preserves, and with satisfying flavor.

1 **thin slice rye bread, toasted**	2 **teaspoons apple butter**
2 **tablespoons low-fat cottage cheese**	

Spread toast with cottage cheese and top with apple butter.

309   ORANGE BREAKFAST SHAKE
Prep: 1 minute   Cook: none   Serves: 1
Calories per serving: 124

A breakfast you sip, satisfying and refreshing, with calories low enough to allow for a slice of toast.

½ **cup ice cubes**	⅓ **cup nonfat dry milk**
3 **tablespoons frozen orange juice concentrate**	2 **tablespoons rice or oat bran**
	½ **teaspoon vanilla extract**

Combine ingredients in order given in a blender container. Cover. Blend about 5 seconds, until frothy.

310   CRISPY OAT BRAN COOKIES
Prep: 15 minutes   Bake: 10 minutes   Makes: 24 cookies
Calories per cookie: 35

For breakfast-cookie lovers, this is a delectable way to enjoy your cereal-in-hand, and extra fiber too!

1¼ **cups quick-cooking oats**	1 **tablespoon lemon juice**
½ **cup oat bran**	2 **teaspoons vanilla extract**
¼ **cup nonfat dry milk**	¼ **cup sugar**
2 **medium egg whites**	1 **teaspoon grated orange zest**
Pinch of salt	

1. Preheat oven to 350°. Combine oats, oat bran, and nonfat milk in a large bowl. Beat egg whites until soft peaks form when the beater is raised, then add salt, lemon juice, and vanilla and beat until stiff. Fold in sugar, 1 tablespoon at a time, then orange zest.

2. Fold egg mixture into oat mixture. Drop by spoonfuls onto cookie sheet lined with parchment paper or aluminum foil. Bake about 10 minutes, until golden. Turn off oven and leave cookies in oven to dry, about 10 minutes. Remove, cool on rack, and store in a tin box.

Chapter 10

Diet Desserts

This book is about enjoyable ways to eat meals you will appreciate even more when you look in the mirror. And this chapter will add a lot to your pleasure. Fruits make a refreshing no-fat ice cream; cake billows with egg whites; choco-holics will be hard-put to choose between meringues, mousse, or soufflé. Here are puddings and sherbets, cookies and straw-berries Romanoff, cheesecake and raspberry soufflé.

Taste—really taste—and savor the flavor, texture, and aroma of each dessert. You'll find that the modest diet por-tions can give real satisfaction. Then turn to the next chapter for a coffee or tea to top off this terrific dessert.

---

311 ANGEL FOOD CUPCAKES
Prep: 20 minutes   Cook: 15 minutes   Makes: 12
Calories per cupcake: 80

The lightest of all cakes, and the lowest in calories. Serve as is, or top with Chocolate Topping (page 183).

¾ **cup cake flour (or ⅔ cup**
   flour plus 1 tablespoon
   cornstarch)
¾ **cup sugar**

7 **medium egg whites**
¾ **teaspoon cream of tartar**
¼ **teaspoon salt**
¾ **teaspoon vanilla extract**

1. Preheat oven to 375°. Sift together flour and 2 tablespoons sugar.

2. Beat egg whites until frothy. Beat in cream of tartar, salt, and vanilla. Beat until peaks fold over slightly when beater is lifted. Sprinkle remaining sugar over surface of egg whites, 2 tablespoons at a time, and fold in with rubber spatula. Sift ¼ cup of flour-sugar mixture over surface and fold in. Repeat until all flour is added.

3. Using a spatula, spoon gently into cupcake pan with pleated paper lin-ers. Bake about 15 minutes, until golden. Cool in pan on rack.

312   APPLE ROLL-UPS

Prep: 15 minutes   Cook: 25 minutes   Makes: 12 slices
Calories per slice: 57

These delicious, flaky-crusted apple-raisin treats are surprisingly easy to make. Check your supermarket for packaged phyllo dough, sold frozen or refrigerated, in a narrow box about 15 inches long. If the box has 2 plastic envelopes, each with 2 sheets, keep one envelope sealed and save for later use.

2 medium Granny Smith or other tart green apples	2 tablespoons stale bread crumbs
2 tablespoons lemon juice	2 tablespoons raisins
2 sheets phyllo dough	2 tablespoons light brown sugar
3 tablespoons butter or margarine, melted	¾ teaspoon ground cinnamon

1. Peel and core apples, cut into ¼-inch dice, and drop into lemon juice combined with cold water to cover.

2. Preheat oven to 400°. Unfold one sheet of phyllo dough on a table or counter. The longer side (horizontal) should measure about 15 inches and should be placed so that it faces you. Brush with 1 tablespoon butter or margarine and sprinkle with bread crumbs. Place second sheet of phyllo dough over first; brush with another 1 tablespoon butter or margarine.

3. Drain apple cubes. Add raisins, 1½ tablespoons brown sugar, and ½ teaspoon cinnamon. Toss all to combine, then spoon apple mixture along long side of phyllo dough nearest you, 1 inch in from the edge. Roll up fairly firmly, like a jelly roll.

4. With a sharp knife, cut roll into 12 1¼-inch slices. Place each slice seam side down on a cookie sheet. Brush tops of slices with remaining 1 tablespoon butter and sprinkle with remaining sugar and cinnamon. Bake about 25 minutes, or until golden brown and crisp.

313   APPLE MERINGUE BAKE

Prep: 25 minutes   Cook: 17 or 53 minutes   Serves: 4
Calories per serving: 122

An impressive dessert, at only 122 calories.

4 medium Rome Beauty or Yellow Delicious apples	½ teaspoon cinnamon
½ cup low-calorie cranberry-apple juice	1 medium egg white
½ cup water	1 tablespoon lemon juice
	2 tablespoons sugar

1. Core apples and peel off upper one-third skin of each. Pour cranberry-apple juice and water into a bowl large enough to hold apples side by side. Add ¼ teaspoon cinnamon and place apples upside down in juice. Cover bowl with microwave-safe plastic wrap or wax paper. Microwave on high 8 minutes, or until apples are tender. Let stand 1 minute, covered. Or bake in a preheated 425° oven 45 minutes, until apples are tender.

2. Uncover apples and turn right side up in liquid to drain tops. Set oven to 325°. Beat egg white until frothy. Add lemon juice and beat until fairly stiff peaks form when beater is raised. Mix sugar with remaining ¼ teaspoon cinnamon. Add to egg whites 1 tablespoon at a time, beating after each addition until whites are stiff. Spread over apple tops, or pipe in a spiral through a pastry bag, over tops. Bake 8 minutes, or until meringue is browned.

---

314 ANGEL FOOD SHORTCAKE
Prep: 5 minutes   Cook: none   Serves: 4
Calories per serving: 88

Make this when you've baked Angel Food Cupcakes and have Whipped Topping on hand.

- 12 **strawberries (1 cup)**
- 1 **tablespoon orange-flavored liqueur**
- 4 **Angel Food Cupcakes (page 163)**

- 1 **cup Whipped Topping (recipe follows)**

1. Hull strawberries and slice. In a small bowl, toss strawberries and liqueur.

2. Remove cupcakes from paper liners. Split in half horizontally. Place bottom half of each on 4 small plates. Cover each with 3 tablespoons sliced berries and a little of the juices and liqueur. Cover with top half of cupcakes. Spoon ¼ cup whipped topping over each and cover with remaining sliced berries, letting them spill over cake.

---

315 WHIPPED TOPPING
Prep: 12 minutes   Cook: none   Makes: 1 cup
Calories per tablespoon: 4

Use this whip as a topping or frosting.

- ¼ **cup instant nonfat dry milk**
- 1 **packet granulated sugar substitute**

- ¼ **cup ice water**
- ¼ **teaspoon vanilla extract**
- 2 **teaspoons lemon juice**

Combine dry milk, sugar substitute, ice water, vanilla, and lemon juice in the bowl of an electric mixer. Beat with whisk attachment on high speed for 10 minutes.

316   APRICOT MOUSSE
Prep: 10 minutes   Cook: 15 minutes   Serves: 4
Calories per serving: 147

Distinctive apricot flavor adds special appeal to a quickly prepared dessert non-dieters will appreciate, too.

6 ounces dried apricots
1½ tablespoons almond liqueur
3 medium egg whites, at room temperature

Optional: 4 teaspoons Light Crème Fraîche (page 143)

1. Place apricots in a small saucepan. Add enough cold water to cover. Cook over medium heat 15 minutes, or until tender. Let apricots cool in cooking liquid, then transfer both apricots and liquid to a blender or food processor and puree until smooth. Turn into a large bowl. Stir in almond liqueur.

2. Beat egg whites until stiff but not dry. Fold about one third of egg whites thoroughly into apricot puree, then fold remaining egg whites until just blended.

3. Divide apricot mousse among 4 individual glass dessert dishes. Top each with 1 teaspoon crème fraîche, if desired.

317   BANANAS FLAMBE
Prep: 2 minutes   Cook: 4 minutes   Serves: 4
Calories per serving: 80

Flaming bananas make a dramatic dessert, so quick you can make it in a flash after the main dish is cleared, and so lean you can enjoy it with pleasure, at under 100 calories.

2 medium bananas (12 ounces total)
1 tablespoon butter or margarine

2 teaspoons lemon juice
1 tablespoon brown sugar
¼ teaspoon cinnamon
1 tablespoon dark rum

1. Peel bananas and cut in half lengthwise. In a medium skillet, melt butter or margarine over medium heat. Add banana halves, cut sides down, and cook for 2 minutes, until warmed through and lightly browned on bottom.

2. Sprinkle lemon juice, brown sugar, and cinnamon over bananas. Shake the pan to distribute evenly.

3. Heat rum in a long-handled metal ladle or butter warmer. When it flames, pour over bananas. Serve warm.

318   CAPPUCCINO GRANITA
Prep: 5 minutes   Cook: none   Serves: 4
Calories per serving: 32

This is the best use we know for instant espresso—an Italian icy dessert that's easy, quick, low-calorie, and Continental in flavor.

4 teaspoons instant espresso coffee powder
½ cup nonfat dry milk
2 cups ice cubes

4 packets granulated sugar substitute*
Cinnamon

Combine all ingredients except cinnamon in a blender or food processor. Process 10 seconds, or until ground to a chunky slush. Spoon into 4 dessert dishes. Sprinkle lightly with cinnamon and serve immediately.

* *Or use 1½ tablespoons sugar and add 72 more calories per serving.*

319   CHEWY COCOA MERINGUES
Prep: 15 minutes   Cook: 2 hours   Makes: 20
Calories per meringue: 18

2 medium egg whites, at room temperature
1 teaspoon vanilla extract
⅛ teaspoon cream of tartar

Pinch of salt
6 tablespoons sugar
¼ cup unsweetened cocoa powder

1. Preheat oven to 200°. In a medium bowl, combine egg whites with vanilla, cream of tartar, and salt. Beat until soft peaks form. Beat in 5 tablespoons sugar, 1 tablespoon at a time. Continue beating until meringue is stiff, smooth, and shiny.

2. Combine remaining 1 tablespoon sugar with cocoa in a sifter and sift over top of meringue. Fold in cocoa mixture until just blended.

3. Line a baking sheet with parchment paper or foil. Drop cocoa meringue by tablespoonfuls onto paper, or pipe into 1½-inch rounds with a pastry bag and star nozzle.

4. Bake about 2 hours, or until meringues are dry and firm and lift easily from paper. Remove from oven and let cool on baking sheet. Store tightly covered in a dry place.

320   FRESH FRUIT TARTS

Prep: 30 minutes   Bake: 8 to 11 minutes   Makes: 10
Calories per tart: 111

Bake tart shells in advance and fill just before serving, with one fruit or an assortment, for an appealing dessert.

**Easy-Roll Pastry
(recipe follows)**

**10 ounces seedless green
grapes, fresh
strawberries, blueberries,
orange sections, or peach
or plum sections**

1. Preheat oven to 400°. Prepare pastry as directed. On a lightly floured surface, roll out pastry to ⅛ inch thickness. With a 3-inch round cutter, cut out as many circles as possible. Gather pastry scraps together, roll out, and cut again to form a total of 10 rounds. Fit each pastry round into a 2-inch tart pan with removable bottom. Prick pastry all over with a fork. Place matching tart pan on top, or fill with aluminum foil and weight down with dried beans or rice. Bake 6 to 8 minutes, or until dry. Uncover and bake 2 to 3 minutes longer, until lightly browned.

2. Fill each tart shell with an arrangement of fresh fruits. (The pastry shells can be baked ahead, but they should be filled with fruit shortly before eating.)

EASY-ROLL PASTRY

Roll this easy-to-stir pastry as thin as possible to stretch the servings and save calories. Use for pie crusts or tarts. And when measuring the flour, be sure to spoon it lightly into the measuring cup and then sweep off the excess.

**1 cup all-purpose flour,
      lightly spooned**
¼ teaspoon salt

¼ cup vegetable oil
**2 tablespoons orange juice or
      skim milk**

1. Combine flour and salt in bowl. Pour oil and juice or milk into a measuring cup; add all at once to flour. Stir with a fork to mix. Press into a smooth ball, then flatten to a 4-inch disk. Wrap in plastic wrap and refrigerate for at least 30 minutes before rolling out.

2. To form pastry into a single crust, cut 2 strips of wax paper, each 12 inches square. Dampen countertop to prevent slipping. Put down one square of paper, set dough on it, then top with second square of wax paper. Roll out gently to edges of paper, to make an 11- to 12-inch circle. Peel off top paper. Invert pastry over pan and ease into place. Trim excess to ½ inch beyond rim and fold edge over. Flute or crimp edge as desired.

321 CHERRY-APPLE PIE
Prep: 15 minutes   Cook: 35 minutes   Serves: 8
Calories per serving: 191

According to the U.S.D.A. a slice of cherry pie (one-eighth of a 9-inch pie) has 308 calories. This one has 191 calories per serving—one third less than the usual.

Easy-Roll Pastry (page 168)
1 **20-ounce can light cherry pie filling**

1 **medium baking apple, peeled and cut into small dice (¾ cup)**
½ **teaspoon almond extract**

1. Preheat oven to 425°. On a lightly floured surface, roll out pastry to an 11- to 12-inch round about ⅛ inch thick. Fit into a 9-inch pan without stretching dough. Press gently against bottom and sides of pan. Trim edges to ½ inch beyond rim. Fold over excess and crimp decoratively. Reserve remainder of pastry for other uses.

2. In a medium bowl, combine cherry pie filling, diced apple, and almond extract. Stir to combine. Pour filling into pie shell.

3. Bake pie in preheated oven for 35 minutes, until crust is golden.

322 CHOCOLATE ANGEL FOOD CAKE
Prep: 21 minutes   Cook: 20 minutes   Serves: 10
Calories per serving: 92

This little cake tastes remarkably like a mousse cake, but there's not a smidgen of cream in the bowl. Prepare to share the recipe with non-dieters, too.

¾ **cup sugar**
½ **cup sifted cake flour**
¼ **cup unsweetened cocoa powder**

5 **medium egg whites**
½ **teaspoon cream of tartar**

1. Preheat oven to 375°. Grease an 8-inch tube pan on bottom only and flour pan. Shake out excess flour. Sift together 2 tablespoons sugar and all the sifted flour and cocoa.

2. Beat whites until frothy. Beat in cream of tartar and continue beating until peaks fold over slightly when beater is lifted. Gradually sprinkle remaining sugar over surface of egg whites, 2 tablespoons at a time, and fold in with rubber spatula. Sift ¼ cup of cocoa mixture over surface and fold in. Repeat until all the mixture is added.

3. Turn batter into prepared pan. Bake 20 minutes. Invert over funnel and let cool in pan before unmolding cake.

323   CHOCOLATE MOUSSE

Prep: 12 minutes   Cook: 4 minutes   Chill: 3 hours   Serves: 4
Calories per serving: 149

Here is a true chocolate mousse that adds up to only 149 calories per serving, compared with about 400 for a conventional mousse. No cream or butter here, and a slightly smaller portion.

3 **ounces semisweet chocolate pieces**
2 **tablespoons strong coffee**
1 **whole medium egg, separated**

2 **medium egg whites**
   Pinch of salt
1 **tablespoon orange liqueur**

1. Heat chocolate with coffee until chocolate is soft, but not fully liquid. Beat the 3 egg whites with the salt until very stiff.

2. Beat egg yolk with the liqueur until very thick, pale, and creamy. Add yolk mixture to the chocolate and stir together. Fold in one fourth of the beaten egg whites lightly but thoroughly. Lightly fold in remaining whites. Refrigerate at least 3 hours, until set.

324   CHOCOLATE SOUFFLE

Prep: 5 minutes   Cook: 20 to 25 minutes   Serves: 4
Calories per serving: 166

5 **medium egg whites**
¼ **teaspoon salt**
¼ **teaspoon cream of tartar**
⅔ **cup sugar**

3 **squares (3 ounces) unsweetened chocolate, melted**

1. Preheat oven to 425°. Beat egg whites until foamy; sprinkle salt and cream of tartar over them and beat until stiff but not dry. Gradually beat in sugar.

2. Fold in melted chocolate. Pour into an ungreased 1-quart soufflé dish. Bake 20 to 25 minutes, or until well puffed and browned. This higher heat produces a soufflé with a thicker crust and a slightly soft, moist center. Serve immediately, with a dollop of Whipped Topping (page 165) or Light Crème Fraîche (page 143), if desired—and don't forget to add the extra calories.

325 COFFEE CHARLOTTE

Prep: 15 minutes   Cook: none   Chill: 3 hours   Serves: 4
Calories per serving: 104

A light and fluffy coffee dessert for a no-bake treat.

2 teaspoons unflavored
    gelatin
¼ cup cold skim milk
½ cup hot strong coffee
1 packet granulated sugar
    substitute*

1 egg white
    Pinch of salt
¼ cup nonfat dry milk
¼ cup ice water
6 ladyfingers, split

1. Soften gelatin in cold milk. Add hot coffee, stirring to dissolve gelatin. Stir in granulated sugar substitute. Refrigerate until mixture begins to thicken enough to coat the spoon, about 30 minutes. Beat egg white and salt until soft peaks form. Fold into gelatin.

2. Combine dry milk and ice water. Beat with electric mixer on high speed until thick as whipped cream. Fold into gelatin mixture.

3. Line 4 sherbet glasses with 3 ladyfinger halves in each. Fill with gelatine mixture. Refrigerate until set, at least 3 hours, or overnight.

* *Or use 2 teaspoons sugar and add 32 calories per serving.*

326 TUILES

Prep: 10 minutes   Cook: 10 to 12 minutes   Makes: 18
Calories per serving: 62

These curved cookies are named for the tiles of a roof, because they are bent to that shape while hot. They are great with coffee.

½ cup sugar
2 medium egg whites
¼ teaspoon vanilla extract
½ cup flour

3 tablespoons butter or
    margarine, melted
¼ cup slivered blanched
    almonds

1. Preheat oven to 400°. Butter a baking sheet. Combine sugar and egg whites in a mixing bowl and beat with whisk until foamy, about 2 minutes.

2. Add vanilla, flour, butter, and almonds and blend well. With a teaspoon, drop batter onto baking sheet about 4 inches apart to allow for spreading.

3. Bake for 10 to 12 minutes, until light brown. While still hot, lift cookies off baking sheet and bend each cookie over a rolling pin, so it curves to the shape of a roof tile. Allow cookies to cool and dry before storing in an airtight container.

327   NUT MERINGUE COOKIES
Prep: 10 minutes   Cook: 3 hours   Makes: 30
Calories per cookie: 10

This meringue cookie has more chew than most, thanks to a few spoon-fuls of nonfat dry milk. If you prefer fruit to nuts, substitute 2 tablespoons chopped dry fruits.

4 **medium egg whites**
1 **tablespoon lemon juice**
   Pinch of salt
1 **tablespoon honey**
1 **tablespoon almond-flavored**
   liqueur

2 **tablespoons nonfat dry milk**
2 **tablespoons chopped**
   walnuts

1. Preheat oven to 200°. Beat egg whites with lemon juice and salt until mix-ture forms soft peaks when beater is raised. Add honey, almond liqueur, and nonfat dry milk, beating constantly until mixture stands in stiff peaks. Fold in walnuts.

2. Spoon into a pastry bag fitted with a ⅝-inch nozzle and pipe 3-inch strips of meringue, or drop into rounds by tablespoons onto a baking sheet lined with parchment baking paper or brown paper. Bake 1 hour.

3. Turn off oven, but leave door closed, and let meringues dry in hot oven 2 hours longer. Remove cookies from paper and store in tightly sealed container.

328   STRAWBERRY-BANANA WHIP
Prep: 5 minutes   Freeze: 2 hours or longer   Serves: 4
Calories per serving: 100

There's no cream in this whip, just frozen pureed fruits. The flavor will make you think otherwise.

2 **very ripe large bananas**
   (1 pound total)

1 **tablespoon lemon juice**
1 **cup strawberries**

1. Peel bananas, remove fibers, and cut into chunks. Dip into lemon juice. Place on cookie sheet and put into freezer. Hull strawberries and place on cookie sheet. Freeze at least 2 hours.

2. Place frozen bananas and strawberries in a food processor and whip until thick and creamy. If desired, return to freezer and whip again before serv-ing.

329   CANTALOUPE SORBET

Prep: 7 minutes   Freeze: about 40 minutes   Serves: 4
Calories per serving: 60

1 **large ripe cantaloupe**	1 **tablespoon lemon juice**
2 **tablespoons sugar**	

1. Halve cantaloupe, remove seeds, and cut pulp from rind. Cut cantaloupe into cubes. Combine in blender or food processor container with sugar and lemon juice. Puree until smooth.

2. Turn into ice cream maker and freeze according to manufacturer's instructions. Or place in freezer until slushy, then beat again before serving.

330   PINK GRAPEFRUIT SORBET

Prep: 2 minutes   Freeze: about 20 minutes   Serves: 4
Calories per serving: 72

2 **tablespoons sugar**	2 **cups pink grapefruit juice**

Stir sugar into grapefruit juice to dissolve. Turn into ice cream maker and freeze according to manufacturer's instructions. Or place in freezer until slushy, then beat again before serving.

331   WATERMELON SORBET

Prep: 7 minutes   Freeze: about 40 minutes   Serves: 4
Calories per serving: 57

3 **cups watermelon cubes, seeded**	2 **tablespoons sugar**

1. Combine watermelon cubes and sugar in food processor or blender. Puree until smooth.

2. Turn watermelon puree into ice cream maker and freeze according to manufacturer's instructions. Or place in freezer until slushy, then beat again before serving.

332   CARAMEL CUSTARD

Prep: 10 minutes   Cook: 10 minutes   Chill: 4 hours   Serves: 4
Calories per serving: 173

This differs from the usual caramel custard, which is far richer in eggs and cream and more than double in calories. Gelatin helps make the texture silky, and the flavor appeal includes the same wonderful contrast of custardy base and caramel sauce, at far fewer calories than usual.

1 **envelope (1 tablespoon)**
 unflavored gelatin
2 **cups cold skim milk**
2 **tablespoons honey**
2 **medium eggs**

1 **teaspoon vanilla extract**
2 **tablespoons Light Crème**
 Fraîche (page 143)
¼ **cup sugar**
1 **tablespoon water**

1. Soak gelatin in cold milk. Add honey and cook, stirring, over moderate heat, until gelatin is completely dissolved, 3 to 4 minutes.

2. Beat eggs in a small bowl. Beat a little of hot milk mixture into eggs, then stir egg mixture into remaining milk in pan. Cook over medium-low heat, whisking constantly, until mixture thickens slightly and coats back of a spoon, about 3 minutes. Remove from heat. Stir 1 minute to cool slightly, then stir in vanilla and crème fraîche.

3. In a small heavy saucepan, combine sugar with water. Cook over moderately high heat, swirling pan occasionally, for about 3 minutes, or until caramel turns a deep amber, smells caramelized, and begins to thicken. Immediately spoon 1 tablespoon caramel into each of 4 custard cups or small deep bowls; tilt to coat bottom of cups. Caramel will harden in cold dish. (Don't worry if coating is uneven; it will dissolve smoothly as dessert cools.)

4. Pour custard over caramel and refrigerate until set, about 4 hours. To serve, run a knife around edges of custard cups to release custard and invert onto individual plates. Caramel will coat top and run down sides.

333   FRESH FRUIT GELATIN

Prep: 10 minutes   Cook: none   Chill: 30 minutes   Serves: 4
Calories per serving: 118

This real-juice gelatin has extra fruit added and is mixed in a dramatic time-saving way, to set in less than a half hour, instead of the usual 3 to 4 hours.

1 **envelope (1 tablespoon) unflavored gelatin**	3 **ice cubes**
¾ **cup cold water**	1 **cup fresh diced apple, sliced grapes, berries, or other fruits, combined**
1 **6-ounce can frozen berry or grape or apple juice concentrate**	

1. In small pan, soften gelatin in cold water. Add juice concentrate and bring to a boil, stirring. Cook until gelatin is dissolved completely. Add ice cubes; stir until smooth and slightly thickened.

2. Pour one quarter of the gelatin mixture into each dessert serving dish. Add ¼ cup fresh diced fruit to each dish, spooning a little of the gelatin mixture over the top of fruit. Place in refrigerator and chill until set, at least 30 minutes.

334   GREEN GRAPES WITH CREME FRAICHE AND BROWN SUGAR

Prep: 5 minutes   Cook: none   Serves: 4
Calories per serving: 111

Cool green grapes lend texture and flavor contrast to a creamy caramel-like sauce.

½ **cup Light Crème Fraîche (page 143)**	¼ **teaspoon cinnamon**
1 **tablespoon dark brown sugar**	2 **cups seedless green grapes**

1. Combine Light Crème Fraîche, brown sugar, and cinnamon. Mix well, cover, and refrigerate.

2. Remove grapes from stems. Wash, drain, and place in individual serving dishes, champagne glasses, or wine goblets. Cover with crème fraîche mixture. Cover and refrigerate until serving time. Serve chilled.

335   LEMON-BANANA WHIP
Prep: 2 minutes   Cook: none   Serves: 4
Calories per serving: 29

No one will believe the calorie count on this dessert, and it can be served all year.

1 **package low-calorie lemon gelatin**	1½ **cups crushed ice**
½ **cup boiling water**	1 **small ripe banana, cut into chunks**

1. Put lemon gelatin in a blender or food processor. Add boiling water. Cover and blend 5 seconds to dissolve gelatin.

2. Add ice and banana chunks. Blend 20 seconds longer, or until smooth and "whipped." Spoon into 4 individual dessert dishes. Cover and refrigerate until serving time.

336   LEMON BAVARIAN CREAM WITH BLUEBERRIES
Prep: 18 minutes   Cook: 12 minutes   Serves: 4
Calories per serving: 158

Here's a traditional dessert made in an untraditional way—creamy tasting without the excess cream calories, thanks to skim milk and low-fat ricotta cheese.

1 **envelope (1 tablespoon) unflavored gelatin**	¼ **cup skim-milk ricotta cheese**
½ **cup cold water**	¼ **cup sugar**
2 **cups skim milk**	2 **medium egg whites**
1 **teaspoon vanilla extract**	2 **tablespoons lemon juice**
1 **whole medium egg, separated**	1 **teaspoon grated lemon zest**
	½ **cup blueberries**

1. In a small bowl, combine gelatin and cold water. Let stand 5 minutes to soften gelatin. In a heavy medium saucepan, heat milk. Add gelatin and vanilla. Stir over medium heat until gelatin dissolves. Reduce heat to low.

2. Place egg yolk in a bowl and beat in a little of hot milk. Return yolk mixture to pan and cook, stirring, over low heat until mixture coats the spoon, 3 to 4 minutes. Do not let the mixture boil. Place saucepan over ice cubes and stir until cool and slightly thickened.

3. In a food processor or blender, combine cooled milk mixture with ricotta cheese and sugar. Puree until smooth.

4. Beat 3 egg whites with lemon juice until stiff but not dry. Stir half the egg whites thoroughly into gelatin mixture. Carefully fold in remaining egg whites along with grated lemon zest. Pour into a soufflé dish or bowl and refrigerate until set. Garnish with blueberries.

337 LIGHT PARTY CHEESECAKE

Prep: 10 minutes   Cook: 14 minutes   Chill: 3½ hours
Serves: 8   Calories per serving: 116

Luscious cheesecake appeal in a low-calorie version you will want to repeat often. A great dessert for a party.

8 **light rye wafers**
2 **tablespoons brown sugar**
   Dash of salt
1 **tablespoon melted butter or margarine**
1 **envelope (1 tablespoon) unflavored gelatin**

¼ **cup sugar**
½ **cup skim milk**
½ **teaspoon grated lemon zest**
2 **tablespoons fresh lemon juice**
1½ **cups low-fat cottage cheese**
1 **medium egg white**

1. Preheat oven to 375°. Place rye wafers in a blender or food processor and whirl to make fine crumbs. Add brown sugar, salt, and melted butter or margarine; blend well. Reserve 2 tablespoons of mixture. Press remaining crumb crust onto bottom and sides of an 8-inch pie pan. Bake for 8 minutes, until set. Let cool.

2. Meanwhile, boil water in bottom pan of a double boiler. Off heat, combine gelatin, sugar, and another dash of salt in top of double boiler. Add skim milk and cook over boiling water stirring constantly, for 6 minutes, until mixture simmers and gelatin dissolves. Remove from heat and let cool.

3. Stir grated lemon zest, lemon juice, and cottage cheese into cooled gelatin mixture. Whirl mixture in blender or food processor for extra creaminess. Cover and refrigerate until cheese mixture begins to thicken, about 30 minutes.

4. Beat egg white until stiff, then fold into cheese mixture. Pour into rye crumb crust. Sprinkle circle of remaining crumbs around outer edge of cake. Refrigerate 3 hours, or until set.

338 APRICOT CREPES
Prep: 5 minutes   Cook: 20 minutes   Serves: 10
Calories per serving: 127

Crepes offer a memorable dessert at affordable calories and are low in cholesterol.

1½ cups skim milk
1 medium whole egg,
   separated
1 medium egg white

1 cup flour
¼ teaspoon salt
Apricot Mousse (page 166)

1. Beat milk, whole egg, and egg white together. Add flour and salt and beat just until fairly smooth.

2. Preheat a 6-inch crepe pan or 7-inch skillet. Spray lightly with nonstick vegetable coating. For each crepe, add about 2 tablespoons batter, tilting pan to coat bottom. Cook over medium heat until browned, about 45 seconds. Turn and cook until spotted brown on second side, about 15 seconds. Flip onto serving plate. Fill with 1 tablespoon Apricot Mousse and roll up. Serve warm or at room temperature. Allow 2 crepes per serving.

CHOCOLATE-FILLED CREPES

Fill crepes with 1 tablespoon Chocolate Mousse (page 170).

339 ORANGE PUDDING CAKE
Prep: 20 minutes   Cook: 35 minutes   Serves: 6
Calories per serving: 120

This delicate pudding separates into two layers as it bakes—a delicate custard layer, topped with a spongelike cake layer. Impressive!

2 tablespoons butter or
   margarine
¼ cup sugar
2 medium eggs, separated
2 tablespoons fresh orange
   juice

1 teaspoon grated orange zest
2 tablespoons flour
1 cup skim milk

1. Preheat oven to 375°. Cream butter; add sugar and beat well. Beat egg yolks until thick and lemon colored. Add to creamed butter mixture. Beat in orange juice and zest. Fold in flour and stir in milk.

2. Beat egg whites until stiff. Fold into orange mixture. Pour into a greased 1-quart heavy baking dish. Bake 35 minutes. Let cool. Refrigerate until chilled before serving.

340 ORANGES IN RASPBERRY SAUCE
Prep: 4 minutes   Cook: none   Serves: 4
Calories per serving: 141

Gild an orange with raspberry sauce, a dessert fit for royalty—and a help in keeping fit.

4 navel oranges   8 mint leaves, if available
1 10-ounce package
   unsweetened frozen
   raspberries, partially
   thawed

1. Peel oranges, removing all the white pith. Cut into thick slices. Divide the slices among 4 dessert plates, overlapping slightly.

2. In a blender or food processor, puree raspberries and their syrup. Measure out 4 tablespoons. Freeze remaining sauce for future use.

3. Pour 1 tablespoon of raspberry sauce over orange slices in each dish. Chill until serving time. Top with mint before serving.

341 MERINGUE PEAR TARTLETS
Prep: 15 minutes   Cook: 2 hours   Serves: 4
Calories per serving: 115

Glazed pear in a meringue shell makes a delectable, dramatic dessert that's easier than it looks.

4 medium egg whites, at room   2 tablespoons nonfat dry milk
   temperature   1 tablespoon brown sugar
   Pinch of salt   2 tablespoons white wine
1 tablespoon lemon juice   2 medium pears, peeled,
2 tablespoons sugar   cored, and thinly sliced

1. Preheat oven to 200°. Beat egg whites with salt and lemon juice until mixture forms soft peaks. Stir sugar together with dry milk and gradually beat into egg whites, 1 tablespoon at a time, until mixture is stiff and glossy but not dry.

2. Spoon meringue mixture into four 4-inch circles onto baking sheet lined with parchment paper or brown paper. Make an indentation with back of a tablespoon in center of each. Bake 1 hour. Turn off heat and let dry in warm oven 1 hour longer.

3. Meanwhile, in a small nonreactive saucepan, heat brown sugar and wine over medium-low heat, stirring until sugar dissolves, about 3 minutes. Add pear slices and cook until tender, 3 to 5 minutes. Remove to a serving plate. Spoon pear slices into meringue shells just before serving.

342   OPEN LEMON TART

Prep: 12 minutes   Cook: 20 minutes   Serves: 6
Calories per serving: 104

Extra flaky crust and wafer-thin lemon slices add up to an unusually delicious dessert—worthy of a pastry chef, yet tartly low-calorie.

2   **sheets phyllo dough**
1½ **teaspoons butter or**
    margarine, melted
2   **large lemons**

2   **tablespoons all-fruit orange**
    spread, melted
2   **tablespoons confectioners'**
    sugar

1. Bring dough to room temperature. Unfold one sheet on a moist towel, long side facing you. Brush 1 teaspoon melted butter over pastry. Top with second sheet of dough, spread lower half of the long side with remaining butter and fold top half of both sheets halfway down over this. Fit into 7-inch tart shell or pie pan, bending crust back under itself to fit into pan. Cover with a damp towel while you prepare the filling.

2. Preheat oven to 400°. Cut peel and white pith from whole lemons and slice lemons into paper-thin rounds (easiest in a food processor fitted with slicing disk). Spread phyllo dough with 1 tablespoon warm all-fruit preserve. Arrange lemon slices in concentric circles and top with remaining 1 tablespoon warm fruit spread; sprinkle with sugar.

3. Bake 20 minutes, until pastry is golden and filling is well glazed. Serve at room temperature or chilled.

---

343   PINEAPPLE SPONGE

Prep: 5 minutes   Cook: 2 minutes   Refrigerate: 3 hours   Serves: 4
Calories per serving: 60

A light and refreshing ending for any meal—and pineapples are now available year-round.

1   **envelope (1 tablespoon)**
    unflavored gelatin
½   **cup cold water**
1   **16-ounce can unsweetened**
    crushed pineapple

2   **packets granulated sugar**
    substitute
2   **medium egg whites**

1. Empty gelatin envelope into cold water to soften gelatin.

2. Heat ½ cup of pineapple juice drained from can. Add gelatin and stir until gelatin is dissolved. Add crushed pineapple with remaining juice and sugar substitute. Refrigerate until mixture begins to set, about 30 minutes.

3. Beat egg whites until stiff but not dry. Fold into pineapple mixture. Spoon into a mold or individual serving dishes and chill for several hours before serving.

344   QUICK LEMON SHERBET

Prep: 4 minutes   Cook: none   Serves: 4
Calories per serving: 45

A sherbet ready in a flash, and deliciously refreshing.

3 **ounces frozen lemonade**
    concentrate (half a
    6-ounce can)

2 **cups crushed ice**
1 **medium egg white**

1. In a blender or food processor, combine lemonade concentrate, crushed ice, and egg white. Cover and blend at high speed until mixture is thick and slushy, scraping down sides, if necessary.

2. Serve at once, or store, covered, in the freezer. Beat again, if necessary, before serving.

345   POACHED PEARS IN WINE SAUCE

Prep: 10 minutes   Cook: 30 minutes   Serves: 4
Calories per serving: 164

Pears in wine are a great dessert to make ahead. They keep well in the refrigerator for a week to 10 days, and take in added mellowness of flavor.

1½ **cups water, or enough to**
     cover pears
1   **cup dry red wine**
4   **whole cloves**
1   **2-inch piece of cinnamon**
     stick

1   **teaspoon vanilla extract**
¼   **cup all-fruit raspberry jam**
     Strips of zest from 1 lemon
4   **medium pears**

1. Combine water, wine, cloves, stick cinnamon, vanilla, jam, and lemon zest strips in a heavy saucepan just big enough to hold the 4 pears.

2. Bring liquid to a boil and cook at high heat for 15 minutes. Meanwhile, peel pears, leaving stem intact and removing blossom end. Insert a clove at blossom end.

3. Reduce heat to a simmer. Add pears to saucepan, cover, and poach pears in wine mixture 15 minutes, or until tender. Remove pan from heat and let pears cool in poaching liquid, then refrigerate until chilled.

4. Place 1 pear on each of 4 serving dishes. Spoon ¼ cup poaching liquid over pears.

346   RASPBERRY SOUFFLE
Prep: 15 minutes   Cook: 15 minutes   Serves: 6
Calories per serving: 112

Just four simple ingredients make this elegant year-round raspberry souf-flé—great for unexpected guests or for a dessert party.

1 **10-ounce package frozen raspberries, thawed**
4 **medium egg whites, slightly warmed**

5 **tablespoons sugar**
6 **tablespoons vanilla ice milk**

1. Preheat oven to 375°. Drain raspberries, reserving syrup. Puree raspberries in food processor or blender until smooth.

2. Beat egg whites until they hold soft peaks when beater is raised. Beat in sugar, 1 tablespoon at a time, and continue beating until eggs are glossy and peaks are stiff. Fold beaten whites lightly into raspberry puree.

3. Pour into six 6-ounce soufflé dishes; bake until puffed and slightly browned, 14 to 15 minutes. Meanwhile, cook reserved syrup to thicken and reduce to about 3 tablespoons. Serve soufflés immediately, topping each with a tablespoon of ice milk and a drizzle of raspberry syrup.

347   STRAWBERRIES ROMANOFF
Prep: 12 minutes   Cook: none   Serves: 4
Calories per serving: 124

This is a heavenly aromatic finale for a meal or a party treat, at affordable calories.

1 **pint strawberries**
2 **tablespoons framboise or strawberry liqueur**
½ **cup Light Crème Fraîche (page 143)**

½ **cup low-calorie ice milk, softened slightly**

1. Select 4 perfect berries for garnish. Hull the remainder and cut in half. Sprinkle berries with 1 tablespoon liqueur. In a small bowl, beat together Light Crème Fraîche, ice milk, and remaining 1 tablespoon liqueur until fluffy. Fold cut strawberries into creamy mixture.

2. Spoon into 4 individual goblets and garnish with whole berries. Cover each goblet snugly with plastic paper and refrigerate until serving time. Uncover just before serving, to release aroma.

348 RUM BALLS

Prep: 15 minutes   Cook: none   Standing time: 30 minutes
Makes: 24   Calories per rum ball: 43

These tasty treats will be enjoyed by the whole family—great for parties, too. Serve with espresso for an after-dinner celebration.

1¼ cups crumbled dry Angel
    Food Cupcakes (page 163)
1 tablespoon unsweetened
    cocoa powder

2 tablespoons honey
¼ cup dark rum
1 tablespoon confectioners'
    sugar

1. Toss crumbs and cocoa to combine. Stir in honey and rum, combining well to make a mixture that holds together when pressed.

2. Place confectioners' sugar on a flat plate or sheet of wax paper. Roll heaping teaspoons of crumb mixture into 1-inch balls, pressing between palms to hold shape. Roll balls lightly in sugar to form a thin coating on each. Set out to dry for 30 minutes—if you can wait!

349 CHOCOLATE TOPPING

Prep: 1 minute   Cook: 1 minute   Makes: ⅓ cup
Calories per tablespoon: 59

This easy topping tastes sinfully chocolaty but the calories make it legal. It also makes a fine glaze for cakes and cookies.

¼ cup semisweet chocolate
    morsels
1 tablespoon strawberry
    liqueur

¼ cup low-fat vanilla yogurt

1. Place chocolate morsels and strawberry liqueur in a small microwavable bowl. Microwave on high until chocolate melts, about 1 minute; stir.

2. Add yogurt and stir mixture until smooth. Refrigerate about 30 minutes, until thickened.

Chapter 11

Slim Sips

This array of refreshing drinks ranges from sparkling bellinis, light mimosas, to spiced apple tea, some wonderful coffees, even the yogurt lassie you enjoyed at an Indian restaurant. We've added shakes and fruit juice spritzers–in some wonderful colors and flavors.

The slim secret: For many of these drinks, we've taken advantage of the greatest, most economical, and, easiest diet drink of all—water. We've added water generously to fruits, maintaining refreshing flavor and lightness, to shakes as ice, and even to buttermilk, for a wonderfully refreshing minted drink.

You can do the same, diluting your favorite juices about half with water, or with seltzer for a salt-free spritzer, (Unlike club soda, seltzer has no salt added.)

We have occasionally used granulated sugar substitute in place of natural sweetener. Here we'd better confess, this is a matter of taste on which we differ. One of us would prefer to have the drink tart; the other wants the substitute or even a teaspoon of sugar at 16 calories. Take your choice. We want you to enjoy the drinks as much as we did the tasting.

---

350   BELLINI LEAN
Prep: 2 minutes   Cook: none   Serves: 6
Calories per serving: 50

Peaches and champagne in a low-calorie version of the flavorful toast popularized in Venice.

1 **very ripe medium peach, peeled and quartered, or 2 water-packed peach halves**	1 **cup liquid drained from peaches, or water** 12 **ounces dry champagne (1 split)**

Combine peaches and liquid in blender or food processor. Puree until smooth. Divide among 6 5-ounce champagne flutes. Top each with 3 ounces champagne.

351 STRAWBERRY COOLER
Prep: 1 minute   Cook: none   Serves: 1
Calories per serving: 42

¼ **cup halved strawberries,**
   hulled

¼ **cup orange juice**
½ **cup low-calorie lemon soda**

1. Place berries and orange juice in a blender and puree until smooth.

2. Put ice in a tall glass. Pour berry-juice mixture over ice and add lemon soda.

352 BLUEBERRY COOLER
Prep: 3 minutes   Cook: none   Serves: 2
Calories per serving: 44

½ **cup skim milk**
½ **cup blueberries, fresh or dry**
   frozen

½ **cup ice cubes**
1 **cup no-calorie ginger ale**

Place milk, berries, and ice cubes in a blender. Blend 30 seconds until thick and smooth. Pour into tall glasses. Top each with ginger ale and stir.

353 CAPPUCCINO FROST
Prep: 3 minutes   Cook: none   Serves: 4
Calories per serving: 28

If you enjoy hot cappuccino, this cold version will be a refreshing discovery.

1 **cup skim milk**
4 **rounded teaspoons instant**
   espresso coffee
2 **packets granulated sugar**
   substitute

1 **cup cold water**
½ **cup ice cubes**
   Powdered cinnamon

1. In a blender, combine milk, instant espresso, sugar substitute, water, and ice cubes. Blend until frothy.

2. Fill 4 8-ounce glasses with ice cubes. Pour cappuccino over the ice and dust with powdered cinnamon.

354   COCOA SHAKE

Prep: 1 minute   Cook: none   Serves: 1
Calories per serving: 50

1 **packet instant low-calorie
   cocoa mix**

¾ **cup cold water**
4 **ice cubes**

Combine all ingredients in a blender or food processor. Blend about 25 seconds until well combined and frothy.

355   FRUIT JUICE SPRITZER

Prep: 2 minutes   Cook: none   Serves: 4
Calories per serving: 27

2 **slices of orange with peel**
2 **cups low-calorie cranberry-
   raspberry drink, chilled**

12 **ounces club soda or seltzer,
    chilled**
    Sprigs of mint

Cut each orange slice in half and put one piece in each of 4 tall glasses. Pour ½ cup cranberry-raspberry drink into each glass and fill with club soda. Garnish with sprigs of mint.

356   HERBED VEGETABLE COCKTAIL

Prep: 2 minutes   Cook: none   Serves: 4
Calories per serving: 38

A savory way to start a meal or enjoy a refreshing pause, and add to the vitamin C count of your day.

12 **ounces tomato juice**
4 **ice cubes**
1 **teaspoon lemon juice**
4 **iceberg lettuce leaves, torn
   into pieces**

1 **small cucumber, peeled and
   seeded**
2 **teaspoons chopped fresh
   dill or basil**
1 **teaspoon minced chives**

Place all ingredients in a blender or food processor and blend until smooth. Serve in 6-ounce glasses.

357　LASSIE
Prep: 3 minutes　Cook: none　Serves: 1
Calories per serving: 65

This yogurt cooler from India is refreshing and satisfying, at lower calories than prepared bottled yogurt drinks.

½　cup plain low-fat yogurt
¼　cup water
½　tablespoon rosewater

1　packet granulated sugar
　　substitute
5　ice cubes

1. Put yogurt, water, rosewater, and sugar substitute in a blender or food processor. Blend until sweetener is dissolved.

2. Add ice cubes and continue blending another 30 seconds, or until yogurt drink is frothy. (Ice cubes will still leave some pieces). Pour, with remaining ice pieces, into a tall glass.

STRAWBERRY LASSIE
84 calories

Prepare as above, adding 5 large strawberries, hulled and halved, to the yogurt mixture.

358　MIMOSA LIGHT
Prep: 2 minutes　Cook: none　Serves: 4
Calories per serving: 48

All the fun and flavor of your brunch-time favorite—at less than half the usual calories, and more refreshing.

1　cup orange juice
12　ounces orange-flavored
　　seltzer

½　cup champagne

Combine orange juice and seltzer in a pitcher. Pour into champagne flutes and top each with champagne.

359   MINTED BUTTERMILK SLIM
Prep: 2 minutes   Cook: none   Serves: 1
Calories per serving: 45

Here's a surprisingly light and refreshing buttermilk drink, for those who have rediscovered this longtime favorite.

½ **cup buttermilk**
½ **cup ice water**

1 **tablespoon crushed fresh mint leaves, or ½ teaspoon dried**

Combine all ingredients in a tall glass and stir vigorously to blend.

360   PEACH MELBA SHAKE
Prep: 2 minutes   Cook: none   Serves: 4
Calories per serving: 64

Like having a glass of peach ice cream, yet affordable in calories.

1½ **cups skim milk**
  2 **ripe peach halves, or 2 water-packed canned peach halves**
  1 **tablespoon all-fruit raspberry spread**

2 **packets granulated sugar substitute**
2½ **cups ice cubes**

Place all ingredients in a blender or food processor. Blend about 20 seconds, until smooth and foamy.

361   SPICED TEA PUNCH
Prep: 2 minutes   Cook: 5 minutes   Serves: 4
Calories per serving: 1

3 **cups water**
2 **cloves**
4 **peppercorns**
  Small piece of cinnamon stick

3 **strips of lemon peel**
4 **teaspoons tea of your choice**

1. Bring water to a boil. Add spices and lemon peel. Reduce heat to low and steep 5 minutes. Add tea. Remove from heat and let steep for 4 minutes. Cool, then strain.

2. Fill 4 tall glasses with ice and pour spicy tea over ice.

362   STRAWBERRY SLIM SHAKE
Prep: 2 minutes   Cook: none   Serves: 2
Calories per serving: 61

Shake up a strawberry drink when you want a distinctive quick pick-up.

1 **cup skim milk**	1 **packet granulated sugar**
½ **cup hulled strawberries**	**substitute (optional)**
½ **teaspoon vanilla extract**	1 **cup ice cubes**

Place milk, berries, vanilla extract, sugar substitute, and ice cubes in a blender or food processor. Blend about 30 seconds, until smooth and foamy.

363   SPARKLING LEMONADE
Prep: 3 minutes   Cook: none   Serves: 4
Calories per serving: 13

A refreshing way to get some extra vitamin C. Sprigs of mint, if you have any, add flavor and color. Delicious with non-carbonated water, too.

3 **lemons**	1 **quart club soda or seltzer**
4 **packets granulated sugar**	
substitute	

1. Squeeze lemons and put juice and rind of one of the lemons in a pitcher with ice cubes. Add sweetener and stir to mix well.

2. Add soda and combine. Serve over ice.

364   SPICED APPLE CIDER
Prep: 2 minutes   Cook: 5 minutes   Serves: 4
Calories per serving: 60

Apple cider muddled with spices and peel takes on added flavor, enough to make up for the addition of water, which reduces calories.

2 **cups apple cider or juice**	4 **whole cloves**
1 **small piece of cinnamon**	3 **strips of orange peel**
stick	2 **cups water**

1. Combine all ingredients and cook for 5 minutes. Remove from heat and let stand another 5 minutes.

2. Strain into mugs and serve hot, or strain into a pitcher, cool, and refrigerate.

365 ALMOND MILK COOLER
Prep: 1 minute   Cook: none   Serves: 1
Calories per serving: 67

Enjoy this as a late-evening beverage—the almond-milk combination seems relaxing.

¾ **cup skim milk**   2 **ice cubes**
½ **teaspoon almond extract**

Place all ingredients in a blender or food processor and blend about 30 seconds, or until frothy.

HOT ALMOND MILK FROTHY
67 calories

Combine ¾ cup skim milk and ½ teaspoon almond extract in a mug. Heat.

CALORIE AND EQUIVALENCY TABLES OF COMMONLY USED INGREDIENTS

Vegetables

Ingredient and approximate weight	Approximate Measure after preparation	Calories
Artichoke, 1 medium, 4½ oz.	—	65
Artichoke heart, 1 oz.	—	7
Asparagus, 5 spears, 3½ oz.	¾ cup	26
Beets, no greens, 4 oz.	½ cup sliced	49
Broccoli, 1 stalk, 3½ oz.	1 cup chopped	32
Cabbage, 1 small head, 1 lb.	4 cups shredded	109
Carrot, 1 medium, 2⅓ oz.	½ cup diced or shredded	32
Cauliflower, ⅛ head, 4 oz.	1 cup florets	27
Celery, 1 outer stalk, 1¾ oz.	⅓ cup chopped	8
Cucumber, 1 medium, 8 oz.	1½ cups sliced or diced	30
Eggplant, 1 small, 1 lb.	1½ cups diced	114
Green Beans, 4 oz.	¾ cup	20
Green Peppers, 1 medium, 5 oz.	⅔ cup diced	23
Lettuce		
Iceberg, 1 head, 1 lb.	6¼ cups	70
Endive, 1 head, 1 lb.	4¼ cups	45
Romaine, 1 lb.	6 cups	82
Mushrooms, 8 medium or 4½ large, 4 oz.	½ to ¾ cup sliced	32
Onion, 1 medium, 3½ oz.	½ cup chopped	38
Potato, 1 medium, 5 oz.	⅔ cup cubed, ½ cup mashed	86
Scallions, bunch of 3, 2½ oz.	½ cup sliced	27
Snow Peas, 2½ oz.	½ cup	30
Spinach, 2 oz.	1 cup chopped	14
Tomato, 1 medium, 5 oz.	1 cup chopped	33
Tomatoes, whole, canned, 1 lb.	2 cups	95
Watercress, 2 oz.	1 bunch	11
Zucchini, 1 small, 6 oz.	1 cup sliced	22

Meats

Ingredient	Uncooked Weight per serving	Calories per cooked serving
Beef		
Flank Steak	4 oz.	149
Minute Steak	4 oz.	141
Round Steak	4 oz.	127
Shoulder Steak	4 oz.	131
Ground Beef, lean	4 oz.	186
Lamb		
Leg Meat	4 oz.	123
Chops, Loin	4 oz.	92
Chops, Shoulder	4 oz.	103
Pork		
Loin, boneless	4 oz.	157
Veal		
Boneless	4 oz.	173
Ground	4 oz.	126

Poultry

Ingredient	Uncooked Weight per serving	Calories per cooked portion
Chicken		
Breast Half, boneless, skinless	4½ oz.	166
Breast Half, bone in, skinless	7 oz.	147
Leg and Thigh, bone in, skinless	6 oz.	151
Broiler	¼ of 2½-lb. chicken	171
Turkey		
Cutlet	3 oz.	117
Breast, bone in, skinless	¼ of 2½-lb. breast	162

Seafood

Ingredient	Uncooked Weight or Measure per serving	Calories per cooked serving
Anchovy, fillet	3 thin fillets, ½ oz.	21
Catfish, fillet	4 oz.	121
Clams, littleneck	6 clams	66
Cod, fillet	4 oz.	96
Flounder, fillet	4 oz.	80
Halibut, fillet	4 oz.	117
Halibut, steak	5 oz.	106
Lobster, in shell	1 lb.	69
Mussels, in shell	8 oz.	63
Ocean Perch, fillet	4 oz.	112
Oysters, small	6 oysters	36
Salmon, steak	5 oz.	152
Scallops, shucked	4 oz.	81
Seabass, whole	¼ of 1½-lb. fish	57
Shrimp, in shell	4 oz.	61
Shrimp, peeled	4 oz.	76
Snapper, fillet	4 oz.	116
Sole, fillet	4 oz.	80
Trout, whole	8 oz.	80

Fruits

Ingredient and approximate weight	Approximate Measure after preparation	Calories
Apple, 1 medium, 5 oz.	1 cup sliced	87
Apricot, 1 medium, 1½ oz.	¼ cup sliced	20
Avocado, 1 medium, 10 oz.	1¼ cups sliced	369
Banana, 1 medium, 6 oz.	1 cup sliced; ⅔ cup mashed	127
Blueberries, 5 oz.	1 cup	87
Cherries, canned, pitted, 16 oz.	1¾ cups drained	195

Fruits, continued

Ingredient and approximate weight	Approximate Measure after preparation	Calories
Grapefruit, 1 medium, 1 lb.	1 cup sections	82
Grapes, seedless, 6 oz.	1 cup	107
Lemon, 1 medium, 4 oz.	3 tablespoons juice	12
	whole lemon	27
Orange, navel, 1 medium, 7 oz.	¼ to ⅓ cup juice	28
	whole orange	71
Peach, 1 medium, 4 oz.	½ cup sliced	38
Pear, 1 medium, 6 oz.	½ cup sliced	100
Strawberries, 6 oz.	1 cup	56

Dairy and Related Products

Ingredient	Amount	Calories
Blue Cheese, low-fat	1 oz.	76
Butter	1 tablespoon	108
Cheddar Cheese, low-fat	1 oz.	80
Cottage Cheese, low-fat	4 oz., ½ cup	82
Cream Cheese, light	1 oz., 2 tablespoons	60
Creme Fraîche, (ours)	1 tablespoon	22
Egg	1 medium	78
Heavy Cream	1 tablespoon	52
Margarine	1 tablespoon	108
Mayonnaise, reduced-calorie	1 tablespoon	50
Milk, skim	1 cup	89
Mozzarella, part-skim	1 oz.	72
Parmesan Cheese, grated	1 tablespoon	23
Ricotta Cheese, low-fat	½ cup	171
Sour Cream, low-fat	1 tablespoon	20
Swiss Cheese, low-fat	1 oz.	80
Yogurt, low-fat	1 cup	123

Note: 1 ounce cheese = ¼ cup grated, shredded or finely diced.

Breads

Ingredient	Amount	Calories
Bagel	1 bagel	165
Crispbread	1 crispbread	25
English Muffin	1 English Muffin	131
French Bread	1 slice	58
Italian Bread	1 slice	55
Phyllo Dough	1 sheet	24
Pita Bread	small (4″)	80
	regular (6″)	130
Pumpernickel (black bread)	1 thin slice	69
Rice Cake	1 rice cake	35
Rye Bread	1 slice	56
White Bread	1 slice	62
	1 slice, reduced calorie	40
Whole Wheat (five-grain)	1 slice	56

Cereals

Ingredient	Measures uncooked	cooked	Calories
Bulgur, 2 oz.	⅓ cup	1 cup	201
Oatmeal, 1 oz.	⅓ cup	¾ cup	104
Rice, 2¼ oz.	⅓ cup	1 cup	164
Macaroni, 1-inch pieces, 2 oz.	½ cup	1⅛ cups	210
Noodles, medium, 2 oz.	1½ cups	1½ cups	220
Spaghetti, 2 oz.	½ cup	1⅛ cups	210

Miscellaneous

Ingredient	Amount	Calories
Broth	1 cup	10
Clams, canned	7½-oz. can	114
Crab, canned, drained	6-oz. can	126
Flour, all-purpose	1 tablespoon	29
	1 cup	400
Gelatin, unflavored	1 envelope	25
Kidney Beans, red, canned	½ cup	115
Mustard	1 teaspoon	4
Popcorn, air-popped, ½ tbs.	1 cup popped	27
Raisins	1 tablespoon	29
Sugar, granulated	1 teaspoon	16
Sugar Substitute, granulated	1 packet	4
Tomato Sauce, canned	1 cup	90
Tuna, canned in water	7-oz. can	251
Vegetable Oil	1 tablespoon	125
Vinegar	1 tablespoon	2
Walnuts, chopped	1 tablespoon	49
Wine, dry white or red	1 cup	194

Index

About the Authors

Sylvia Schur, cookbook author, food consultant, and founding member of Les Dames d'Escoffier, is director of Creative Food Service.

Dr. Vivian Schulte is a registered dietician who has studied at the Cordon Bleu and La Varenne in Paris.

To order any of the
365 Ways Cookbooks
visit your local bookseller or call 1-800-321-6890

Our bestselling **365 Ways Cookbooks** are wire-bound to lie flat and have colorful, wipe-clean Kivar® covers.

Each **365 Ways Cookbook** is $16.95 plus $3.50 per copy shipping and handling. Applicable sales tax will be billed to your account. No CODs. Please allow 4-6 weeks for delivery.

> Please have your VISA, MASTERCARD or AMERICAN EXPRESS card at hand when calling.

• 365 •

Easy Italian Recipes 0-06-016310-0
Easy Low-Calorie Recipes 0-06-016309-7
Easy One-Dish Meals 0-06-016311-9
Great Barbecue & Grilling Recipes 0-06-016224-4
Great Chocolate Desserts 0-06-016537-5
Quick & Easy Microwave Recipes 0-06-016026-8
Snacks, Hors D'Oeuvres & Appetizers 0-06-016536-7
Ways to Cook Chicken 0-06-015539-6
Ways to Cook Fish and Shellfish 0-06-016841-2
Ways to Cook Hamburger & Other Ground Meats 0-06-016535-9
Ways to Cook Pasta 0-06-01865-4
Ways to Wok 0-06-016643-6

FORTHCOMING TITLES

Easy Chinese Recipes 0-06-016961-3
Great Cookies and Brownies 0-06-016840-4
Great Dessert Recipes 0-06-016959-1
Mexican Recipes 0-06-016963-X
Meatless Recipes 0-06-016958-3
20 Minute Menus **1** 0-06-016962-1
Soups and Stews 0-06-016960-5
Ways to Prepare for Christmas 0-06-017048-4

Also available in a wire-bound format are:

The Bartender's Bible 0-06-0616722-X $12.95
The Best Bread Machine Cookbook Ever 0-06-016927-3 $15.95